Crony Capitalism

Why has the literature on Asian development not addressed the issue of money politics in Korea? How can we reconcile the view of an efficient developmental state in Korea before 1997 with reports of massive corruption and inefficiency in that same country in 1998 and 1999? Politics is central to the answer. In this book Kang makes two arguments. First, political – not economic – considerations dominated policy making in both Korea and the Philippines. Second, if there is a balance of power among a small and stable set of government and business elites, money politics can actually reduce transaction costs and promote growth. Focusing on the exchange of favors for bribes between state and business, Kang argues that politics drove policy choices, that bureaucrats were not autonomous from political interference in setting policy, and that business and political elites wrestled with each other over who would reap the rents to be had. Even in Korea, corruption was far greater than the conventional wisdom allows – so rampant was corruption that we cannot dismiss it; rather, we need to explain it.

David Kang is Associate Professor of Government, Adjunct Associate Professor at the Tuck School of Business, Fellow at the Center for Asia and the Emerging Economies, Dartmouth College, and an Adjunct Fellow with the Center for National Policy, Washington, DC.

T0370746

Cambridge Studies in Comparative Politics

General Editor
Margaret Levi   *University of Washington, Seattle*

Associate Editors
Robert H. Bates   *Harvard University*
Peter Hall   *Harvard University*
Stephen Hanson   *University of Washington, Seattle*
Peter Lange   *Duke University*
Helen Milner   *Columbia University*
Frances Rosenbluth   *Yale University*
Susan Stokes   *University of Chicago*
Sidney Tarrow   *Cornell University*

Other Books in the Series

List continues on page following Index

Crony Capitalism

CORRUPTION AND DEVELOPMENT IN SOUTH KOREA AND THE PHILIPPINES

DAVID C. KANG

Dartmouth College

CAMBRIDGE UNIVERSITY PRESS
Cambridge, New York, Melbourne, Madrid, Cape Town, Singapore, São Paulo

Cambridge University Press
The Edinburgh Building, Cambridge CB2 2RU, UK

Published in the United States of America by Cambridge University Press, New York

www.cambridge.org
Information on this title: www.cambridge.org/9780521808170

First published 2002

A catalogue record for this publication is available from the British Library

Library of Congress Cataloguing in Publication data
Kang, David C. (David Chan-oong), 1965–
Crony capitalism : corruption and development in South Korea and the Philippines /
David C. Kang.
p. cm. – (Cambridge studies in comparative politics)
Includes bibliographical references and index.
ISBN 0-521-80817-0 – ISBN 0-521-00408-X (pb.)
1. Political corruption – Korea (South) 2. Political corruption – Philippines. 3. Korea
(South) – Economic policy – 1960– 4. Philippines – Economic policy. I. Title.
II. Series.
JQ1725.A55 K36 2001
320.95195 – dc21   2001025806

ISBN-13 978-0-521-80817-0 hardback
ISBN-10 0-521-80817-0 hardback

ISBN-13 978-0-521-00408-4 paperback
ISBN-10 0-521-00408-X paperback

Transferred to digital printing 2006

Contents

Figures

Tables

Tables

Acknowledgments

I owe a tremendous debt to my mentors and colleagues at various institutions around the world. This book began as a dissertation at Berkeley. Vinod Aggarwal, Hong-yung Lee, and Oliver Williamson were both engaged in my work and patient with my progress. Vinnie was a superb advisor: He left me alone when I needed to think, he gave me intense attention at important moments, and he supported me institutionally and personally throughout the entire dissertation process. I also benefited greatly from the support of my other committee members, Hong-yung Lee and Oliver Williamson. Hong-yung Lee was my conduit to Korea, providing invaluable guidance and advice to an overeager student. Oliver was patient in trying to push me to be more rigorous and to think more clearly.

A number of scholars have been generous with their time and energy in wading through drafts of the manuscript. Lots of thanks to Bill Bernhard, Victor Cha, Bruce Cumings, Rick Doner, Paul Hutchcroft, Jongryn Mo, Gabriella Montinola, Katherine Moon, Peter Moore, Greg Noble, Frances Rosenbluth, Ssang-yong Ryu, Dick Samuels, David Waldner, and Meredith Woo-Cumings. Thanks are also due to Chung-in Moon, who has been very generous with his time, energy, and support. I'd also like to thank colleagues who commented on various incarnations of the ideas in this book: Dennis McNamara, Ansil Ramsey, Robert Bates, Mike Thies, Stephan Haggard, Atul Kohli, David Lake, Tun-jen Cheng, David Stuligross, and Barry Weingast. Lew Bateman's and Margaret Levi's guidance at Cambridge has helped improve the book immeasurably. I would especially like to thank Bob Bullock: Through years of spirited conversations and arguments in Seoul, Tokyo, and the States, Bob has remained that rarest of combinations – a wonderful friend and a devastating critic.

Dartmouth provided both the time and the support that allowed me to turn an idea into a book. Linda Fowler, Mike Mastanduno, Anne Saadah, Dean Spiliotes, and Alex Wendt were all supportive and challenging colleagues. Particular thanks go to my research assistants over the years: Dave Moran (twice!), Esther Lee, Arlene Lim, Rachel Kim, Anne Kanyusik, Scotty Martin, Scott Lollis, Heesun Byon, Eunsun Hwang, Hyeran Jo, Sarah Snip, and Susan Sanders.

This work was supported by numerous grants over the years. A Fulbright fellowship allowed me to spend a year in Korea, and the Social Science Research Council provided additional dissertation funds that allowed me to conduct research both abroad and in the States. At Berkeley, a John L. Simpson fellowship allowed me to complete the dissertation. The Northeast Asia Council of the Association for Asian Studies supported a further trip to Asia to conduct interviews. The Dickey Center at Dartmouth was generous with its support, allowing me to return to the Philippines, and the Rockefeller Center at Dartmouth supported trips to the Philippines and Korea.

I owe my Asian colleagues an enormous debt for allowing me to ask naive questions and continually pester them. I would like to thank Korea University for inviting me to be a visiting professor there in 1995 and to thank the Kyungnam University Institute for Far Eastern Studies in Seoul for allowing me to spend a year in the relatively clean air of Samchung-dong during 1992–1993. Kyongsoo Lho has been a steadfast mentor ever since I met him when I was an undergraduate at Stanford, and I owe him a deep debt of gratitude. In addition, for their perceptive insights into Korean life, thanks to Park Ungsuh, Kim Kihwan, Lee Han-bin, Oh Young-ju, Chang Seok-myung, Song In-sang, Lee Duksoo, Kim Kwang-soo, Ahn Young-ok, Kim Ho-won, and Kim Chung-sik. Finally, many thanks to Cholsoo Lho for years of guidance throughout this project.

In the Philippines I benefited enormously from my interactions with the Asian Institute of Management. Ateneo University provided me with institutional support and library access. For their insights into Philippine life, thanks to Yeng Felipe, Chito Salazar, Vicente Paterno, Washington SyCip, Roberto Ocampo, Frankie Roman, Victor Venida, Pamela De La Paz, Tony Gatmaitan, Sedfrey Ordonez, Fiona Paua, and Ricardo Saludo. Thanks especially to Paul Hutchcroft and Rick Doner for their advice. In both Korea and the Philippines there were those who wished to remain anonymous, and I thank them for their time and insights.

Acknowledgments

My brother Steven Chan-ho and my sister Laura Chan-ju were helpful throughout this process, with their constant encouragement and – in the case of my sister – expert editorial advice. Finally and most importantly, this book could never have been written without the unwavering support of my parents. It is to them that I dedicate this book.

1

The Puzzle and the Theory

I am convinced, therefore, that Korean politics will not be reformed unless the standards of the people are raised, a change of generations is promoted, the contents of elections are studied, and an open system for the procurement of political funds is worked out by means of consistent policies.

– Park Chung-hee

Have we earned the right to continue to demand . . . continued trust and confidence in us? Unless we can confidently answer these questions, we dare not proceed. . . . Now is the time to cut off the infected parts of society from active public life, before they endanger the entire body politic.

– Ferdinand Marcos

When the Hanbo Steel Company of South Korea went bankrupt in early 1997, an inquest discovered that at least two billion dollars had evaporated from its accounts, most likely ending up in the pockets of political or business elites.[1] Upon his arrest for bribery, Hanbo's chairman, Chung Tae-soo, privately let it be known that if the government pressed its case against him too vigorously he would unleash an "atomic bomb" (*poktan*) and implicate bankers and politicians who had been involved with Hanbo over the years.[2] Chung was convicted, although the case was not pursued with particular vigor. While numerous observers professed to be shocked – Shocked! – at the revelations, in reality such scandals are a recurrent theme in Korean political history, and the exchange of money for political influence has been not just an open secret, it has been common knowledge. Since independence in 1948, Korea has seen a seemingly endless flow of

---

[1] Yoon Young-ho, "Chŏng Tae-su wa kŏmŭn ton" (Chung Tae-soo and black money), *Shindonga* (March 1, 1997): 201.
[2] From a businessman close to the investigation, March 1997.

corruption scandals bring down scores of elites. Among those who have served time in jail or been exiled are former presidents Chun Doo-hwan and Roh Tae-woo, members of many presidential staffs, and a slew of military officers, politicians, bureaucrats, bankers, businessmen, and tax collectors.[3]

For decades the scholarly literature largely ignored the prevalence of money politics as inconsequential or as peripheral to the "real story" of South Korea: economic growth led by meritocratic technocrats and austere military generals. Growth was so spectacular that the reality of corruption was concealed or was dismissed out of hand. The rapid growth of the Asian economies evoked a mixture of wonder and fear. Sometimes called miracles, or Tigers, countries such as Korea, Taiwan, Singapore, and Hong Kong leapt from poverty to riches within a generation. And until late November 1997 and the stunning fall of the Korean *won*, observers argued that better government in Asia was a prime reason for that region's spectacular growth. This perspective held up Asia's seemingly neutral bureaucracies, effective politicians, and hardworking businessmen as central factors in economic growth.[4]

In contrast, scholars have held up the Philippines as the paradigmatic corrupt state, typified by its former president Ferdinand Marcos. The Philippines failed to develop rapidly because of government meddling, powerful business sectors that reaped windfall gains from government largess, and incompetent civil servants. The entire world knows about Imelda Marcos's 2,000 pairs of shoes and about the abuses that occurred at the Malacañang presidential palace. The Philippines, to this day, has a public image of cronyism, corruption, and bad government retarding its development.

The Asian financial crisis of late 1997 abruptly changed the West's view of Asia. Overnight, Korea was lumped in with the Philippines and roundly criticized for cozy government-business relationships that – in the pierc-

---

[3] For good overviews of the 1995 scandals, see Ahn Byoung-yong, "pichagǔm kwa taekwǒn yokǔi chuakhan janch'i" (The disgusting feast of illicit funds and presidential hunger for power), *Shindonga* (December 1995): 112; and Kim Yong-suh, "No Tae-u kusokgwa YS ǔi sǒntaek" (The detention of Roh Tae-woo and Kim Young-sam's choices), *Sisa Wolgan* (December 1995): 56–65.

[4] For representative views, see Peter Evans, *Embedded Autonomy* (Princeton: Princeton University Press, 1995); Alice Amsden, *Asia's Next Giant* (Cambridge: Cambridge University Press, 1989); and Chalmers Johnson, "Institutions and Economic Performance in South Korea and Taiwan," in *The Political Economy of the New Asian Industrialism*, edited by Frederic Deyo (Ithaca: Cornell University Press, 1987), pp. 152–155.

ing hindsight of instant experts – were obviously corrupt, inefficient, and backward. Focused only on explaining successful outcomes, the conventional model provided no analytic way to make sense of the 1997 crisis. Countries previously regarded as miracles now were nothing more than havens for crony capitalists who got rich the easy way. The result was a scramble to reinterpret the newly industrializing countries. But the pendulum may have swung too far – from excessive praise for the Asian juggernaut in the 1980s to excessive contempt for Asian business practices in the 1990s.

How can we reconcile rapid growth in East Asia before 1997 with reports of extensive money politics in those same countries in 1998 and 1999? How do we explain extensive money politics in Asia? How does money politics affect our understanding of the developmental state?

I. The Argument

Politics is central to the answer. In this study I make two arguments. First, both Korea and the Philippines experienced significant corruption throughout the postindependence era. Second, political – not economic – considerations dominated policy making in both countries. Focusing on the exchange of favors for bribes between state and business, I argue that politics drove policy choices, that bureaucrats were not autonomous from political interference in setting policy, and that business and political elites wrestled with each other over who would reap the rents to be had. Even in Korea, corruption was far greater than the conventional wisdom allows – so rampant was corruption that we cannot dismiss it; rather, we need to explain it.

Although money politics – corruption and cronyism – is generally seen as inhibiting economic growth, there are certain conditions in which it can actually be beneficial. Developing countries typically have weak institutional structures. In that case, *if there is a balance of power among a small and stable set of government and business elites, money politics can actually reduce transaction costs* and make long-term agreements and investments more efficient, even while enriching those fortunate few who collude together.[5]

---

[5] For overviews of transaction costs, see David C. Kang, "South Korean and Taiwanese Development and the New Institutional Economics," *International Organization* 49, no. 3 (Summer 1995): 555–587; Oliver E. Williamson, *The Economic Institutions of Capitalism* (New York: The Free Press, 1985); Douglass North, "A Transaction Cost Theory of

This political hypothesis can differentiate Korea and the Philippines while also bridging the boom years and the crisis.[6] For too long scholars have focused on bureaucrats and on outcomes. To understand the contrasting economic outcomes of Korea and the Philippines, one must directly address corruption and politics.

The crisis was not caused overnight, and the historical structures that led to the crisis will endure long after the events of 1997 have faded from memory. Using Korea and the Philippines as case studies, I explore the politics of the developmental state by focusing on the interplay of institutions and money politics. In both countries, growth and corruption existed side by side for decades. Even in the period of rapid Korean growth, a political calculus, not economic efficiency, was the crucial factor in determining economic policy. But the configuration of actors that facilitated rapid growth in Korea in the 1960s was undermined by its very success and eventually led to the crisis of 1997. In the Philippines, a different configuration of actors retarded development for decades. It seems finally to have altered, and perhaps the strong growth of the 1990s is the beginning of an upward trend.

The political hypothesis advanced in this study suggests a new direction for our research about the developmental state. Situated at the intersection of international relations and comparative politics, and comprising a set of ideas about institutional arrangements and policy choices, the developmental-state perspective held up Asia's seemingly neutral bureaucracies, effective politicians, and consistent trade policies as central factors in economic growth.[7]

Politics," *Journal of Theoretical Politics* 2, no. 4 (1990): 355–367; and Barry Weingast, "Constitutions as Governance Structures: The Political Foundations of Secure Markets," *Journal of Institutional and Theoretical Economics* 149 (March 1993): 286–311.

[6] For a study with the same goal as mine but for Japan, see Robert Bullock, "Politicizing the Developmental State: Agriculture and the Conservative Coalition in Postwar Japan" (MS, U.C. Riverside, 2001).

[7] The focus on state institutions includes Weberian bureaucracies that are autonomous from political and social interference. Among many who hold this view, Peter Evans has argued that "highly selective meritocratic recruitment and long-term career rewards create commitment and a sense of corporate coherence." Evans, *Embedded Autonomy*, p. 12. Alice Amsden also writes that "economic success in Korea challenges the assumption . . . that government intervention degenerates into 'rent-seeking.'" Amsden, *Asia's Next Giant*, p. 327. For other specific instances, see Karl Fields, "Strong States and Business Organization in Korea and Taiwan," in *Business and the State in Developing Countries*, edited by Sylvia Maxfield and Ben Ross Schneider (Ithaca: Cornell University Press,1997), p. 126; Johnson,

However, the literature on the developmental state led us down the wrong analytic path. This literature implied that corruption and growth simply cannot coexist. As a result, our view of Asia has become excessively focused on explaining either why these countries were not corrupt or why growth was not as spectacular as popularly believed.[8] South Korea has reported phenomenal growth over the past thirty-five years; the Philippines has not. Working backward from successful economic outcomes, one easily falls into the presumption that Korea *must* have had less corruption and better government than the Philippines merely because it had such rapid growth.[9]

This is not to argue that there has been no scholarship on Asian corruption. Especially in the wake of the 1997 financial crisis, the past few years have seen a number of studies that have begun to address the issue of corruption in Asia. These works, however, have tended to concentrate on two areas of research that have generally not responded to each other. The first area has focused on explaining different types of corruption, with only passing reference to how this affects our understanding of economic growth.[10] The second area has largely been focused on assessing whether and to what extent corruption was a factor contributing to the 1997

"Institutions and Economic Performance in South Korea and Taiwan," p. 152; and Ziya Önis, "The Logic of the Developmental State," *Comparative Politics* 24 (1991): 114. The major policy focus is on export-oriented industrialization, with a state that "in direct exchange for subsidies . . . exacts performance standards from firms." Amsden, *Asia's Next Giant*, p. 146.

[8] On rent seeking, see James Buchanan, Robert Tollison, and Gordon Tullock, eds., *Towards a Theory of the Rent-Seeking Society* (College Station: Texas A&M University Press, 1980); and Anne O. Krueger, "The Political Economy of the Rent-Seeking Society," *American Economic Review* 64 (1974): 291–303. For a revisionist view of Asian growth, see Alwyn Young, *Lessons from the East Asian NICS: A Contrarian View* (NBER Working Paper 4482, 1993).

[9] "If *H*, then *I*. *I* is true, therefore *H* is true." Carl Hempel, *Philosophy of Natural Science* (Englewood Cliffs, NJ: Prentice-Hall, 1966), p. 7. On selection bias, see Gary King, Robert Keohane, and Sidney Verba, *Designing Social Inquiry* (Princeton: Princeton University Press, 1994).

[10] See Byeong-Seog Park, "Political Corruption in South Korea: Concentrating on the Dynamics of Party Politics," *Asian Perspective* 19 (Spring/Summer 1995): 163–193; Beatrice Weder, *Model, Myth, or Miracle: Reassessing the Role of Governments in the East Asian Experience* (New York: United Nations University Press, 1999); Richard Mitchell, *Political Bribery in Japan* (Honolulu: University of Hawaii Press, 1996); and Jeffrey A. Winters, "Suharto's Indonesia: Prosperity and Freedom for the Few," *Current History* 94 (1995): 420–424.

financial crisis.[11] For example, Stephan Haggard writes that "in Western commentary, these [causes] are frequently reduced to corruption, cronyism, and nepotism . . . but the sources of vulnerability . . . sprang from the political commitments of governments."[12] But this body of literature tends not to explore how the Asian countries experienced rapid growth in the first place. Whereas both strands of research are important, an extended dialogue about the relationship between money politics and Asian development has only begun to occur, and a comprehensive treatment of the issue has yet to appear.[13]

The Korean and Philippine experiences suggest broader implications for the study of government-business relations in developing countries. Most important, a model of politics is central to understanding the developmental state. We cannot assume benevolence on the part of the developmental state. A "hard" view of the developmental state – that the state is neutral, picks winners, and provides public goods because the civil service is insulated from social influences – is difficult to sustain empirically. However, even the "soft" view – that governments can have a beneficial effect however government action is attained – needs a political explanation. The Korean state was developmental – it provided public goods, fostered investment, and created infrastructure. But this study shows that this was not necessarily intentional. Corruption was rampant in Korea, and the state intervened in the way that it did because its doing so was in the interests of a small group of business and political elites. The production of public goods was often the fortunate by-product of actors' competing to gain the private benefits of state resources.

---

[11] On cronyism and corruption as causes of the financial crisis, see Giancarlo Corsetti, "Paper Tigers? A Model of the Asian Crisis," *European Economic Review* 43, no. 7 (June 1999): 1211–1236; Gerald Segal and Davis Goodman, eds., *Towards Recovery in Pacific Asia* (London: Routledge, 2000); Callum Henderson, *Asia Falling: Making Sense of the Asian Crisis and Its Aftermath* (New York: McGraw-Hill, 1998); and T. J. Pempel, ed., *The Politics of the Asian Financial Crisis* (Ithaca: Cornell University Press, 1999). For a counterargument, see Ha-joon Chang, "The Hazard of Moral Hazard: Untangling the Asian Crisis," *World Development* 28, no. 4 (April 2000): 775–788.

[12] Stephan Haggard, *The Political Economy of the Asian Financial Crisis* (Washington, DC: Institute for International Economics, 2000), p. 10.

[13] Two good works in this vein are Richard Doner and Ansil Ramsey, "Thailand: From Economic Miracle to Economic Crisis," in *Asian Contagion: The Causes and Consequences of a Financial Crisis*, edited by Karl D. Jackson (Boulder, CO: Westview Press, 1998); and Andrew Wedeman, "Looters, Rent-scrapers, and Dividend-collectors: Corruption and Growth in Zaire, South Korea, and the Philippines," *Journal of Developing Areas* 31 (Summer 1997): 457–478.

It is unwise to focus on individual policy choices (for example, export-oriented industrialization, or EOI) or specific institutional arrangements (the bureaucracy) as isolated issues. Institutions and policies are intervening variables, and the larger institutional environment – in this instance the government-business relationship – affects any specific issue.[14] Both institutions and policies comprise a wide range of issues. Institutions are more than just the organization of the state – they can be legal or corporate as well – whereas policies comprise trade, regulatory and financial policies. A distorted picture will emerge if we focus mainly on state institutions and ignore industrial organization, or if we focus on trade policy and ignore lax regulatory and financial policies. The case studies in this book show that political and economic entrepreneurs are quite resourceful and that institutional design or policy choices are subject to manipulation, evasion, and modification.[15]

Additionally, transaction costs – the costs of making, monitoring, and enforcing agreements between actors – are affected by the larger institutional environment. This study shows that certain configurations of government and business elites (what I call "mutual hostages") can reduce transaction costs and actually promote growth. The argument that follows suggests that to understand policy making in developing countries, one must first understand, for each country, the particular political challenges faced by individual leaders, and their close supporters, and the manner in which business attempts to influence policies. The strategic allocation of economic policy and benefits is an important political resource. The relationship between government and business elites differs in each country, and another source of constraints is the international system. Different countries face different international pressures, and not all countries race from the same starting line nor run under similar conditions. Most important in the international system are the external threats that can cause leaders to pay more attention to growth and efficiency.

One reason that scholars have not dealt with these issues in detail has been an overwhelming preoccupation with explaining economic outcomes. Those analysts who are not trying to explain growth tend to paint a far

---

[14] Douglass North, "The New Institutional Economics," *Journal of Theoretical and Institutional Economics* 142 (1986): 230–237; and Oliver Williamson, "Comparative Economic Organization: The Analysis of Discrete Structural Alternatives," *Administrative Science Quarterly* 36 (1991): 269–296.

[15] Oliver Williamson, *The Economic Institutions of Capitalism* (New York: Free Press, 1985).

darker and more abusive picture of Korean politics than those trying to explain why what was essentially gangster rule in Korea was actually good for growth. Mark Clifford describes Korea as a "culture of rage," Gregory Henderson depicts Park Chung-hee's rule as a swirl of factions unable to cohere, and Bruce Cumings sees a pattern of authoritarian strongmen.[16] Although it may be difficult to describe Korean politics in such pejorative terms and then explain Korea's remarkable economic outcomes, we must avoid falling into the trap of deciding a priori that Korean politics cannot have been corrupt because the country experienced strong growth. Alternatively, we need to explain the pattern of money politics in the Philippines, not just assert its existence.

I begin with an overview of Korea and the Philippines in which I emphasize both similarities and differences between the two countries. Domestic politics, the organization of society in both countries, has been more similar than is generally recognized, and much of the early economics in both countries was also similar. However, Korea and the Philippines differ in how both colonialism and the external environment at independence affected them. In Korea, Japanese and U.S. influences tended to disrupt the old order, and a severe threat from North Korea provided an impetus for growth. In contrast, in the Philippines, Spanish and American colonialism tended to reinforce traditional political and economic patterns, and the absence of any realistic threat provided Philippine leaders with little incentive to alter the existing arrangements.

This study next focuses on the role of the bureaucracy. One of the core tenets of the developmental-state perspective is the important role of the bureaucracy. However, the bureaucracy under Park Chung-hee was not substantially more autonomous or coherent than that under Syngman Rhee or Ferdinand Marcos. In addition, Korea did not have a "pilot ministry" directing development. Finally, government subsidies were not exchanged for performance standards – the endemic overcapacity of Korean industry is prima facie evidence that economic policy decisions were made for political reasons. In contrast, the Philippine bureaucracy was far more competent than is popularly believed. In both Korea and the Philippines rulers have reigned *and* ruled, and the bureaucracy has not been autonomous from political regime interests. The difference in quality

---

[16] Mark Clifford, *Troubled Tiger* (New York: M. E. Sharpe, 1994), p. 11; Gregory Henderson, *The Politics of the Vortex* (Cambridge, MA: Harvard University Press, 1967); and Bruce Cumings, *Korea's Place in the Sun* (New York: W. W. Norton, 1997).

between the Philippine and Korean bureaucracies is overstated. Although the Philippines suffers from poor political leadership, the bureaucrats themselves are well-trained and dedicated.

I then turn to domestic politics. The relative strength of the state and the business sector determines the form and level of money politics, which in turn has an impact on a country's development trajectory. I provide a model built upon an analogy with the economic example of markets to describe the pattern of corruption in Korea and that in the Philippines. This highly stylized model of corruption relies on the analogy between state/business to producers/consumers. Looking at the business sector as either concentrated or dispersed, and at political leadership as either coherent or fractured, leads to a matrix that predicts levels and types of corruption. In the most interesting combination, both state and business are strong and concentrated, leading to a situation of "mutual hostages" where both sides potentially benefit, and opportunism and exploitation are constrained.

Governments engage in three generic types of economic policy: trade policy, financial policy, and regulatory policy. In Korea, although trade policy in the 1960s was generally supportive of exports, financial and regulatory policies tended to work at cross-purposes. State control of the financial sector created incentives for business to focus on expansion over efficiency, and extensive and contradictory regulatory and tax policies gave the state discretionary power over the firms. The few dominant firms in Korea (the *chaebol*) thus nurtured their political connections as an important component of business strategy. The coherence of the state and the business sector prevented either from dictating events, and although money politics existed, it was constrained.

Understanding policy decisions requires understanding the political incentive structure within which actors make economic decisions. Political leaders use both pork and public goods strategically: neither pork nor policy is preordained, and both have political benefits and costs. Korea under Park may not have been different from Korea under Syngman Rhee in the extent to which the bureaucracy was politicized. However, whereas Korea has plenty of corruption and politicization in public works contracts and loan allocations, pockets of the bureaucracy were staffed with educated and trained people recruited through a competitive examination process. Park Chung-hee created a bifurcated bureaucracy that allowed him to meet his patronage requirements and still pursue economic efficiency. Such a bifurcation allowed Park to follow both an internal agenda aimed at retaining political power and "buying off" supporters and an external agenda focused on economic development.

Although the Philippines has exhibited some of the classic traits of a weak and predatory state, important distinctions also exist. The democratic era in the Philippines saw corruption, jurisdictional battles between the executive and the legislature, and a bureaucracy permeated by outside interests. The state was unable to formulate consistent or coherent economic policies. Under Marcos, however, the state became both more coherent and more autonomous from social interest groups. The problem under martial law was not a lack of state strength but the uses to which such strength was put. Marcos, like Park, followed an explicit political strategy, destroying the most potentially dangerous elite families, co-opting others, and ignoring the rest. Marcos's strategy temporarily succeeded; there was substantial acquiescence to his rule for the first half of martial law. However, Philippine governmental policies always remained subject to manipulation, with trade policies focused on import substitution, financial policies never consistently implemented, and regulatory policies often a contradictory mix of special dispensations to favored cronies.

The pattern of Philippine money politics swung like a pendulum from excessive bottom-up rent seeking by society during the democratic period, to excessive top-down predation by Marcos and his cronies under martial law. From 1946 to 1972, particularistic demands from business overwhelmed the ability of the state to meet them, leading to corruption and incoherent policy making. With martial law beginning in 1972, the direction of corruption reversed, and Marcos used the power of the state to expropriate wealth for himself and his associates. Under Marcos, the Philippines had the potential to pursue a more disciplined developmental path, with a coherent bureaucracy and considerable state power. But Marcos lacked any constraint on his excesses, and as a result the Philippines lost its opportunity to grow rapidly.

The patterns in both Korea and the Philippines changed significantly with their democratic transitions in the mid-1980s. In Korea, the transition to democracy in 1987 diffused the power of the state. This led to increased demands for political payoffs as politicians began to genuinely compete for electoral support and to decreased ability of the state to resist or contain the demands of the business sector. The small number of massive Korean firms, unrestrained by any market forces because of their size, made increasingly risky decisions. Thus "too much" democracy combined with a still collusive business-government relationship resulted in increasingly ineffectual policy making, and the Asian financial crisis of 1997 brought this to light.

In contrast, by the early 1980s Ferdinand Marcos had run the Philippines into the ground. The dramatic uprising of "People Power" in 1986 leveled the playing field for both state and business. As the Philippines slowly recovered, state and business were less powerful and less coherent, leading the Philippines in the early 1990s to begin a painful restructuring process. The Philippines was less affected by the crisis of 1997 because some of those collusive government-business ties had been broken by the downfall of Marcos, speeding the process of reform. Largely owing to policy reforms and increased regulation of the financial sector, the Philippines fared relatively well in the crisis of 1997. The prospect for continued economic and political growth appears, if not inevitable, quite likely.

This book is about politics, and it centers on explaining the patterns of money politics. The argument adduced here, however, leads naturally to a question about economic growth. If both Korea and the Philippines experienced extensive corruption, why did Korea grow much faster than the Philippines? In the concluding section of the book I shift the emphasis from explaining money politics to exploring the relationship between money politics and development. Simply put, the balance of power among elites in Korea reduced transaction costs, while bandwagoning politics in the Philippines raised transaction costs. Although an imbalance between economic and political elites can lead to corruption spiraling out of control and choking off growth, where a rough balance does exist, corruption is contained. However, corruption is only one of many variables that affect development, and to answer the larger question of why Korea has developed but the Philippines has not we must be sensitive to a number of other factors that existed in Korea but not in the Philippines, including an external threat, extensive U.S. aid, and land reform, in addition to the balance that limited corruption and that is described in this book.

Leaders of states make deliberate choices about whether to constrain their ability to steal domestic capital. Standing at the intersection of domestic and international politics, and restrained by domestic institutions and international pressures, the leaders must deal with foreign countries, survive in domestic politics, and also craft economic policies. In making sense of why Korea initially succeeded, but the Philippines did not, we have to understand the broad contours of the relationship between big business and the state. By comparing the two countries, this book not only sharpens our perspective on the individual countries but also leads to further comparative research on politics, corruption, and development.

II. The Theory: Money Politics, Rent Seeking, and Corruption

I focus on the rent seeking and corruption that occur between public and private actors. At the heart of the model is the idea that those actors with excessive power will tend to abuse it. The dependent variable is the exchange between state and business of favors for bribes. The independent variable is the relationship between state and business. My analytic focus is on this larger institutional environment – the actual institutions of governance all exist within this larger relationship, and each specific institution is affected by this environment.

I use the term "money politics" because it is less normative than "corruption" and also because it highlights public-private interaction. Both "corruption" and "rent seeking" are broader terms, describing activities that can occur at the private-private level as well as vis-à-vis the state. James Buchanan defines "rent seeking" as "that part of the payment to an owner of resources over and above that which those resources could command in any alternative use."[17] Thus rents are created when an actor manipulates prices and causes them to diverge from competitive levels, and the existence of rents can lead to corruption by various actors attempting to gain access to the rents. By manipulating prices, the actor himself, or some other actor on whose behalf the price manipulator is acting as an agent, is able to reap "excess profits."[18]

Rents can be created in a number of ways, but a principal way is through state intervention.[19] The state uses its power to manipulate prices and

[17] James Buchanan, "Rent Seeking and Profit Seeking," in *Towards a Theory of the Rent-Seeking Society*, edited by James Buchanan, Robert Tollison, and Gordon Tullock (College Station: Texas A&M University Press, 1980), p. 3.
[18] Pranab Bardhan, "Corruption and Development: A Review of Issues," *Journal of Economic Literature* 35 (1997): 1320–1346; Serguey Braguinsky, "Corruption and Schumpeterian Growth in Different Economic Environments," *Contemporary Economic Policy* 14 (1996): 14–25; Kofi O Nti, "Comparative Statics of Contests and Rent-Seeking Games," *International Economic Review* 38, no. 1 (1997): 43–59; and Yoram Barzel, "Measurement Cost and the Organization of Markets," *Journal of Law and Economics* 25 (1982): 27–48.
[19] Ha-joon Chang, *The Political Economy of Industrial Policy* (New York: St. Martin's Press, 1994); Susan Rose-Ackerman, *Corruption: A Study in Political Economy* (New York: Academic Press, 1978); Andrei Shleifer and Robert Vishny, "Corruption," *Quarterly Journal of Economics* 108 (August 1993): 599–617; Margaret Levi, *Of Rule and Revenue* (Berkeley: Uni-

markets to generate rents. For example, import licenses confer rents by restricting the amount of goods that come into a country; actors who can import the restricted goods are able to sell those goods at a higher than market price, thereby obtaining rents.[20] By intervening, the government creates incentives for business to try to influence policy decisions. Corruption occurs when businessmen use bribery, personal connections, or some other means to attempt to influence policy decisions and gain rents. The distribution and volume of rents are thus a function of the relative strengths of the state and the business sector.

1. The Politics of Corruption

Were there no government distributing rents, there would be no corruption, and thus a key issue is how to model the government-business relationship. In examining both the supply and the demand for political corruption, this simplified model of the government-business relationship necessarily abstracts from a rich reality.

Following Shleifer and Vishney, a state can range from coherent to fractured.[21] A state is coherent if it can formulate preferences independent of social influences and if political leaders have internal control over their bureaucrats.[22] Although there are many possible configurations of the relationship among political leaders, bureaucrats, and political organizations (domestic politics: parties, associations, etc.), for the sake of simplicity I

versity of California Press, 1988); Paul Milgrom and John Roberts, "Bargaining Costs, Influence Costs, and the Organization of Economic Activity," in *Perspectives on Positive Political Economy*, edited by James E. Alt and Kenneth A. Shepsle (Cambridge: Cambridge University Press, 1990); Parimal Kanti Bag, "Controlling Corruption in Hierarchies," *Journal of Comparative Economics* 25 (1997): 322–344; and Mushtaq Khan, "The Efficiency Implications of Corruption," *Journal of International Development* 8, no. 5 (1996): 683–696.

[20] Corruption is thus a subset of rent seeking. Rents may be allocated purely on merit, or they may be allocated toward bribes.

[21] Shleifer and Vishney model different types of government structures, but they avoid studying how business organization may affect corruption. Shleifer and Vishney, "Corruption." Susan Rose-Ackerman discusses types of state organization similar to my work, although she does not use the terminology I employ here. See Rose-Ackerman, *Corruption*.

[22] On autonomy and state strength, see Peter Katzenstein, ed., *Between Power and Plenty: Foreign Economic Policies of Advanced Industrial States* (Madison: University of Wisconsin Press, 1978). On internal control (agency costs), see Matthew McCubbins and Thomas Schwartz, "Congressional Oversight Overlooked: Police Patrols versus Fire Alarms," *American Journal of Political Science* 28 (1984): 165–179; and Frances Rosenbluth and Mark Ramseyer, *Japan's Political Marketplace* (Cambridge, MA: Harvard University Press, 1993), Chs. 6 and 7.

focus on only two polar cases. The most coherent situation exists when political leaders have full control over their political organizations and their bureaucrats, and in this case leaders actively use domestic politics as a means of ensuring continued rule. At the other pole, the most fractured situation exists when leaders survive only tenuously, when they engage in constant conflict with political organizations over the form and content of the state, and bureaucrats can play off "multiple principals" to their own advantage.[23] At the heart is the question of control.

It is the interaction of government and business that is of interest, however, and we therefore need to understand business organization as well as government organization. My view of the business sector builds on the work of Michael Shafer.[24] He argues that the organizational charac- teristics of the predominant economic sector (e.g., mining or agriculture) have different implications for its relationship to the state. In sectors with high asset specificity and high production inflexibility, companies will be less responsive to market signals, and it will be harder for them to adjust quickly to exogenous shocks, either political or economic. These types of firms will have more incentive to resist attempts by the state to intervene. Alternatively, in sectors with low asset specificity, low production inflexi- bility, and low factor inflexibility, firms will be more easily influenced by exogenous forces.

The approach used here examines business more broadly than does Shafer. In this model, a strong concentrated business sector is the diver- sified business group, comprised of well-organized firms that cover many sectors of the economy.[25] As Ben Ross Schneider puts it, "big (and encom- passing) is beautiful."[26] This definition of diversified firms is one in which companies cover many sectors rather than one, may have import- competing subsidiaries as well as export-oriented subsidiaries, and may have agricultural and urban firms. Given their cross-ownership of various subsidiaries and the range of their interests, these firms' interests cannot be neatly categorized. In addition, the larger that diversified business

[23] Pablo Spiller, "Politicians, Interest Groups, and Regulators: A Multiple-Principals Agency Theory of Regulation, or 'Let Them Be Bribed,'" *The Journal of Law and Economics* 33 (April 1990): 65–101.
[24] Michael Shafer, *Winners and Losers: How Sectors Shape the Developmental Prospects of States* (Ithaca: Cornell University Press, 1994).
[25] Amsden, *Asia's Next Giant*, p. 8.
[26] Ben Ross Schneider, "Elusive Synergy: Business-Government Relations and Develop- ment," *Comparative Politics* 31, no. 1 (October 1998): 109.

state

	coherent	fractured
small-N (concentrated)	I: mutual hostages type: PD collusion amount: medium	II: rent seeking type: bottom-up amount: large
large-N (dispersed)	III: predatory state type: top-down amount: large	IV: laissez-faire type: residual amount: small

business

PD = Prisoner's Dilemma

Figure 1.1. The Four Types of Corruption

groups are relative to the economy as a whole, the more they are likely to attempt to influence government policy and the more they are likely to wield political influence. These conglomerates can be differentiated from single-sector, smaller, and less-diversified firms. On a spectrum, we might put individual artisans at one end, with Japanese *keiretsu*, Korean *chaebol*, Philippine family conglomerates, and Mexican *grupos* at the other end.[27]

We can now build the analogy for politics and corruption, with a coherent/fractured state along one axis and a concentrated/dispersed business sector along the other (Figure 1.1). In this model I take as given the initial distribution of rights and the type of actors. These are exogenous to the model, and I remain agnostic as to why and how society came to look a certain way.

2. Types of Corruption: Bottom-Up or Top-Down

Although the model is a simplified abstraction of the government-business relationship, it allows us to parsimoniously capture the underlying dynamics of how corruption occurs. There are two analytically distinct types of

---

[27] On Latin American conglomerates, see Kurt Weyland, "'Growth with Equity' in Chile's New Democracy?" *Latin American Research Review* 32 (1997): 37–68.

corruption: the top-down predation by a strong state on society, and the bottom-up rent seeking of powerful groups that overwhelm the ability of the state to contain and channel their demands. Neither one of these is analytically prior to the other, and both can occur under the right circumstances.

Top-down corruption has been best explicated in the notion of a "predatory" state.[28] The predatory state is one in which the state takes advantage of a dispersed and weak business sector. Political elites pursue outright expropriation; they also solicit "donations" from businessmen who in turn are either "shaken down" by the regime or who volunteer bribes in return for favors, and employ other means as well.[29] In contrast, bottom-up corruption occurs when social actors have the power to overwhelm the state. When the strength of the business sector is enough to force concessions from the state, rent seeking behavior results. Potential state influence over economic life is vast, and those businessmen or groups privileged enough to receive low-interest loans or import quotas will benefit at the expense of others.[30] Indeed, a typical problem in developing countries is being able to resist society's demands on the state.[31] When rent seeking demands become too onerous, the state is incapable of implementing decisions and growth is stifled.

The first two possibilities I consider are analogous to either a predatory state or a rent-seeking business sector. The typical case is that some group or segment of society has far more access to power than others, as in Cell III. When a country has a coherent state and a dispersed business sector, the result is predatory behavior by the state (top-down behavior) in which political elites can scrape off rents in a predatory manner. Political elites presiding over a coherent state will have the opportunity to take advantage of a fractured business sector.

Alternatively, when a concentrated business sector and a fragmented state exist, as in Cell II, the result is rent seeking (bottom-up behavior).

[28] Levi, *Of Rule and Revenue*, pp. 32–45.
[29] Charles Tilly, "The State as Organized Crime," in *Bringing the State Back In*, edited by Peter B. Evans, Dietrich Rueschemeyer, and Theda Skocpol (Cambridge: Cambridge University Press, 1985).
[30] For an interesting discussion along these lines, see Milgrom and Roberts, "Bargaining Costs, Influence Costs, and the Organization of Economic Activity"; and Chang, *The Political Economy of Industrial Policy*.
[31] Joel Migdal, *Strong Societies and Weak States: State-Society Relations and State Capabilities in the Third World* (Princeton: Princeton University Press, 1988).

Here rents created by the state flow to business, because the latter has colonized the former and transformed it into a sort of "executive committee." A business sector composed of strong interest groups may overwhelm the state with its various demands, leading to either policy incoherence or policy indecision. Many analyses of third-world countries emphasize that the state is a relatively recent, and hence weak, addition to the political scene. Strong interest groups may be able to capture control of the state and use the power of the state for their own ends.

Two other possibilities exist. In Cell IV there are numerous interest groups and diffuse power within the state. In this situation, no single group could have too much influence, and the "political market" would come close to clearing. This builds on Susan Rose-Ackerman's notion that "the role of competitive pressures in preventing corruption may be an important aspect of a strategy to deter bribery."[32] When both state and business are weak, rents are all but eliminated. Neither state nor business is powerful enough to take advantage of the other, and so exploitation is difficult. Many of the advanced industrial democracies – at least when compared with less-developed countries (LDCs) – may approximate this situation. As bureaucrats compete with each other to offer policy, thus driving the cost of a bribe toward zero, numerous capitalists also compete with each other for the policy, also driving the price toward zero. In Cell IV, corruption is lowest.

The final and most interesting case is Cell I, where both government and business are equally strong: there is a relatively coherent state but also a small number of powerful interest groups. In this instance, the level of rents is limited and the division relatively equitable. The result is "mutual hostages" in which the state and those powerful groups may collude with one another, but neither has the advantage. Cell I reflects the old saw: "If you owe the bank a little money, the bank owns you. If you owe the bank a lot of money, you own the bank." In this mutual hostage situation, both the political and economic elites are powerful enough to harm the other but are deterred from such actions by the damage that the other side can

---

[32] Susan Rose-Ackerman, "Bribery," in *The New Palgrave Dictionary of Economic Thought*, edited by John Eatwell, Murray Milgate, and Peter Newman (London: Macmillan, 1988), p. 278. See also Christopher Bliss and Ragael Di Tella, "Does Competition Kill Corruption?" *Journal of Political Economy* 105, no. 5 (1997): 1001–1023; and Shleifer and Vishney, "Corruption."

inflict.[33] As will be argued more fully in Chapter 7, this situation reduces transaction costs for both government and business elites.

In Cell I, rents can be had and corruption can occur, but the level of rents is constrained by the power of the other group. Small-N (business concentration) reduces transaction costs, and hence rent seeking, because a small-N eases monitoring and enforcement costs. In this situation, although there are rents to be earned by both business and state, the amount will be less than in the polar cases where one group dominates the other, and more than in the case where both groups are dispersed into a large number of small actors.

In this sense, strategic interaction between state and business corresponds to a prisoner's dilemma. Although in the short run either actor may be better off by defecting and gaining all the rents, the other actor retains the ability to punish defection over time, and thus grudging cooperation may ensue.[34] Cooperation in the strong/strong (Cell I) is not automatic. As in a prisoner's dilemma, both sides are better off defecting and grabbing all the rents for themselves. Indeed, Cell I could lead to a war of attrition, with both sides slugging it out. Even without active cooperation, however, exploitation will be limited by the power of the other side. In the Korean example, we will see that Park initially tried to take advantage of the business sector but then realized he was unable to do so.[35]

Thus the least corruption would occur in situations where both state and business are weak and disorganized, for neither group could take advantage of the other and all the groups would compete against each other, driving the price of corruption close to zero. The most corruption would occur when only one side is coherent, either state or business. A middle position exists when both state and business are strong and can take partial but not total advantage of each other.

3. Measurement

The theoretical concepts in this book are widely accepted and used in the social sciences, even though the difficulty in measuring them is also widely

---

[33] This is based on the idea of bilateral monopoly. See David Kreps, *Microeconomic Theory* (Princeton: Princeton University Press, 1992), pp. 551–573. See also Roger Blair, David Kaserman, and Richard Romano, "A Pedagogical Treatment of Bilateral Monopoly," *Southern Economic Journal* 55, no. 4 (April 1989): 831–841.
[34] Robert Axlerod, *The Evolution of Cooperation* (New York: Basic Books, 1984).
[35] The 1961 "Illicit Wealth Accumulation Act," or *puch'ŏng ch'uk'je an*, is an example of this.

acknowledged.[36] Recognizing this difficulty, in this study I focus on the polar cases in an attempt to lay out the ranges of the variables and test the model's plausibility.

Measuring the dependent variable of corruption and influence peddling is difficult. By their very nature these are acts that their actors wish to keep hidden. Although other scholars have used as evidence polls of perceptions of corruption, traced one pattern of corruption, or relied on corruption scandals, there is no comprehensive indicator of corruption.[37] But a variety of indicators can give us a sense of the size and pattern of corruption.[38] Occasional scandals reveal the pattern of influence. Estimates of campaign spending, kickbacks, and secret funds are useful first approximations. Tracing patronage and cronyism requires deep ethnographic knowledge.

Measuring the independent variables is only marginally easier. To measure the strength of the business sector I focus on a series of indicators, including sectoral concentration, employment, sales, and peak associations. Firms' value added as a proportion of gross domestic product (GDP) gives an indicator of their market and political power, and the

---

[36] See Stephen Krasner's discussion in *Defending the National Interest: Raw Materials Investments and U.S. Foreign Policy* (Princeton: Princeton University Press, 1978), esp. Ch. 1.

[37] Daniel Treisman, for example, uses the Transparency International index of perceived corruption as his measure of actual corruption in "The Causes of Corruption: A Crossnational Study" (MS, UCLA, 1997); Robert Wade traces the sale of office in India in "The Market for Public Office: Why the Indian State is Not Better at Development," *World Development* 13, no. 4 (April 1985): 467–497; and Chalmers Johnson follows the corruption scandals in Japan in "Tanaka Kakuei, Structural Corruption, and the Advent of Machine Politics in Japan," *Journal of Japanese Studies* 12, no. 1 (Winter 1986): 1–28. Other theoretically informed empirical work includes Stephen D. Morris, *Corruption and Politics in Contemporary Mexico* (Tuscaloosa: University of Alabama Press, 1991); Richard Doner and Ansil Ramsey, "Rents, Collective Action, and Economic Development in Thailand," paper prepared for presentation at the conference on "Rents and Development in Southeast Asia," Kuala Lumpur, August 27–28, 1996; Edgar Kiser and Xiaoxi Tong, "Determinants of the Amount and Type of Corruption in State Fiscal Bureaucracies: An Analysis of Late Imperial China," *Comparative Political Studies* 25, no. 3 (October 1992): 300–331; Richard Levy, "Corruption, Economic Crime, and Social Transformation since the Reforms: The Debate in China," *Australian Journal of Chinese Affairs* 95, no. 33 (1994): 1–25; and Andrew Wedeman, "Systemic Change and Corruption in China," paper delivered at the 95th Annual Meeting of the American Political Science Association, Atlanta, GA, September 2–5, 1999.

[38] Paul Hutchcroft, "Obstructive Corruption: The Politics of Privilege in the Philippines," in *Rent-Seeking and Development: Southeast Asia's Political Economies*, edited by K. S. Jomo and Mushtaq Khan (forthcoming); Wayne Sandholtz and William Koetzle, "Accounting for Corruption: Economic Structure, Democratic Norms, and Trade" (MS, UC Irvine, 1998).

19

composition and concentration of their bank loans indicate the firms' vulnerability to the state and other actors. Measuring state strength is necessarily more qualitative. To measure state coherence and low agency costs, I rely mainly on detailed case studies that follow the process of policy making, and I do not attempt to provide a single quantifiable measure for the variables. Case studies can reveal whether leaders act on their parties and domestic politics or whether they respond to them. Process tracing of both policy decisions and institutional origins can reveal whether there is agency slack between leaders and bureaucrats.

III. Conclusion

Korea and the Philippines both had extensive corruption that permeated the normal politics of elections, economic policy making, taxation, and the day-to-day running of the country, and similar institutional structures led to similar patterns of money in both countries. However, Korea and the Philippines had different social organizations and different constraints and incentives that affected their pattern of money politics. Corruption in Korea, although endemic, was constrained by the collusion of a powerful business class and a coherent state. Each major group was able to benefit from its close relationship with the other, but neither could ever gain the upper hand. Despite each group's constant bemoaning of its counterpart's utter lack of qualifications, each needed and relied upon the other. In contrast, corruption in the Philippines swung like a pendulum. As one group or the other gained predominant power, it would busily set about lining its own pockets, aware that in the next round its fortunes might well be reversed.

The key to understanding patterns of money politics is the government-business relationship. Too much power in the hands of either political or economic elites invites abuses in the form of rent seeking and corruption. A balance between elites allows less discretion and less abuse. To explore the abstract propositions presented in this chapter, we now turn to a detailed study of Korea and the Philippines.

2

Comparing Korea and the Philippines

[Martial law] was a liberation – particularly for the business community. . . . it meant an equalization of opportunity, a breaking down of the old bastions of privilege that had kept political power a captive of economic monopolies. . . . Having finally freed ourselves from the stranglehold of the old oligarchy, we must see to it that we neither resurrect it nor replace it with a new oligarchy through a cartelization of economic privilege.

– Ferdinand Marcos

Imagine an Asian country that has enjoyed significant American patronage over the decades. Its people are hardworking and value education and the family. Family ties are so important that scholars and journalists call clans the basic building block of the country, and who one knows matters far more than what one can do. This country has a long history, consisting mostly of being colonized by outside powers. Since World War II, the country has been ruled by a set of elites – quasi dictators and their rich businessmen friends. Within the country its politicians switch parties at the drop of a hat. Party identification means nothing; ideology and programmatic differences are almost absent in elections; political success hinges on personalities, political manipulation, and pork-barrel politics. With episodic regularity, the country's leaders and economic elites have been either arrested or forced into exile because of recurrent corruption scandals. The local press calls corruption "our disease," and one of the most popular topics of conversation in local drinking halls is the utter lack of qualified leadership in both the economic and the political spheres. Privilege is measured by the extent to which one is an exception to the rules. Thousands of this nation's residents emigrate every year to the United States either to study or to live permanently, and the American presence is everywhere – from the style of advertising on television, to popular music, to the latest clothing worn by stylish college girls. The U.S. presence is also ubiquitous at the political and economic levels: the shape and form of the government bears an American imprint, the United States has been by far the most important ally, and for the past fifty years almost nothing has happened without tacit or explicit U.S. consent.

I am writing, of course, about both Korea and the Philippines. Far too often these countries have been considered to be different. The Philippines has been called a "Latin American" country, given its Spanish colonial heritage and large, landed plantations.[1] In many ways the Philippines and Korea are indeed quite different: Korea is ethnically homogenous, Confucian, and geographically peninsular, whereas the Philippines is multiracial, culturally diverse, and a series of islands. Philippine national identity begins at the earliest with the Spanish period; the Koreans can trace an identifiable, distinct political unit back to the unified Silla dynasty of the seventh century.

Yet despite their very real differences, the Philippines and Korea are remarkably similar along many other dimensions – dimensions that are important for the questions I seek to answer in this book. Both countries have been occupied by the Japanese, and both have had U.S. soldiers stationed on their territory after World War II. Since the end of World War II, both the Philippines and Korea have relied heavily upon external finance to fund their economic activity. During the 1960s and 1970s similarities between South Korea and the Philippines continued. Both states were capitalist and authoritarian: Park Chung-hee declared martial law in Korea in October 1972 after closely watching the U.S. reaction to Marcos's declaration of martial law in the Philippines in the previous month.

One easily glosses over similarities and differences among countries, assuming that all LDCs are basically the same. This is certainly not so for Korea and the Philippines, and understanding whether, how, and in what ways they are similar and different has an impact on our understanding of the political and economic trajectories that they have followed. In this chapter I provide an overview of Korea and the Philippines, highlighting the similarities and differences between the two countries. The historical legacy and international threats were different in Korea and the Philip-

---

[1] See, among others, Gretchen Casper, *Fragile Democracies: The Legacies of Authoritarian Rule* (Pittsburgh: University of Pittsburgh Press, 1995); and Walden Bello, David Kinsely, and Elaine Elinson, *Development Debacle: The World Bank in the Philippines* (San Francisco: Institute for Food and Development Policy, 1982), p. 128.

pines, whereas their domestic politics and society – and to some extent their economies – show some surprising similarities.

I. Contrasting Colonial Legacies

Nations do not begin the path to development from the same starting line, and the historical experiences of Korea and the Philippines were different, especially with respect to their colonial legacies.[2] During the past century, Korea and the Philippines were subject to powerful international pressures, and contrasting colonial experiences set the stage for both Korean development and Philippine underdevelopment. The United States had a formative – and opposite – impact on these countries. Whereas in Korea events tended to destroy the old order, in the Philippines they reinforced it. Philippine elites tended to be legitimized by having close relations to the U.S. imperialists. In contrast, Korean elites were delegitimized by their relations with the Japanese colonizers. Thus the U.S. colonization of the Philippines reinforced the existing structures, whereas Japanese colonialism caused Korea's existing political structures to wither away. In terms of the model, the distribution of rights upon independence in the late 1940s was far more fluid in Korea than in the Philippines. Traditional Filipino elites retained power and influence, but in Korea some of those rights exclusively enjoyed by *yangban* (landlords) had begun to dissipate.

A common argument holds that Japanese colonialism set the stage for Korea's subsequent development.[3] Not only did Japanese imperialism effect a profound transformation of the Korean economy *at the time*, but it contributed to Korea's long-term growth.[4] To this impact we must also add the U.S. influence. Korea and the Philippines are the only countries in Asia to bear an American institutional imprint; indeed, both nations

[2] An excellent history of the Philippines is Stanley Karnow, *In Our Image* (New York: Random House, 1989). On Korea, see Bruce Cumings, *Korea's Place in the Sun: A Modern History* (New York: W. W. Norton, 1997).
[3] See Atul Kohli, "Where Do High Growth Political Economies Come From? The Japanese Lineage of Korea's 'Developmental State,'" *World Development* 22, no. 9 (September 1994): 1269–1293; Carter Eckert, *Offspring of Empire: The Koch'ang Kims and the Colonial Origins of Korean Capitalism, 1876–1945* (Seattle: University of Washington Press, 1991); and Dennis McNamara, *Colonial Origins of Korean Enterprise, 1910–1945* (New York: Cambridge University Press, 1990).
[4] For more on this debate, see Stephan Haggard, David Kang, and Chung-in Moon, "Japanese Colonialism and Korean Development: A Critique," *World Development* 27, no. 6 (June 1997): 867–881.

23

have presidential systems modeled on that of the United States. Everything has historical roots – the question is how to distinguish what is general from what is specific. For Korea, a fifteen-year hiatus existed between the end of Japanese colonial rule and the first spurt of growth. Nevertheless, given that Japanese colonialism was followed in rapid-fire succession by three wrenching and significant historical events – World War II, the hostile American occupation, and the peninsular war – the combined impact of Japanese and U.S. influence was transformative in Korea. A largely peasant and rural society with traditional tenancy relations was upended, with massive internal migration and a subsequent loosening of the old order. Korea in 1953 was a nation in which the economic and political playing field had been leveled to a significant degree.[5]

In the Philippines, the contrasting argument that colonialism hindered development is more plausible. The Philippines was a Spanish colony from 1521 to 1898 and a U.S. colony from 1898 to 1946. Spanish colonialism was extractive and repressive, and even the U.S. administration that followed was not profoundly transformative. From the arrival of the Spanish conquistadors in 1521, Filipinos from the age of nineteen to sixty were levied tribute "for the privilege of being royal subjects."[6] The various Catholic orders (Franciscan, Jesuit, Dominican, and Augustinian) had acquired vast haciendas, on which the native Filipinos worked as tenant farmers. By the nineteenth century, these religious orders owned 40 percent of the surface area of Bulacan, Rizal, Cavite, and Laguna.

The late nineteenth century saw Spanish power waning around the globe, and the Filipinos themselves date their independence from June 12, 1898, with the declaration by Emilio Aguinaldo, who would be elected the new nation's first president. The United States had other ideas, however, and declared the Philippines a U.S. colony after Dewey landed in Manila (Table 2.1).

The United States fought an eight-year war of counterinsurgency against the Philippines from 1898 to 1906, killing over two hundred thousand Filipinos. U.S. colonial administration followed. The Japanese invaded in 1941, and General MacArthur's decision in 1944 to free the

---

[5] United States Armed Forces in Korea, *South Korean Interim Government Activities* (Seoul: prepared by the National Economic Board, November–December 1948); and Charles R. Frank Jr., Kwang Suk Kim, and Larry E. Westphal, *Foreign Trade Regimes and Economic Development: South Korea* (New York: Columbia University Press, 1975).

[6] Mariel N. Francisco and Fe Maria C. Arriola, *The History of the Burgis* (Manila: GCF Books, 1997), p. 25.

Comparing Korea and the Philippines

Table 2.1. *Korea and the Philippines: A Chronology*

Korea	Philippines
1398–1910: Choson dynasty	1521–1898: Spanish colony
1910–1945: Japanese colony	June 12, 1898: Declaration of Independence
	1898–1906: U.S. war of suppression
	January 23, 1899: Emilio Aguinaldo inaugurated as first president of the Republic of the Philippines
August 15, 1945: independence and partition into North and South Korea	1898–1946: U.S. colony
1945–1948: U.S. military government in Korea (USAMGIK)	1941–1945: Japanese conquest
1948: independence; Syngman Rhee elected president of 1st Republic	July 4, 1946: independence from the U.S.; Roxas inaugurated as first president of sovereign Philippines
June 25, 1950–1953: Korean War	1948: Roxas outlaws Hukbalahap movement; Quirino sworn in as president after Roxas dies of heart attack
1950–1954: land reform	1953: Ramon Magsaysay elected president
	1954: Luis Taruc surrenders to Aquino, ending Huk insurgency
	1957: Carlos Garcia sworn in as president after Magsaysay dies in plane crash; Garcia reelected
April 19, 1960: student uprising to oust Rhee 1960–1961: 2nd Republic under Chang Myon	1961: Macapagal defeats Garcia
May 16, 1961: coup d'état by Park Chung-hee	1965: Marcos defeats Macapagal in election for president
1963: 3rd Republic: Park elected president	1966: Marcos meets U.S. president Johnson in Manila; agreements include reduction in bases lease from 99 to 25 years
	1968: battalion of engineers to Vietnam
1971: Park barely wins election against Kim Dae-jung	1969: Marcos reelected president
1972–1979: 4th Republic: martial law	September 22, 1972: declaration of martial law

(continued)

Table 2.1. (*continued*)

Korea	Philippines
October 1979: Park assassinated	August 21, 1983: Benigno Aquino returns to Manila, assassinated leaving the plane
December 1979: coup by Chun Doo-hwan; initiates 5th Republic	February 7, 1986: Aquino widely believed to have won election for president against Marcos
1980: Kwangju uprising	February 1986: "People Power" uprising at Edsa
1987: democracy movement ousts Chun; Roh Tae-woo elected president, 6th Republic	February 26, 1986: Marcos leaves for asylum in Hawaii
	1986–1992: Cory Aquino president
	September 1991: U.S. bases lease not renewed by Philippines
1992: Kim Young-sam elected president (first nonmilitary president since 1960)	1992–1998: Fidel Ramos president
December 1997: Korea seeks IMF protection; Kim Dae-jung elected president	May 1998: Joseph Estrada elected president

Philippines led to brutal fighting that devastated much of the islands. On July 4, 1946, the United States granted the Philippines independence, making it the first country to be voluntarily freed by its colonial master.

Filipino leaders have always been caught between the pull of rewards for accommodating the imperial powers and the desire for independence. Even Aguinaldo, the first Philippine president, upon his election in 1898, had picked men for his cabinet who were "distinguished persons," drawn from the upper classes, many of whom just months before had been members of the Spanish Consultative Assembly and against independence. Francisco and Arriola write that "farmers and military officers were useful in the Revolution, he [Aguinaldo] felt, but they were lacking in education and social graces."[7]

The arrival of the Americans did little to transform this pattern of relations. The United States did plant on the Philippines institutions that were American in imprint, notably the educational, political, and legal systems.

[7] Francisco and Arriola, *The History of the Burgis*, p. 71.

And the United States introduced the use of English and encouraged a focus on the West. But in political and economic terms, the Americans did little to transform the existing Philippine power structures. The *ilustrados*, or rich intelligentsia, were conservative elites who had gained power by assimilating to the Spanish ways. These landowners had no interest in implementing reforms that would curb their prerogatives, preferring instead to preserve a feudal system. As Stanley Karnow notes, "American officials, long aware of these inequities, only began to suggest improvements in the 1930s."[8] By then, however, it was too little, too late. The influence of the United States was so pervasive that Filipino elites naturally gravitated to the Americans. And the Americans, from William Taft (the first civilian governor of the Philippines) to General Douglas MacArthur, tended to feel most comfortable with those landed, educated elites who spoke English and had adopted Western practices. From Sergio Osmeña and Manuel Quezon to Ramon Magsaysay and later Marcos and Aquino, Filipino elites either were the virtual creation of their American mentors, or they used their close relations with the United States to preserve their power and privilege. American colonization was pervasive and yet, ultimately, nontransformative.

When the Philippines gained independence in 1946, the existing power structure merely took over the institutions of wealth and power in the new republic, with little potential for transforming property rights and other privileges. In contrast, Korea, in the first half of the twentieth century, did see a profound transformation of its property rights broadly defined. Korea also benefited from a formative U.S. influence that included imposed land reform and aid and funding policies that helped shape economic policy in both the Rhee and Park eras. Thorough land reform was carried out in the early 1950s in Korea, while even in the 1990s countries such as the Philippines have not instituted general and consistent land reform. This transformation of property rights in Korea was critical in helping to set the stage for growth and was originally enforced by the U.S. military government. Land reform is important for a number of reasons. First, land reform increases agricultural productivity. Second, land reform frees up labor, as peasants previously tied to the land in sharecropper arrangements are now free to move to the city. Finally, land reform breaks the power of the landed oligarchy, who traditionally oppose most industrialization policies.

[8] Karnow, *In Our Image*, p. 15.

In Korea, land reform proceeded in two stages. The first stage was administered by the United States Army Military Government in Korea (USAMGIK), and entailed distribution of land previously owned by the Japanese, amounting to 13 percent of South Korea's total farmland.[9] The second stage was undertaken by Syngman Rhee as a means of breaking the power of the local oligarchs. The National Assembly passed a land reform bill on February 2, 1950, that provided landowners with government bonds that could be used to purchase the vested Japanese industries. By 1954, 40 percent of total farmland in Korea was subject to redistribution.[10] Despite its being partial and gradual, South Korean land reform was successful in destroying the centuries-old feudal land-tenure system. This initial act of redefining property rights was central to Korean development.

In stark contrast, land reform has been an abortive issue in the Philippines since before World War II. Breaking the power of the agricultural plantations has proven enormously difficult. Under U.S. colonial administration, land reform was ignored because the Americans were reluctant to upset the existing arrangements, and by 1946 the tenancy rate in the Philippines was *higher* than it had been under the Spaniards.[11] Since independence, privileged elites in the Philippines have been able to successfully resist most attempts to redistribute land and free up tenant farmers. All Philippine presidential candidates since the 1950s have run on platforms offering vague promises of land reform, but attempts to implement reform have never been pursued with vigor. After declaring martial law in 1972, Ferdinand Marcos promised land reform as its centerpiece, although he never pursued such reform either. Mark Thompson writes that "land reform came to a standstill after the first few years of martial law; it had served largely to undermine Marcos' landlord opponents, not to lessen inequality in the countryside."[12] Even the subsequent administrations, from Cory Aquino to Fidel Ramos, failed to push vigorously for land reform. During the Ninth Congress (elected in 1992), twenty-seven members from the agricultural province of Mindanao introduced House Bill (HB) 1967. Claiming that land reform hindered industrial develop-

---

[9] Sang-Chul Yang, *The North and South Korean Political Systems: A Comparative Analysis* (Boulder: Westview Press, 1994), p. 618.

[10] Sang-Chul Yang, *The North and South Korean Political Systems*, p. 619.

[11] Sterling Seagrave, *The Marcos Dynasty* (New York: Harper and Row, 1988), p. 13.

[12] Mark Thompson, *The Anti-Marcos Struggle: Personalistic Rule and Democratic Transition in the Philippines* (Quezon City: New Day Publishers, 1996), p. 57.

ment, HB 1967 suspended the implementation of agrarian reform until the year 2020.[13]

There is an inherent attraction to the argument that the farther back in history one goes, the more fundamental the explanation of the present will be. For better or for worse, the impact of Japan and the United States on Korea during the first half of the century – capped by a peninsular war – upset the old structures, leveled the economic playing field, and weakened or destroyed the traditional social order. As for the Philippines, perhaps the legacy is the path not taken: centuries of colonization did little to transform the political, economic, and social hierarchy in the Philippines.

II. The Role of External Threats

Another difference between Korea and the Philippines was the role of the external threat. Central to my argument is the constraining effect that the international security environment has upon a leader's ability to make a credible commitment to domestic actors. In countries lacking a significant external threat, the leader has less incentive to make a credible commitment, whereas a genuine security threat both increases the leader's incentives to monitor bureaucracies and reduces opportunism by economic actors.[14]

Threats reduce opportunism because domestic policy is nested within the larger context of security concerns.[15] Unless concerned with an external threat, the leader will have little incentive to move from predatory to productive practices, and the leader's actions will be less credible.[16] The leader now must not only retain power but also be prepared to face an

---

[13] Eric Gutierrez, *The Ties that Bind: A Guide to Family, Business, and Other Interests in the Ninth House of Representatives* (Manila: Philippine Center for Investigative Journalism, 1994), p. 40.

[14] O. E. Williamson, "The Institutions and Governance of Economic Development and Reform" (MS, Berkeley, 1992), p. 28.

[15] Virod Aggarwal, *Liberal Protectionism. The International Politics of Organized Textile Trade* (Berkeley: UC Press, 1985). For other scholars who acknowledge the role of threats, see Chalmers Johnson, *MITI and the Japanese Miracle* (Stanford: Stanford University Press, 1982); and Jung-en Woo, *Race to the Swift* (New York: Columbia University Press, 1991), Chs. 3 and 4.

[16] Robert Powell, "Absolute and Relative Gains in International Relations Theory," *The American Political Science Review* 85 (December 1991): 1303–1320; and Duncan Snidal, "Relative Gains and the Pattern of International Cooperation," *American Political Science Review* 85 (September 1991): 701–726.

adversary, and thus the leader's choices are much more constrained. Specifically, economic policies devoted to support-maximization now must be undertaken with an eye to either economic growth or diminishing interdependence, as the state of a nation's economy will have serious consequences for the leader's ability to wage a war.[17] External threats provide the leader with an incentive to support a stronger economy.

For the three decades following independence, the Philippines and South Korea were in radically different geostrategic situations. Whereas the Philippines was the location for massive U.S. military deployments at the Subic and Clark bases, as well as protected by the Pacific Ocean from any realistic attack, South Korea sat uneasily in the shadow of North Korea, China, and the Soviet Union. Such marked contrasts in the level of external threat induced differences in domestic policies in the two countries.

1. No Threat to the Philippines

Postindependence Philippines was ensconced in a cocoon of U.S. protection. This meant that Philippine elites were not forced to make the hard choices and trade-offs necessary for growth, especially when the U.S. commitment provided them with access to largesse and markets. The U.S. provision of a security umbrella, and all the attendant riches that the U.S. bases gave to the Philippines, provided little incentive for *any* Filipino ruler to upset this goose laying the golden egg.[18] After independence, the Philippines remained a virtual colony of the United States, with both positive and negative aspects for the Philippines. On the positive side, the U.S. creation of Clark and Subic bases as the main American naval positions in Asia eliminated virtually any external threat against the Philippines. At the height of its operations, Subic Bay Naval Base was the largest naval support base in the Pacific and the largest naval base in the world outside of the

[17] See Joel Migdal, *Strong Societies and Weak States: State-Society Relations and State Capabilities in the Third World* (Princeton: Princeton University Press, 1988), p. 21; Douglass North, *Structure and Change in Economic History* (New York: Norton, 1981); James Goldgeier and Michael McFaul, "A Tale of Two Worlds: Core and Periphery in the Post-Cold War Era," *International Organization* 46 (Spring 1992): 467–491; and Paul Kennedy, *The Rise and Fall of the Great Powers: Economic Change and Military Conflict from 1500 to 2000* (New York: Random House, 1987), pp. 70–71.

[18] David Wurfel, *Filipino Politics: Development and Decay* (Ithaca: Cornell University Press, 1988), p. 177.

United States. Occupying over thirty-six thousand acres of land, Subic Bay employed up to thirty thousand Philippine workers in 1972.[19] The United States got ninety-nine-year leases on the Subic and Clark military bases; in return, the Philippines received a free trade agreement that ensured it continued access to and dependence on the U.S. market.

On the negative side, the Philippines signed a free trade agreement with the United States (the Bell Act) that allowed significant U.S. corporate presence in the islands. Although the Philippines received considerable aid, the Bell Act also forced the Philippines to make major concessions to the United States on trade and investment in order to receive that aid. Claude Buss notes that "a pound of flesh was the price extracted for American capital."[20] U.S. companies quickly dominated the Philippine market in such diverse sectors as automobiles, power generation, textiles, and consumer goods.

Although an external threat may have been absent in the Philippines, an internal threat to democracy did exist. This threat, from the Huk movement, was largely eliminated by the mid-1950s, after which rather than representing a genuine threat to the Republic it was used more as an excuse for repressive measures. Although the United States and the Philippine elite attempted to label the guerrilla movement a communist infiltration, the reality was that Huk agitation was a result of the long-standing grievances of peasants over their treatment by landlords – a nationalist movement.[21] The benefits of education, opportunity, and wealth remained firmly in the hands of the elites, and the gap between peasant and landlord grew.[22]

The nascent Philippine Republic undertook a campaign to suppress the Huk movement in the 1950s. With the collaboration of the CIA, and with U.S. military aid and advisors, the Philippine government suppressed the Huk rebellion. Ramon Magsaysay, appointed secretary of national defense

[19] U.S. Congress, Senate, Staff Report, Committee on Foreign Relations, *Korea and the Philippines: November 1972*, Committee Print, 93rd Congress, 1st session, February 18, 1973, p. 41.
[20] Claude Buss, *The United States and the Philippines: Background for Policy* (Stanford: Hoover Institution, 1977), p. 21.
[21] Luis Taruc, *Born of the People* (New York: International Publishers, 1953), pp. 26–51.
[22] For a good overview of the origins of the Huks, see U.S. Department of State, Office of Intelligence Research, *The Hukbalahaps*, OIR Report No. 5209, September 27, 1950, cited in *The Philippines Reader: A History of Colonialism, Neocolonialism, Dictatorship, and Resistance*, edited by Daniel Schirmer and Stephen Rosskamm Shalom (Boston: South End Press, 1987), p. 118.

in 1950, was put in charge of the suppression movement.[23] Magsaysay emphasized the political as well as the military aspect of the Huk suppression: he forced his soldiers to befriend the peasants in the field, and he offered land and a new life to those peasants who would surrender. Magsaysay also reorganized the Department of Defense, purged the army of its worst leaders, and attempted to clean up the election process. Under his leadership, the Huk movement was largely subdued.

Although by the late 1950s the Huks were silenced, another, more obviously pro-Communist movement grew up in its stead. The New People's Army (NPA), formed by Jose Maria Sison in the late 1960s, began organizing small groups of workers and students around nationalist, economic, and political issues. Inequities between the United States and the Philippines, the war in Vietnam and the Cultural Revolution in China, and the continuing inequity in landownership all combined to keep alive a small guerrilla movement. Even here, however, the perception of instability was worse than the reality. By 1967 there were fewer than 170 communist guerrillas in the entire country.[24] In 1972 the Communist Party of the Philippines (CPP) had only two thousand members, and the NPA was almost nonexistent.[25] Indeed "amateurish attempts to adopt Chinese and Vietnamese communist tactics ended in demoralizing failures."[26] Just two days before the declaration of martial law on September 22, 1972, the executive session of the Philippine National Security Council had been briefed on internal security. "Security conditions were reportedly described at that meeting as between 'normal' and 'Internal Defense Condition No. 1' (the worst or most unstable security condition is No. 3)."[27]

Rhetoric mattered more than reality, however, and for Marcos the "communist" insurgency was more than a minor irritant; it was also a convenient excuse for martial law and repression. In 1972, Marcos was able to restrict the news media on the grounds of communist subversion of the press, and although the press did have a nationalistic (and sometimes

---

[23] Stephen R. Shalom, "Counter-Insurgency in the Philippines," *Journal of Contemporary Asia* 7, no. 2 (1977): 153–172.

[24] Figure taken from William H. Overholt, "The Rise and Fall of Ferdinand Marcos," *Asian Survey* 26, no. 11 (November 1986): 1137–1163. Even by 1972 there were only 800 guerrillas, according to an interview with the chief of staff of the Armed Forces of the Philippines (p. 1140). Gregg Jones puts the number at 300 in 1972. See Gregg R. Jones, *Red Revolution: Inside the Philippine Guerrilla Movement* (Boulder: Westview Press, 1989), p. 45.

[25] For a fascinating account of the guerrilla movement, see Jones, *Red Revolution*.

[26] Jones, *Red Revolution*, p. 6.

[27] Senate, Staff Report Committee on Foreign Relations, *Korea and the Philippines*, p. 2.

Marxist) bent, there was no real danger of creeping communism in the media.[28] The United States also knew that in the late 1960s the threat was nonexistent. An exchange at a U.S. congressional hearing is revealing:

> *Senator Symington*: What is the capacity of the Red Chinese today in the Pacific to menace the Philippines from a military standpoint?
> *Admiral Kauffman*: I would say at the moment, sir, very small.
> *Senator Symington*: What you . . . are actually saying, militarily speaking, is that there is no threat to the Philippines, are you not? . . . The truth of the matter is that the principal threat to the Government of the Philippines comes from the Filipinos who do not agree with the Government in the Philippines, is that not a fair statement?
> *Admiral Kauffman*: I am loath to give a positive yes on that, sir, because it implies that I am seriously worried about the internal threat, and I am not.[29]

In fact, the Philippine government staged a series of incidents that were used to justify martial law. For example:

Government soldiers shot the empty white Mercedes Benz of Minister of Defense Enrile full of holes, and the government announced that communist guerrillas had attempted to assassinate the Defense Minister. Under orders, a sergeant from the Firearms and Explosives unit of the Philippine Constabulary blew up a series of minor power pylons and other targets around Manila, and the government announced that communist guerrillas were threatening the security of Manila itself. Using such threats to justify his policy, Marcos declared martial law in 1972.[30]

The United States was fully aware that it was guaranteeing Marcos's survival. As Senator Fulbright said in 1969, "[I]s it not inevitable that . . . we would always use our influence for the preservation of the status quo? We will always resist any serious change in political and social structure of the Philippine government."[31]

---

[28] David A. Rosenberg, "Liberty versus Loyalty: The Transformation of the Philippine News Media under Martial Law," in *Marcos and Martial Law in the Philippines*, edited by David A. Rosenberg (Ithaca: Cornell University Press, 1979).

[29] U.S. Congress, Senate, Committee on Foreign Relations, Subcommittee on United States Security Agreements and Commitments Abroad, *United States Security Agreements and Commitments Abroad: The Republic of the Philippines* (September–October 1969), pp. 60–61, 67–68.

[30] Overholt, "The Rise and Fall," p. 1141.

[31] From Senate, Committee on Foreign Relations, Subcommittee on United States Security Agreements and Commitments Abroad, *United States Security Agreements and Commitments Abroad*, p. 69.

Since independence, no external threat has forced Philippine leaders to make difficult choices. Nor were internal threats a major concern or U.S. support likely to be withdrawn. This lack of external threat allowed Philippine elites to be concerned only with an internal agenda aimed at maximizing U.S. aid. Under these circumstances, the impetus to make policy directed toward development was absent, and the status quo was rarely threatened. Entrenched elites were able to sabotage reform, and what minimal international pressures were placed on the Philippines never became linked to efficiency.

2. Severe External Threat to South Korea

In contrast to the Philippines, Korea did face a serious external threat, which induced Koreans to focus on industrial "national champions" and on maintaining positive military and economic ties to the United States Into the 1980s South Korea depended on extensive U.S. support, and yet the U.S. commitment to the South fluctuated over time. This weak commitment by the United States to the defense of South Korea forced Syngman Rhee and Park Chung-hee to envision two possible worlds, one in which the United States was committed to South Korea and one in which the United States was absent from the peninsula. Such uncertainty gave the South Korean state the incentive to develop domestic capacities for both economic production and fighting wars, induced compliance within the populace, and justified any number of repressive measures designed to provide security.

Into the mid-1970s the North Korean economy was performing at a level similar to that in the South on a per capita GNP basis (Table 2.2). In absolute size, the GNP of North Korea grew more rapidly than that of the South until 1960, and even in 1975 it remained at almost half the size of that of the South. More important than the objective size of the economy, however, was the perceived North Korean threat.[32] After 1950 North Korea seriously hoped to invade the South; tensions remained high along the De-Militarized Zone (DMZ) for decades. In 1968 the North captured the U.S. ship *Pueblo* and held its crew hostage. In that same year a suicide commando group from North Korea attempted to assassinate Park Chung-hee at the Blue House, South Korea's presidential mansion.

[32] David C. Kang, "Rethinking North Korea," *Asian Survey* 35, no. 3 (March 1995): 253–267.

Table 2.2. *Comparison of GNP and Per Capita GNP,*
North and South Korea (billions of U.S. dollars)

Year	GNP		Per Capita GNP	
	North	South	North	South
1953	0.44	1.35	58	76
1960	1.52	1.95	137	94
1970	3.98	7.99	286	248
1975	9.35	20.85	579	591
1980	13.5	60.3	758	1,589
1985	15.14	83.4	765	2,047
1990	23.1	237.9	1,064	5,569

Source: *Vantage Point* 18, no. 3 (March 1994): 18.

The North had modernized its military and had accepted military and economic aid from both China and the Soviet Union.[33] Incidents along the DMZ reached a peak during the mid-1960s, further increasing South Korean fears that the North was planning some preemptive move against the South (Table 2.3).[34]

Despite the perceived threat against the South from North Korea, the United States has never been comfortable with its own military presence on the peninsula. This basic fact has been one of the root causes of South Korean fears, and it has changed the South's perception of the nature of the North Korean threat. In 1948 the United States had withdrawn its troops except for a small Korean Military Advisory Group (KMAG) and did not consider South Korea to be a significant ally. American decision makers argued that the United States had "little strategic interest in Korea, or maintaining troops or bases in Korea . . . and the Soviet threat is not

[33] For works on North Korea, see Peter Hayes, *Pacific Powderkeg: American Nuclear Dilemmas in Korea* (Lexington, MA: Lexington Books, 1990). For other excellent works, see Dae-sook Suh, *Kim Il-Sung, the North Korean Leader* (New York: Columbia University Press, 1988); Kong-dan Oh, *North Korea in the 1990s: Implications for the Future of the U.S.-South Korea Security Alliance* (Santa Monica: RAND note N-3480-A, 1992); and Robert Scalapino and Chong-sik Lee, *Communism in Korea*, 2 vols. (Berkeley: University of California Press, 1972).

[34] An excellent discussion of consistent border incidents is found in *UNCURK, Report 1970* (25th session, supplement 26). Cited in Jong-chung Back, *Korean Reunification: Conflict and Security* (Seoul: Research Center for Peace and Unification of Korea, 1988), p. 182.

Table 2.3. *North Korean Military Activity, 1965–1970*

Incident	1965	1966	1967	1968	1969	1970
DMZ	42	37	445	486	87	66
ROK	17	13	121	143	24	47
Exchange of fire in the DMZ	23	19	122	236	55	42
Exchange of fire in the ROK	6	11	96	120	22	26
TOTAL INCIDENTS	88	80	784	985	188	181
Casualties						
North Koreans killed in the ROK	4	18	228	321	55	46
North Koreans captured in the ROK	51	21	57	13	6	3
UN military personnel killed in the ROK	21	35	131	162	15	9
UN military personnel wounded in the ROK	6	29	294	294	44	22
ROK police and civilians killed	19	4	22	35	19	7
ROK police and civilians wounded	15	5	53	16	17	17
TOTAL CASUALTIES	116	112	785	841	156	104

Source: UNCURK, *Report 1970* (25th session, supplement 26). Cited in Jong-chung Back, *Korean Reunification: Conflict and Security* (Seoul: Research Center for Peace and Unification of Korea, 1988), p. 182.

immediately serious."[35] Yet the outbreak of the Korean War forced the United States to decide whether or not to fight a "monolithic communist menace," and by 1953, the United States was entangled in defending South Korea as part of broader U.S. geopolitical interests. Korea thus became the proving ground for the U.S. policy of communist containment, and this switch by the United States had more to do with its decision to "contain and eventually roll back" communism across the globe than with any inherent desire to protect South Korea.

[35] U.S. Department of State, RG 59, box #7394, 895.01/2-2547, "Memorandum for the Secretary of State and the Secretary of War," p. III-A, cited in Yeonmi Ahn, "The Political Economy of Foreign Aid: The Nature of American Aid and Its Impact on the State-Business Relationship in South Korea" (Ph.D. diss., Yale University, 1992), p. 66.

Because the United States defended Korea for broad geopolitical reasons, Korean leaders were always acutely aware that the U.S. commitment to Korean defense could change at any time. Even in 1972, the United States was asking: "Should we wish to be automatically involved in another Korean War were it to break out?"[36] For South Korean leaders the worst-case scenario was the total withdrawal of U.S. troops from the peninsula, and they planned accordingly.

In the mid-1950s Rhee had the advantage of a relatively clear and stable U.S. commitment, and this provided him with an international setting different from, and less threatening than, the setting within which Park Chung-hee was to rule after him. As Jung-en Woo writes, "Once the Korean war was over, with the United States unequivocally committed in Korea, Rhee switched from obsequiousness to recalcitrance."[37] Rhee's unwillingness to increase taxes and reduce government spending created conflicts with the Americans. A U.S.-ICA evaluation in early 1958 shows the depth of the U.S. commitment: "From the point of view of the United States, we have no alternative to continuing to work with Syngman Rhee. There are many things about Rhee's regime that can be criticized but no one can impugn his patriotism or his anti-Communism. As already indicated, the United States has a big stake in Korea. It is therefore to our advantage not to withdraw our support from Rhee's government . . ."[38]

In addition, in the early postwar era, the United States aim was to build up Korea from a military perspective rather than an economic one. A 1955 International Cooperation Administration (ICA) study put it well:

Because of world conditions following the armistice in Korea, the decision was made in favor of a rapid buildup of ROK [Republic of Korea] military strength instead of rapid reconstruction. The ensuing strain on the ROK economy necessitated an increase in saleable commodity imports, to generate local currency counterpart funds for defense support, at the expense of capital investment projects.[39]

[36] Senate, Staff Report, Committee on Foreign Relations, *Korea and the Philippines*, p. 47.
[37] Woo, *Race to the Swift*, p. 52.
[38] U.S.-ICA Evaluation of Korea Program, April 1958. Quoted in David Satterwhite, "The Politics of Economic Development: Coup, State, and the Republic of Korea's First Five-Year Economic Development Plan (1962–1966)" (Ph.D. diss., University of Washington, 1994), p. 217.
[39] International Cooperation Administration, Non-Military Section of the Mutual Security Program, Far East, FY 1957 Budget Bureau Presentation: Korea, November 10, 1955, "Narrative Statement," p. VI-5. Quoted in Satterwhite, "The Politics of Economic Development," p. 240.

By the late 1950s, however, the situation had begun to change. The North was recovering faster than, and beginning to pose a genuine threat to, the South. North Korean leader Kim Il-sung, who had survived the devastation of the war and had purged his rivals, was calling for armed overthrow in the South. By then, too, the United States had grown weary of South Korea's halting efforts at development and planned to reduce economic assistance. Woo notes that American economic advisors referred to South Korea as a "rat hole" and a "bottomless pit" and had begun to search for ways to influence South Korea other than through aid.[40]

Whereas Rhee had been the beneficiary of a stable though grudging U.S. commitment, by the time Park Chung-hee took power, through a coup on May 16, 1961, the geopolitical situation in Asia was changing. The attention of the United States was increasingly diverted to Southeast Asia and the conflict in Vietnam, and thus Park had to be more concerned than had Rhee with an external threat. One of Park's most important moves was the dispatch of South Korean troops to Vietnam. In the early 1960s, U.S. officials had considered transferring the Seventh and Second Divisions from Korea to Vietnam if more troops were needed. Thus the deployment of two Korean divisions solved both the American problem of reinforcement in Vietnam and the Korean problem of keeping U.S. troops in Korea.

Eventually, forty-eight thousand South Korean troops were based in Vietnam, the "White Horse" and "Tiger" divisions. The Americans agreed that if South Korea were to contribute more troops to Vietnam, the United States would not withdraw any of its own troops from Korea without consultation. In addition, the U.S. Agency for International Development (USAID) would provide $150 million specifically for Korean economic development, and the United States would pay the cost of basing the South Korean troops in Vietnam.[41] Additionally, any South Korean goods sent to Vietnam in support of the troops would be paid for by the United States and considered South Korean exports to Vietnam. Thus in 1966, 80 percent of all Korean earnings in Vietnam returned to Korea. Similarly, Korea's exports to Vietnam were $36 million, or 8 percent of its total exports.[42] According to Sungjoo Han, between 1965 and 1969 total Korean

[40] Woo, *Race to the Swift*, p. 46.
[41] Kim, Se-jin, "South Korea's Involvement in Vietnam and Its Economic and Political Impact," *Asian Survey* 10, no. 6 (1970): 519–532.
[42] *Chungang Ilbo*, November 11, 1969; *Donga Ilbo*, September 17, 1968.

earnings from South Korea's involvement in Vietnam were $546 million, 16 percent of its total foreign receipts for that period, and its financial gains from 1965 to 1973 were estimated at $1 billion.[43] Such gains were crucial in helping South Korea meet the goals of the Second Five-Year Plan of 1967–1971.

Park never felt completely comfortable relying on a tepid U.S. commitment to Korea's defense, and yet his need to rely on the U.S. persisted. By the late 1960s, it had become clear that the United States was no longer willing to subsidize the Korean economy to the same level as it had under Rhee, and, as the United States withdrew almost half its military forces under the "Nixon shock" of 1969, the Park regime was forced to cast about for new directions. Two facts became increasingly apparent to Park. First, the U.S. commitment to Korea's defense was waning. The days of a "free ride" were over for South Korea, and the long-expected U.S. pullout had begun. Second, South Korea needed to upgrade its indigenous defense capabilities, both industrial and military. As Park said in a New Year's speech in 1970: "The forthcoming seventies will become one crucial era of our country's national security . . . we must at least prepare ourselves to deter and annihilate by our own capacity an independent military aggression by the North. We should also modernize our military equipment . . . and promote defense industries . . . Today, we can hardly think of national security and war without a basis in economic power."[44]

For Park, the lessons of the Vietnam War and the reduction of troops were clear. First, South Korea's security could no longer be entrusted principally to the United States. Its security ties to the United States had served as a deterrent in the past, but a strengthened and modernized South Korean army was now an imperative if the nation's long-term security was to be assured. Second, Park believed that South Vietnam would not have collapsed, even in the face of an American retreat, had the Thieu regime succeeded in building a cohesive domestic political and economic base.[45] The Korean focus on heavy industry and chemical manufacturing in the 1970s was largely a result of Park's perception of the deteriorating international situation.[46]

---

[43] Sungjoo Han, "South Korea's Participation in the Vietnam Conflict," *Orbis* (1978): 898.

[44] Park Chung-hee, "New Year's Presidential Press Conference," January 9, 1970.

[45] *Washington Post*, May 31, 1969, p. 4.

[46] Jung-ho Yoo, "The Industrial Policy of the 1970s and the Evolution of the Manufacturing Sector in Korea" (Seoul: Korea Development Institute, KDI Working Paper No. 90–17, October 1990).

The international situations in which the Philippines and Korea found themselves throughout their early existences were almost polar opposites. Korea faced an intense security threat from the North and relied heavily on the United States to deter Northern aggression against it. In contrast, the Philippines had no identifiable external threat, and the internal threat was largely marginal. These conditions had consequences for domestic economic policy, with Korea focusing on national champions and heavy industry, whereas in the Philippines economic policy was not closely tied to national defense and survival.

III. Economic Performance

For the Philippines and South Korea, the differences in initial conditions, the historical legacies, and the roles of external threats are clear, as is the difference in economic outcomes. By 1980, South Korea had become a truly impressive success story, whereas the Philippines remained a developmental laggard. However, when we examine the economic story more closely, we find that this disparity has not been constant and is relatively recent. In 1955, the Philippines had a gross national product (GNP) of $4.7 billion (U.S. dollars), whereas Korea's GNP was only $2.3 billion; moreover, on a per capita basis the Philippines was roughly twice as rich as Korea. By the early 1980s, the situation had changed dramatically. Korea was considered a model of development, whereas the Philippines was widely regarded as a political and economic failure. By 1985, South Korea's per capita GNP was approaching $2,200; the Philippines lagged far behind, at $599. Table 2.4 compares the basic economic performance of the two countries. What is notable is that both Filipino per capita and absolute GNP remained higher than Korea's into the late 1960s. It was only in the 1970s that Korea began to quickly outdistance the Philippines.

To these compelling numbers may be added an additional measure: per capita income as a percentage of that in the United States. One of the goals of development is, after all, to begin catching up with the already high-income economies in the West. Figure 2.1 uses the United States as a reference point, and we see that although the Philippines began the last half of the twentieth century with a marginal edge over South Korea, by the early 1970s South Korea's per capita income had drawn level with that in the Philippines and afterward had accelerated even more sharply in narrowing the gap with the United States.

Table 2.4. *Comparative Economic Performance: Korea and the Philippines (GNP in billions of U.S. dollars at current exchange rates; population in millions)*

	1955	1965	1975	1985	Avg. Annual Growth Rate 1955–1975	Avg. Annual Growth Rate 1975–1985
Korea						
GNP	2.3	3.0	20.9	88.8	11.7	15.6
Population	21.5	28.3	35.3	41.2	2.5	1.5
GNP/capita	107	106	590	2,155	8.9	13.8
Philippines						
GNP	4.7	5.9	15.9	32.6	6.2	7.5
Population	23.6	31.8	42.0	54.4	2.9	4.8
GNP/capita	199	188	375	599	3.2	4.8

Source: IMF, *International Financial Statistics* (Washington, DC: International Monetary Fund, various years).

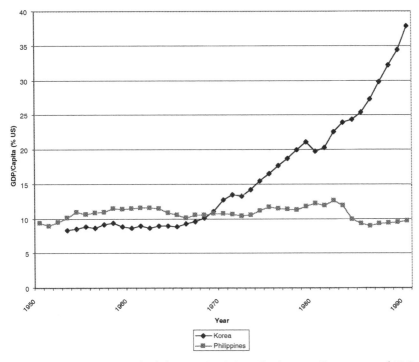

Figure 2.1. Korean and Philippine GDP Per Capita as a Percentage of U.S. GDP Per Capita (1951–1990). *Source*: Penn World Tables, http://www.nber.org

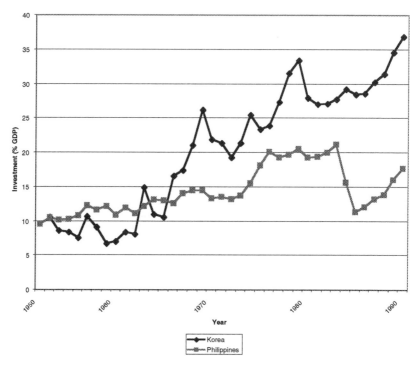

Figure 2.2. Real Investment as a Percentage of GDP. *Source*: Penn World Tables, http://www.nber.org

1. Investment and U.S. Aid

Figure 2.2 shows that real investment as a percentage of GDP was far greater in South Korea than in the Philippines. Although investment in both countries during the 1950s hovered in the single digits, by the late 1960s South Korea was investing almost 20 percent of its GDP, whereas the Philippines was mired in the low teens.

As Jonathan Temple notes, however, "[T]his does not get us very far. It merely pushes the demanding question down a rung, from explaining growth to explaining investment."[47] In the case of Korea, the underlying source of investment was U.S. aid and international borrowing. Table 2.5

---

[47] Jonathan Temple, "The New Growth Evidence," *Journal of Economic Literature* 37 (March 1999), p. 121. See also Robert Barro, *Determinants of Economic Growth: A Cross-Country Empirical Study* (Cambridge, MA: MIT Press, 1997).

Comparing Korea and the Philippines

Table 2.5. *U.S. Aid Received, Various Countries, 1946–1980 (in millions of U.S. dollars)*

	Postwar Relief Period (1946–1948)	Marshall Plan (1949–1952)	Mutual Security Act (1953–1961)	Foreign Assistance Act (1962–1980)	Total Less Repayments and Interest (1946–1980)
Vietnam			2,197.4	21,811.4	22,873.5
Israel		86.5	508.0	17,881.3	15,781.5
South Korea	181.2	498.1	4,364.1	8,681.6	12,738.5
Taiwan	643.7	743.1	3,039.0	2,205.2	5,820.0
Philippines	329.3	712.5	499.9	1,658.0	2,822.6
Indonesia	67.7	111.6	270.1	2,815.4	2,687.7
Brazil	19.9	32.3	520.9	2,642.4	2,287.0
Thailand	6.2	104.1	570.4	1,797.6	2,262.7
Colombia	1.8	5.0	156.7	1,563.6	1,188.0
Chile	4.0	8.9	235.0	1,187.7	944.2
Peru	7.5	8.6	175.0	754.0	706.5
Kenya			7.2	390.7	355.0
Liberia	7.5	2.3	31.5	301.6	303.6
Mexico	42.6	51.3	44.1	220.3	241.0
Argentina			55.5	447.9	185.6
Malaysia			23.3	215.0	120.8
Saudi Arabia	4.3	0.4	99.9	223.7	66.8

Source: Office of Planning and Budgeting, Bureau for Program and Policy Coordination, U.S. Agency for International Development, *U.S. Overseas Loans and Grants and Assistance from International Organizations, July 1, 1945–September 30, 1980* (Washington, DC: U.S. Government Printing Office, 1981).

shows that Korea and the Philippines both were among the five highest recipients of U.S. aid from 1946 to 1980. The others were Vietnam, Israel, and Taiwan. However, over the period in question, Korea received almost six times as much aid as the Philippines. All the major recipients were of geostrategic importance to the United States, and it is no surprise that Vietnam and Israel did comparatively less with their windfall than did Korea or Taiwan. Both Israel and Vietnam endured almost constant conflict during this time, and countries fighting wars tend to concentrate on day-to-day survival rather than on designing long-term development strategies. On a per capita basis, Taiwan's aid levels were similar to that received by Korea.

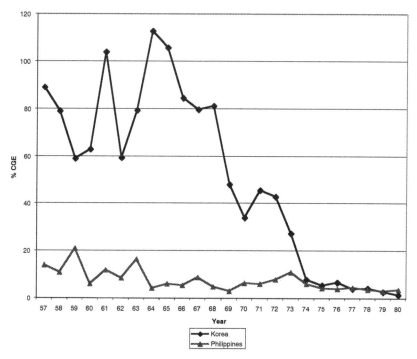

Figure 2.3. U.S. Aid as a Percentage of Central Government Expenditure (CGE) in Korea and the Philippines, 1957–1980. *Sources*: Office of Planning and Budgeting, Bureau for Program and Policy Coordination, U.S. Agency for International Development, *U.S. Overseas Loans and Grants and Assistance from International Organizations, July 1, 1945–September 30, 1980* (Washington, DC: U.S. Government Printing Office, various years), and IMF, *International Financial Statistics Yearbook*, various years. Chart is patterned after John Linantud, "Backs against the Wall? The Impact of Foreign Threat on Dictatorship and Democracy in Philippines, South Korea, and Thailand, 1950–95," paper presented at the annual meeting of the American Political Science Association, September 2, 1999.

The amount of aid for Korea contrasts even more sharply with that given the Latin American countries. For example, from 1946 to 1980 Korea received over $12 billion in U.S. aid, whereas Mexico received only $241 million.

Even more indicative of the differences between Korea and the Philippines is the ratio of U.S. aid to central government expenditures. Figure 2.3 shows Korea and the Philippines from 1957 to 1980. To answer Jonathan Temple's challenge, whereas Korea at times received over

Table 2.6. *Growth Effect of Foreign Capital (percentage)*

	1962–1966	1967–1971	1972–1976	1977–1982	Average over 1962–1982
GNP growth rate (A)	7.9	9.7	10.2	5.6	8.2
Incremental Capital-Output Ratio (ICOR)	2.3	3.1	3.4	5.0	3.4
GNP growth rate without savings (B)	3.8	4.9	6.9	4.1	4.9
Growth effect of foreign capital (A – B)	4.1	4.8	3.3	1.5	3.3

Source: Yoon-je Cho and Joon-kyung Kim, *Credit Policies and the Industrialization of Korea* (Seoul: KDI, 1997), p. 103.

100 percent of its central government expenditures as aid, ratios for the Philippines remained small, typically under 20 percent. Given these levels of U.S. involvement, it is no surprise that Korea grew faster than the Philippines.

The Korean advantage in accruing external financing continued for its foreign borrowing. A study by the Korea Development Institute estimates that foreign capital was responsible for over forty percent of Korean growth from 1962 to 1982 (Table 2.6). Cho and Kim write that "Korea would not have been successful otherwise: its highly repressive financial policy . . . limited the mobilization of domestic resources, and Korea would have experienced slower economic growth."[48] Table 2.6 also estimates the amount of investment required for an additional unit of output (the "incremental capital-output ratio," or ICOR), and shows that the ICOR grew steadily over time, indicating that Korean productivity decreased over time.

One widely cited explanation for Korea's growth, a high savings rate, does not appear to have been significant. In fact, savings in Korea and the

---

[48] Yoon-Je Cho and Joon-Kyung Kim, *Credit Policies and the Industrialization of Korea* (Seoul: KDI, 1997), p. 13.

Table 2.7. *Savings as a Percentage of Gross Domestic Product (average annual percentage)*

	1960–1964	1965–1969	1970–1974	1975–1979	1980–1984
Korea	4.1	11.8	18.2	25.3	25.2
Philippines	15.3	15.4	21.5	24.7	21.8

Source: IMF, *International Financial Statistics*, various years.

Philippines were similar until the late 1960s, and it appears that rather than causing high growth, a high savings rate was the result of higher income in Korea. An American assessment of the economic situation in Korea in 1972 noted the low savings rate compared with that in other developing countries.[49]

The savings situations are more similar than different, however. In South Korea a high savings rate appears to follow, rather than lead, rapid increases in GDP. This is what one would expect according to basic economic reasoning. In general, poorer families tend not to save, and only as income rises do individuals begin to save and invest. In Korea, savings clearly accelerate *after* the onset of high growth. Table 2.7 shows that the savings rate in Philippines has consistently been either higher than or roughly equivalent to that in South Korea.

2. Agriculture and Exports

Some scholars have argued that Korea caught up so quickly with the Philippines because agriculture played a far larger role in the Philippine political economy than in Korea's.[50] They argue that nations like the Philippines, with abundant natural resources, have less incentive to develop manufacturing and industrial bases than nations such as Korea, which lack natural resources. Rent seeking and corruption will be higher in the resource-abundant nation because there is a larger "pie" to

[49] Senate, Staff Report, Committee on Foreign Relations, *Korea and the Philippines*, p. 16.
[50] Jeffrey Sachs and Andrew Warner, "Natural Resource Abundance and Economic Growth," Development Discussion Paper 517a (Cambridge, MA: Harvard Institute for International Development, 1995).

Table 2.8. *Origins of GNP for Korea and the Philippines*
(average annual percentage)

	1960	1965	1970	1975	1980
Korea					
Agriculture	46	44	33	29	20
Manufacturing	17	21	25	31	35
Services	36	34	42	40	45
Philippines					
Agriculture	29	30	32	33	28
Manufacturing	24	23	26	29	29
Services	46	50	42	38	43

Source: United Nations Statistical Yearbook, various years.

divide up initially and because the incentive to create wealth through manufacturing is less pressing. Although this argument is plausible, it does not explain the slower economic growth in the Philippines than in Korea.

Table 2.8 shows the sectoral distribution of GNP for Korea and the Philippines. Note that in 1960 the Philippines was *more* industrialized than was Korea. In fact, agriculture remained a larger share of Korea's GNP until 1975, or after Korea had come to be considered a "successful case of development." In contrast, manufacturing's share in the Philippines was higher than in Korea until 1975.

Thus in relative terms the Philippines was as industrialized as Korea, although overall economic growth was far higher in Korea from 1960 on. Perhaps the important factor was agricultural exports and less so the makeup of gross domestic product. Here differences between the two countries do exist (Table 2.9). In South Korea, agriculture accounted for 12 percent of exports in 1952, whereas in the Philippines agriculture was 38 percent of exports in 1949. However, in 1960 agriculture made up 30 percent of Korean exports, before dropping to under 9 percent in 1975. In contrast, agriculture remained over 20 percent of Philippine exports until 1980. Thus Korea has relied less on agriculture than has the Philippines in its export drive, although the differences are not as dramatic as generally believed.

Table 2.9. *Korean and Philippine Exports by Sector*
(as percentage of total exports)

	Agriculture		Manufacturing	
	Korea	Philippines	Korea	Philippines
1949	12.1*	38	6.7*	3.2
1955	5.6	34.9	17.6	7.7
1960	30.4	33	19.8	10.9
1965	16.1	26	62.6	19.2
1970	7.8	26	80.1	19.8
1975	8.9	22.9	89.7	62.5
1980	5.3	11.2	94.2	70.8
*1952				

Source: IMF, *International Trade Statistics Yearbook* (Washington, DC: International Monetary Fund, various years).

Manufacturing in South Korea, however, grew from 17 percent of exports in 1955 to 80 percent of exports by 1970, whereas in the Philippines manufacturing was 7 percent of exports in 1955 and 19 percent of exports in 1970. Surprisingly, manufactures from the Philippines soared after 1970, to 70 percent of exports by 1980.

Another economic difference between South Korea and the Philippines is the size of exports in each economy. Scholars from both the free market school and in the statist school have argued that a single-minded focus on exports has fueled growth in Korea and in the other high-growth Asian economies. Yet, as Figure 2.4 shows, exports in the Philippines were also fairly large – larger, in fact, than exports in another "success story," Brazil.

3. Economic Policies

Although I will discuss these policies in detail in later chapters, here I provide a brief overview of the economic policies pursued after independence in both Korea and the Philippines. Although Korea followed a trade policy of import substitution in the 1950s, it had, by the mid-1960s, begun to orient its trade policies toward export-oriented industrialization (EOI). Korea also maintained high import barriers and heavily restricted direct foreign investment. The Park regime's financial policies directed lending to favored firms through a complex mix of investment incentives and

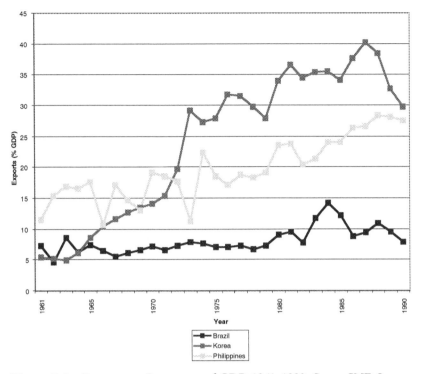

Figure 2.4. Exports as a Percentage of GDP, 1961–1990. *Source*: IMF, *International Financial Statistics, Yearbook*, various years

government guarantees over foreign loans.[51] Regulatory policies in Korea were poorly enforced and contradictory, creating opportunities for influence peddling.

The Philippines, in contrast, could never implement coherent and systematic policy reforms. Throughout the postindependence era, the Philippine banking system remained subject to manipulation and mismanagement.[52] Government-directed lending, although a goal under most presidents, was inconsistent. In trade, the Philippines – for reasons to be discussed later – pursued an import-substitution policy. Foreign direct

[51] For overviews of economic policies in Korea, see Stephan Haggard, *Pathways from the Periphery* (Ithaca: Cornell University Press, 1990), and Peter Evans, *Embedded Autonomy* (Princeton: Princeton University Press, 1995).

[52] Paul Hutchcroft, *Booty Capitalism: The Politics of Banking in the Philippines* (Ithaca: Cornell University Press, 1998).

investment, mainly by U.S. and Japanese firms, was extensive. The economy was a mix of selectively implemented and contradictory regulatory policies.

Thus, there have been some notable differences between Korea and the Philippines, particularly in the realms of investment, trade policies, and foreign aid. Still, much of the conventional wisdom does not stand up to scrutiny: savings rates, agricultural shares of GDP, exports, and manufacturing exports all appear more similar than different in Korea and the Philippines over the period in question. The overriding difference is in investment. When we turn our attention to politics and society, the similarities are even more pronounced.

IV. Politics and Society

Korea and the Philippines have similar domestic politics and societies. Postindependence Philippine history consists of three main periods. The first, democratic, period, lasted from 1946 to 1972. The two main political parties in Filipino politics were the Nacionalistas and the Liberals. They traded power, and elections during this period – although marred by sporadic violence and vote buying – were considered legitimate. Ferdinand Marcos's declaration of martial law in 1972 ushered in the next, darker, phase of Philippine history. Having ransacked the nation, Marcos left office only in 1986 when the famous "People Power" movement and resulting loss of U.S. support left him vulnerable. In the third period, from 1986 to the present, the Republic of the Philippines has moved slowly but steadily toward a genuine democracy with fair elections and increasingly stable legal and political institutions.

In contrast to the Philippines, Korea has a long history as a nation. The Unified Silla dynasty (666–932) united the peninsula's three separate kingdoms. The Choson dynasty (1398–1910) fell into decay, and Korea withdrew into itself. In 1910, Japan formally colonized Korea, relinquishing its hold only in 1945.

Constant conflict bordering on chaos has marked Korea's postindependence history. Far from having a consensual social structure, Korea seems to be eternally at the boiling point. Since 1948, the first president to leave office voluntarily and without facing massive uprisings was Roh Tae-woo in 1992. Syngman Rhee was ousted in student uprisings in 1960, Chang Myon was evicted from office by a coup d'état in 1961, Park Chung-hee was assassinated by his CIA head in 1979, and Chun Doo-hwan left office after massive uprisings in 1987. In addition, each new president has inaugurated a new constitution, to the point that political parties have had to consistently reconstitute themselves.

Ostensibly quite different, Korea and the Philippines share a number of traits. In the social realm, the importance of families and education is similar in both countries. In the political realm, the style of politics again is similar. Politics and policy making in Korea and in the Philippines are dominated by oligarchic families. The composition of these elite families, their interests, and their political and economic calculations depend largely on their relations with other elite families. Although more "objective" interests exist – such as import-competing and export-oriented firms, or urban and rural firms – essentially, politics is the function of large families. Most elites know one another, attended school together, and see each other regularly.

1. Oligarchs and Networks

The basic units in the Philippine political economy are extended families. The Philippines does not have import-competing and export-oriented sectors that are coherent and form sustained interests, nor does it have easily identifiable manufacturing or agricultural sectors or functional sectors such as steel or electronics. Philippine society is not easily viewed as differentiated by labor and capital. Instead, the Lopez, Cojuangco, and Soriano clans are the famous and powerful families that have influenced political and economic policy for the past century. As Paul Hutchcroft writes:

> The basic building blocks of the political economy of the Philippine oligarchy are not "elite segments" but extended families. . . . The state is much more likely to be responding to families than to any other coherent segments. Patrons, who historically had relied on their own local resources, found expanded opportunities in obtaining external and office-based resources.[53]

In the early twentieth century, political unrest became more prevalent, and crime and protests also increased. The traditional power of the landholding elite waned during this period; in many ways, the increased unrest

---

[53] Paul Hutchcroft, "Oligarchs and Cronies in the Philippine State: The Politics of Patrimonial Plunder," World Politics 43 (April 1991): 422. See also David Wurfel, "Elites of Wealth and Elites of Power, the Changing Dynamic: A Philippine Case Study," Southeast Asian Affairs 1979 (Singapore: Institute of Southeast Asian Studies, 1979): 233–245.

of the Huks and the agrarian unrest of the 1920s and 1930s in Central Luzon were indicators of the weakening landlord-tenant ties. In addition, the commercialization of agriculture, growth in population, and postwar economic development program that focused on manufacturing all further weakened this once-powerful class.[54]

An instructive example is the Lopez clan from Iloilo, originally the leading family of the "sugar bloc." By the 1950s, Eugenio Lopez had diversified the family interests into many other sectors, including banks, a newspaper (*The Manila Chronicle*), radio and television stations, and an airline company. The family's political connections included Fernando Lopez, Eugenio's brother, who was vice-president under both Quirino and Marcos. Alfred McCoy writes that "Lopez mastered the logic of political investment, risking great capital in presidential campaigns and reaping even greater rewards."[55] Such was the clan's influence that by the 1970s Marcos was referring to the Lopez family when he referred to "oligarchs."[56] Although the Lopez clan suffered spectacularly under Marcos, they survived and have made a comeback.

The oligarchy did not comprise a static set of families. There was considerable dynamism, with new families rising as their own fortunes followed political fortunes. As manufacturing became increasingly important in the postwar era, and agriculture lost its preeminence, new families rose to prominence. The resulting mix of old and new oligarchs, however, although diversifying within business sectors, actually produced more conformist attitudes about economic policy.[57] The families tended to engage in agricultural, commercial, real estate, and manufacturing ventures focused around a bank. But in diversifying, the families no longer had clear sectoral interests; instead, many families came to share similar goals for macroeconomic policy, and their sectorally based conflicts became subdued. David Wurfel wrote in 1979 that "the occasional policy conflicts between industry and export agriculture which have flared in the past are

---

[54] Amando Doronila, *The State, Economic Transformation, and Political Change in the Philippines, 1946–1972* (Singapore: Oxford University Press, 1992), p. 94.

[55] Alfred McCoy, "Rent-Seeking Families and the Philippine State: A History of the Lopez Family," in *An Anarchy of Families: Political Elites and the Philippine State*, edited by Alfred McCoy and Michael Cullinane (Madison: University of Wisconsin Center for Southeast Asian Studies, 1993), p. 395.

[56] Wurfel, "Elites of Wealth and Elites of Power, the Changing Dynamic," p. 239.

[57] This section relies on Hutchcroft, "Predatory Oligarchy, Patrimonial State," pp. 122–135.

therefore muted" by family ties. "For those who wish to see developments of rational policy based on clear conceptions of group interest, the complicated kinship dimension is unfortunate."[58] In fact, 50 percent of the members of the Philippine Congress in 1970 had relatives holding elective office.[59]

This description of the Philippines can also be applied to a great extent to Korea. Koreans have always been clannish, and so important is the notion of family in Korea that not until 1997 was the law changed to allow men and women with a similar surname to marry. Bruce Cumings writes:

The latticework of Korean society in the Chosun period consisted of "highly structured patrilinear descent groups" – families in the great chain linking past and present.... The lineage group organized society at the top, in such a way that most of the Chosun elite came from a relative handful of eminent families. And it organized society at the bottom, with many Korean villages having but one clan.[60]

The family-based nature of Korean society survived the transition to modernity and extends, naturally enough, to both politics and the economy. Although one tends to discuss "Hyundai" or "Samsung," in reality one is talking about the Chung Ju-yong family or the Lee Byung-chull family, respectively.[61] Understanding this "keeping up with the Kims" explains a good deal about the overcapacity of the large *chaebol*. Firms are family run and owned and are passed on from generation to generation. Table 2.10 shows that of the top fifty *chaebol* in 1984, only two were run by nonfamily members. As one businessman has noted: "Korea is run by fewer than 100 families. The bureaucrats are charged with managing their affairs."[62]

Table 2.11 shows the highest position of the founder's second generation for the 50 largest *chaebol* in Korea in 1984. Chapter 5 will show that Philippine business is also largely a family affair.

---

[58] Wurfel, "Elites of Wealth and Elites of Power," p. 244. See also Nowak and Snyder, "Clientelist Politics in the Philippines: Integration or Instability," *American Political Science Review* 68, no. 3 (Autumn 1974): 1148.
[59] Stephen E. Frantzich, "A Comparative Study of Legislative Roles and Behavior" (Ph.D. diss., University of Minnesota, 1971), p. 228.
[60] Cumings, *Korea's Place in the Sun*, pp. 49, 51.
[61] Baek Sung-yol, *Chaebŏl ka ŭi saram dŭl: 22 tae chaebŏl kŭrup ŭi ch'angŏp, sŏngjang, hyŏnhwang, inmaek, honmaek story* (The men of the *chaebol*: The story of the founding, growth, present condition, personal relations and marriage relations of the 22 largest chaebol groups) (Seoul: Dosuh Chulpansa, 1991).
[62] Author's anonymous interview, September 12, 1995.

Table 2.10. *Origins of Chairmen of the Fifty Largest* Chaebol *(ranked by 1984 sales)*

	Top 10	Top 11–20	Top 21–30	Top 31–40	Top 41–50	Total
Founder	5	4	4	6	8	27
Founder's son	4	5	5	3	2	19
Founder's brother	1	0	1	0	0	2
Professional manager	0	1	0	1	0	2[a]

[a] Kia Group and Samyang Food Group.

Source: Minho Kuk, "The Governmental Role in the Making of *Chaebol* in the Industrial Development of South Korea," *Asian Perspective* 19, no. 1 (Summer 1995): 127.

Table 2.11. *Highest Positions of the Founder's Second Generation in Each* Chaebol *Group (50 largest* chaebol *ranked by 1984 sales)*

	Top 10	Top 11–20	Top 21–30	Top 31–40	Top 41–50	Total
Chairman	4	5	5	3	2	19
Vice-chairman	3	0	2	0	4	9
President	0	1	2	3	1	7
Vice-president	0	0	0	0	2	2
Lower than vice-president	2	0	1	2	0	5
No position	1	4	0	2	1	8

Source: Minho Kuk, "The Governmental Role in the Making of *Chaebol* in the Industrial Development of South Korea," *Asian Perspective* 19, no. 1 (Summer 1995): 127.

The clannishness of Korean society extends to politics as well. Park Chung-hee was related by marriage to Kim Jong-pil (along with Park, a member of the 1961 coup; later, a prime minister), and also to the Poongsan group, whereas Kim Jong-pil has ties through marriage to the Kolon group. Former prime ministers and foreign ministers are related to *chaebol* and back; they are so intertwined that, as the large families send their offspring into politics and business, the drawing of a relational map quickly becomes confusing.[63] And whereas individual families may suffer

[63] An excellent diagram can be found in Kang Chol-gyu, Choi Jong-pyo, and Jang Jisang, *Chaebŏl: sŏngjang ŭi chuyŏk inka t'amyŏk ŭi hwasin inka* (*Chaebol*: Pivotal role in growth or paragon of greed?) (Seoul: Gyongje Jongui Chonsiminyonhab, 1991), pp. 80–81.

Table 2.12. *Educational Attainment of Top Philippine Officials, 1946–1963*
(percentage)

	College Graduate (4 Years or More)	College (1–3 Years)	High School Graduate	Less than High School
Presidents, vice-presidents, and Cabinet members	96.7	3.3	0.0	0.0
Senators	96.0	4.0	0.0	0.0
Representatives	92.3	3.7	4.0	0.0
Supreme Court justices	100.0	0.0	0.0	0.0

Source: Dante Simbulan, "A Study of the Socio-economic Elite in Philippine Politics and Government" (Ph.D. diss., Australian National University, 1965), p. 159.

in the short term if they fall into disfavor with the current political leadership, these families invariably resurface later. As one businessman noted, "Clearing your reputation in Korea takes only a few weeks!" For example, Lee Byung-chull was widely reputed to have personal difficulties with Park Chung-hee, and as a result, Samsung profited less dramatically than the other *chaebol* during the 1960s and 1970s.

2. Education

The next great source of networks is elite education. In both Korea and the Philippines elites attend the same schools and know each other. In the Philippines, many of the elites come from the University of the Philippines (UP), Ateneo de Manila University, De La Salle University, and the University of Santo Tomas. The UP has more of a radical or left-wing reputation than the other schools, and Ateneo is known to produce business managers. Politicians overwhelmingly come from elite backgrounds. Over half of all members of Congress in the 1960s had graduated from the University of the Philippines, and of those graduates over two-thirds had studied law.[64] As Table 2.12 shows, from 1946 to 1963, 96 percent of senators and over 90 percent of representatives were college graduates.

[64] Wurfel, "Elites of Wealth and Elites of Power," p. 235.

55

Table 2.13. *College Attendance of Various Philippine Elites, 1963 (percentage)*

	Political Elite	Who's Who Elite	Carroll's Business Elite[a]
Private (religious)			
U. of Sto Tomas	15.5	13.1	7.7
Ateneo de Manila	9.3	7.1	15.4
Letran, De La Salle, San Beda	2.2	6.0	6.6
Private (nonsectarian)			
Philippine Law and U. of Manila	15.2	10.0	2.2
Jose Rizal College	1.7	1.7	7.7
Public			
University of the Philippines	25.7	24.5	20.8
Abroad	14.2	20.8	20.8
TOTAL	83.8	83.2	81.2
Others	16.2	16.8	18.8

[a] John Carroll, "The Filipino Manufacturing Entrepreneur: A Study of the Origins of Business Leadership in a Developing Economy" (Ph.D. diss., Cornell University, 1962).

Source: Dante Simbulan, "A Study of the Socio-economic Elite in Philippine Politics and Government" (Ph.D. diss., Australian National University, 1965), p. 164.

Philippine elites, like elites in most countries, overwhelmingly attended just a few colleges (Table 2.13). Dante Simbulan used three measures to assess the educational background of economic and political elites in the Philippines and found that over 80 percent of the elites in 1963 either had attended one of nine domestic universities or had studied abroad. As Simbulan notes, this finding is remarkable "when the fact is considered that there were in 1946, for example, 498 private colleges and five public schools."[65]

In Korea as well, the elites tend to graduate from the same schools and work with each other over time. Tables 2.14 and 2.15 show the educational backgrounds of economic and political elites in Korea. A remarkable 67 percent of all economic elites and 73 percent of higher civil servants in the economic ministries had attended one of the three major universities in Korea (Seoul National, Korea, or Yonsei).

[65] Dante Simbulan, "A Study of the Socio-economic Elite in Philippine Politics and Government" (Ph.D. diss., Australian National University, 1965), p. 163.

Table 2.14. *Education of Officials at the Ten Largest Korean* Chaebol, *1989* (*percentage in parentheses*)

	Seoul National	Yonsei U.	Korea U.	Others	Total
Chairman, vice-chairman, president	104 (51.0)	27 (13.2)	12 (5.9)	61 (29.9)	204
Vice-president	81 (48.5)	17 (10.2)	20 (12.0)	49 (29.3)	167
Managing director	187 (47.6)	44 (11.2)	22 (5.6)	140 (35.6)	393
TOTAL	372 (48.7)	88 (11.5)	54 (7.1)	250 (32.7)	764

Source: Kang Chol-gyu, Choi Jong-pyo, and Jang Jisang, *Chaebŏl: sŏngjang ŭi chuyŏk inka t'amyŏk ŭi hwasin inka* (*Chaebol*: Pivotal role in growth or paragon of greed?) (Seoul: Kyongje Chongui Chonsiminyonhab, 1991), p. 76.

Table 2.15. *Education of Higher Civil Servants in Korean Economic Ministries, 1989* (*above the level of section chief*)

	Finance	Economic Planning Board (EPB)	Construction	Total (%)
Seoul National	75	49	45	169 (53.8)
Yonsei U.	6	10	5	21 (6.7)
Korea U.	16	14	12	42 (13.4)
Others	22	31	29	82 (26.1)
TOTAL	119	104	91	314

Source: Kang Chol-gyu, Choi Jong-pyo, and Jang Jisang, *Chaebŏl: sŏngjang ŭi chuyŏk inka t'amyŏk ŭi hwasin inka* (*Chaebol*: Pivotal role in growth or paragon of greed?) (Seoul: Kyongje Chongui Chonsiminyonhab, 1991), p. 76.

The stereotype in the West of the importance of education in Asia needs little emphasis here. Koreans (and Asians in general) often speak of how much they value education. Moreover, although popular images may differ, scholars have long noted that Filipinos value education too.[66] The half-century of American rule (1898–1946) saw massive investment in infrastructure and education in the Philippines. Under the U.S. colonial

---

[66] See Doronila, *State, Economic Transformation, and Political Change* p. 21; and Renato Constantino, *Dissent and Counter-consciousness* (Quezon City: Malaya Books, 1970), p. 114.

Table 2.16. *Spending on Education as a Percentage of Central Government Expenditures, Korea and the Philippines, 1950–1980*

	Korea	Philippines
1950	8.2	n.a.
1955	4.8	25.4
1960	15.1	28.1
1965	13.6	29.1
1970	21.4	24.4
1975	11.6	11.4
1980	14.1	10.3

Source: United Nations Statistical Yearbook, various years.

administration, between 20 and 25 percent of government expenditure was on education. In 1957, Filipinos had a higher literacy rate than most of their fellow Asians and ranked second only to the United States in rates of enrollment in higher education among 121 countries.[67] By 1960 more than 70 percent of the Philippine population was literate. John Carroll found that 72 percent of entrepreneurs had a college education,[68] and a 1984 UNESCO study remarked that "a passion for education is one of the unique characteristics of the Filipino."[69]

If spending patterns reveal anything about a government's priorities, the Philippine government and the Korean government look more similar than different in their emphasis on education. Table 2.16 reveals that the Philippines actually outspent Korea on education until the mid-1970s, certainly as a percentage of central government expenditures. Also of interest is that in both Korea and the Philippines, under martial law in the 1970s the priorities of the governments, as reflected in the budgetary allocations to defense and industry, shifted away from education.

[67] Figures from "Basic Data for Cross-National Comparisons: Provisional Profiles," Research Monograph no. 1, Yale University Political Data Program, 1963, cited in Carl H. Lande, "The Philippines," in *Education and Political Development*, edited by James S. Coleman (Princeton: Princeton University Press, 1965), p. 335.

[68] John Carroll, *The Filipino Manufacturing Entrepreneur, Agent and Product of Change* (Ithaca: Cornell University Press, 1965).

[69] UNESCO, *The Literary Situation in Asia and the Pacific: Country Studies* (Bangkok: UNESCO, 1984), p. 1.

Table 2.17. *Educational Levels in Korea and the*
Philippines, 1950–1980

	Korea	Philippines
Primary		
1950	53	74
1955	54	54
1960	60	56
1965	63	97
1970	96	n.a.
1975	100	96
1980	100	92
Secondary		
1950	20	22
1955	36	25
1960	32	25
1965	43	24
1970	38	n.a.
1975	53	n.a.
1980	72	44

Note: Figures for Korea 1950–1965 and Philippines 1950–1960
represent adjusted school enrollment ratios; after these dates the
figures represent net enrollment ratios.
Source: UNESCO, *Statistical Yearbook*, various years.

Table 2.17 shows that until the 1970s the prevalence of people with a
primary education as a percentage of the population was actually greater
in the Philippines than in Korea – indeed, educational levels appear to
follow, rather than to lead, development in Korea. Typically, as a country
becomes richer, more of its population have the opportunity to receive
primary and secondary educations. It should be noted, however, that the
overall educational level of the Philippines has also continued to rise;
although less than one-quarter of the population had received a secondary
education in 1950, by 1980 almost half of the population had a secondary
education.

A full understanding of the differences in education and in social structure deserves more attention than I can devote to it here. My basic point
in this brief section has been that Korea and the Philippines are strikingly
similar in some ways, more similar than we might have initially thought
possible.

Cultural differences can be profound and important, and I certainly would not argue that the Philippine and Korean cultures are the same. Rather, they have traits that are similar, and as Korea and the Philippines are both Asian nations, I would also argue that they are not entirely different. The key causal connection is how these cultural values manifest themselves in the political and economic spheres, and, as I have shown in this section, these two countries exhibit patterns of social organization and cultural behavior that are similar in many ways.

V. Conclusion

This broad comparison of Korea and the Philippines reveals a number of similarities. The patterns of politics, some of the social structure, and the importance of family-based conglomerates are similar in the two countries. Yet there are differences as well. Because of geopolitics, Korea received more U.S. aid, and hence Korea invested more than the Philippines, has a different colonial past, and grew far more quickly over the past four decades. With this background, I turn now to patterns of politics in the two countries and focus on explaining how and why money politics is different in the two countries.

3

Institutions: Bureaucrats and Rulers

Why do we use the civil service examination to identify potential civil servants, anyway? These days those examinations test candidates on their ability to write according to the currently accepted essay format. . . . People study the essay format from childhood and finally pass the examination when they are old and gray. The examination system thus selects men who are useless, and it does so on the basis of useless writing.

— Pak Chega, circa 1775

To tell the truth, gentlemen, I should like to continue being President of the Philippines if I were sure I would live one hundred years. Have you ever known anyone who voluntarily renounced power? Everybody likes power.

— Manuel Quezon

In 1989, almost two-thirds (63%) of the bureaucrats in Korea's Ministry of Finance and almost half (47%) of Economic Planning Board (EPB) civil servants over the level of *samugwan* (Grade III) had graduated from Seoul National University (SNU). Normally these statistics are used as evidence of the superior quality of the SNU students. What tends to be less well known, however, is that faculty members at SNU's Graduate School of Public Administration are often asked to help write the national civil service exam (*haengchŏng kosi*, or *haengsi*). Although this circumstance does not diminish the accomplishment of those who pass the exam and enter the civil service, it does provide a clue that not all is as it appears within the vaunted Korean bureaucracy.

We begin our exploration of money politics by focusing on bureaucracy. The developmental statist explanation for growth centers on the hypothesis that in successful countries bureaucracies are more efficient than they are in less successful countries. The basic search has been for those institutional arrangements that have enhanced cooperation and information

while minimizing graft and inefficiency. However, there is no perfect institution that will minimize corruption and ensure bureaucratic efficiency
and smooth control of all actors. As Gary Miller has argued:

[T]he internal logic of self-interested behavior by both subordinates and superiors cannot be shown to sustain a vision of hierarchy as smoothly running, efficient
machine. On the contrary, results described in the literature of social choice theory,
principal-agency theory, and incentive compatibility reveal built-in logical in-
consistencies that make it impossible to design an incentive/control system that
simultaneously disciplines the self-interested behavior of both superiors and
subordinates. For every incentive system that has other desirable characteristics,
there will always be an incentive for some individuals to "shirk" – to pursue a nar-
rower definition of interest that results in equilibrium outcomes that everyone in
the organization can recognize as deficient.[1]

In this chapter I focus on the analytic issue of bureaucratic autonomy
and argue that identifying organizational attributes does not allow us to
make *ex ante* predictions about the developmental efficiency of a particular state. As noted in Chapter 1, many scholars have focused on the period
of rule by Park Chung-hee (1961–1979) and its strong state – its relatively
uncorrupt, autonomous, and insulated bureaucracy; its rational economic
planning; and its unselfish leadership – as central to South Korea's economic development. In contrast, scholars generally regard the Philippines
as an example of a predatory "weak state," in which under Ferdinand
Marcos the plunder and patronage were the supreme political and economic goals. But preferences are only a part of the story: we need to look
at how preferences are translated into policy, and that means we need to
look at institutions.

Unfortunately, the literature does not do a good job of describing the
actual organizational attributes of the developmental state. Although much
of the research on both the Philippines and Korea uses the state as an
important actor in explaining both economic policy and the politics behind
policy choices, few researchers have systematically examined the internal
workings of these governments.[2] To the extent that the literature exam-

[1] Gary Miller, *Managerial Dilemmas: The Political Economy of Hierarchy* (Cambridge: Cambridge University Press, 1992), p. 3.
[2] For example, see Yung-whan Rhee, Bruce Ross-Larson, and Gary Pursell, *Korea's Competitive Edge: Managing the Entry into World Markets* (Baltimore: Johns Hopkins University
Press, 1984); Jung-en Woo, *Race to the Swift* (New York: Columbia University Press, 1991);
Alice Amsden, *Asia's Next Giant: South Korea and Late Industrialization* (Oxford: Oxford
University Press, 1989); Peter Evans, *Embedded Autonomy* (Princeton: Princeton Univer-

ines the state, it tends to imply that bureaucracies have been autonomous from political influences in South Korea, but in the Philippines they have not. Thus the following questions arise: was the South Korean bureaucracy autonomous from politics? If so, how did this bureaucracy function effectively? What differentiates the bureaucracies in South Korea from those in the Philippines? What is the actual process by which policy preferences are implemented?

I make one overarching argument in this chapter while addressing three related sets of issues. The main argument is that in both Korea and the Philippines, rulers have reigned *and* ruled, and the bureaucracy has been distinctly subordinate to political regime interests. In bureaucratic arrangements the key difference between Korea and the Philippines was not state autonomy – in both countries politicians oversaw the bureaucracy, including staffing. A technocratic view of public administration ignores the political milieu within which bureaucrats operate. Overlooking politics is particularly problematic for Korea, because the structure of its bureaucracy was such that the Korean president had full control over many bureaucracies, minimizing their ability to operate independently, make meritocratic appointments, and remain protected from societal interests. The organization of the bureaucracy was much less significant for Korean and Philippine development than was politics: the nature of the political leadership that sat atop the bureaucracy in both countries and the social forces the leaders sought to organize and disorganize in order to maintain power.

The first set of related issues concerns the distinction between patronage and politicization in the bureaucracy.[3] Park may not have been different from Syngman Rhee or Ferdinand Marcos in the extent to which he politicized the bureaucracy. However, clearly Korea does differ from the Philippines in the use of patronage. Although Korea had plenty of corruption and politicization in public works contracts and loan allocations, pockets of the bureaucracy were staffed with educated and trained people recruited through a competitive examination process. Park Chung-hee

sity Press, 1995); Frederic Deyo, "State and Labor," in *The Political Economy of the New Asian Industrialism*, edited by Frederic Deyo (Ithaca: Cornell University Press, 1987), p. 182; Stephan Haggard, *Pathways from the Periphery* (Ithaca: Cornell University Press, 1990), p. 45; and James Cotton, "Understanding the State in South Korea: Bureaucratic Authoritarian or State Autonomy Theory," *Comparative Political Studies* 24, no. 4 (January 1992): 512–531.
[3] Barbara Geddes, *The Politician's Dilemma* (Berkeley: University of California Press, 1994).

created a bifurcated bureaucracy that allowed him to meet his patronage requirements and still seek economic efficiency. Such a bifurcation allowed Park to pursue both an internal agenda aimed at retaining power and "buying off" supporters and an external agenda aimed at realizing economic growth at home and increasing Korea's economic and political independence from other nations.

The second set of issues concerns the Philippines. Although the Philippines has exhibited many of the "classic" traits of a weak state and incompetent bureaucracy, some important distinctions exist. The quality and educational level of higher Filipino bureaucrats have generally been quite good. The issue has been interference by political superiors. The democratic era in the Philippines saw corruption, jurisdictional battles between the executive and the legislature, and a bureaucracy permeated by special interests. Under Marcos, however, the state became both more coherent and more autonomous from social interest groups. The problem under martial law was not a lack of state strength, but the uses to which such strength was directed.

The third set of issues concerns Syngman Rhee, South Korea's first leader (1948–1960). This chapter begins the process of "rehabilitating" Rhee. With the welcome exception of Jung-en Woo, most work on the 1950s in South Korea has laid the blame for slow development and incoherent economic policies squarely on Rhee's shoulders.[4] I examine the institutional constraints that Rhee faced and show that, in many ways, his relations with and style of ruling over the bureaucrats were similar to those of Park Chung-hee.

As this brief comparison will make clear, there is little evidence that Park Chung-hee treated bureaucrats differently than did either Rhee or Marcos. In all three administrations, power remained firmly in the hands of the executive and was not delegated to meritocratic technocrats. By the period of martial law, the bureaucracy in both countries had become autonomous from societal interests, but not from regime interests.

Bureaucratic arrangements in the two countries were largely similar and do not explain much about the policy process or economic outcomes.

---

[4] To my knowledge, Jung-en Woo's *Race to the Swift* is the only major English-language publication that attempts to find a "method to Rhee's madness." See also Chung-in Moon and Sang-young Rhyu, "Overdeveloped State and the Political Economy of Development in the 1950s: A Reinterpretation" (MS, Seoul, Yonsei University, 1997).

This chapter begins with a comparison of Korea's first two rulers, Syngman Rhee and Park Chung-hee, showing that many of the supposed reforms under Park were less transformative than the current literature has stated. The second section examines the Philippines, emphasizing the many ways in which the South Korean and Philippine bureaucracies look similar. In the third section, I show that what actually was different in Korea under Park Chung-hee was a separation of political and economic bureaus. A final section focuses on the Economic Planning Board as a "pilot ministry" and shows that Park in Korea, like Marcos in the Philippines, made shifts in response not to bureaucrats, but to business and regime interests.

I. Personnel Policy and the Organization of the Civil Service in South Korea

The problem of selection bias introduced in Chapter 1 is particularly acute when discussing the Korean bureaucracy. Authors of all stripes have labeled the Rhee period (1948–1960) as "weak" and the Park Chung-hee period (1961–1979) as "strong." In general this perception has arisen because of economic performance, generating the following tautology: South Korea under Park experienced rapid economic development; therefore, Park *must have* presided over a strong state. In contrast, because of poor economic outcomes, Syngman Rhee has been criticized in the literature for using the bureaucracy as a place for his patronage appointments and for subordinating bureaucratic consistency to political expediency.[5]

In explaining South Korean development, many scholars have centered their analysis on the period following Park Chung-hee's 1961 coup d'état.[6] This has led to a curious lacuna in the literature, where the Syngman Rhee period either is dismissed as aberrant because of Rhee's personality or is overlooked altogether. Although personality played a role, Rhee and Park also operated in different geopolitical and domestic contexts. Scholars have generally described the Rhee regime as despotic, rent seeking, and

---

[5] Lee Hahn Been, *Future, Innovation and Development* (Seoul: Panmun Book Co., 1982); Bark Dong-suh, "Haengchŏng kwallyo ŭi hyŏngsŏng" (The Formation of bureaucrats), *Shindonga* (October 1982); and Kim Kwang-woong, *Hankuk ŭi kwallyo chedo yŏnku* (Research on the Korean bureaucracy) (Seoul: Taeyong Munhwasa, 1991).

[6] Amsden, *Asia's Next Giant*, pp. 25–54.

incoherent, characterized by using the bureaucracy to siphon off funds and buy supporters.[7] Conventional wisdom portrays Rhee as a ruler who was less concerned with the country's economic development than he was with maximizing the amount of foreign aid Korea received from America. This view also sees President Rhee as generally staffing the civil service with uneducated or ill-suited cronies who were personally loyal to him. Under Rhee, the argument goes, corruption in the state was high: an overvalued exchange rate and a complex licensing system for imports led to a lax allocation of USAID dollars and to speculation, kickbacks, and over-pricing. Planning was ignored, and development took a back seat to political goals.

It is especially ironic that in discussing the bureaucracy Western scholars have focused on the meritocratic and competent Korean bureaucracy, whereas Korean scholars have focused on twenty years of corruption.[8] But when we actually compare the political institutions under Park and Rhee, many of the indicators that might reveal comprehensive reform of the bureaucracy under Park Chung-hee are ambiguous at best. Rhee was creating a nation and filling an entire bureaucratic apparatus from scratch, and the few bureaucrats who had worked under the previous Japanese administration tended to be low-level functionaries, unsuited to running bureaucracies.[9] Rhee needed to fill the rest of the bureaucracy with appointments, as the exam system could not provide enough civil servants to staff the entire apparatus.

---

[7] Stephan Haggard, Byung-kook Kim, and Chung-in Moon, "The Transition to Export-led Growth in South Korea," *Journal of Asian Studies* 50 (1991): 850–873; and Jon Huer, *Marching Orders: The Role of the Military in South Korea's "Economic Miracle," 1961–1971* (New York: Greenwood Press, 1989).

[8] Yi Munyong, "Kongmuwŏn pup'ae isipnyŏnsa" (Twenty years of civil service corruption), *Sasang'gye* (March 1966); Cho Suk-chun, "Hankuk kunsa chŏngbuha ŭi issŏsŏ ŭi tu kaji kwanhan pigyo yŏnku" (A comparative study of two adminstrative reforms under the Korean military government), *Hanguk Hengchŏng Nonchŏng* (Korean journal of public administration) 6, no. 2 (1968): 98–121; Bark Dong-suh, *Hanguk kwallyo ch'edo-ui yokssajok kaebal* (The historical development of the Korean bureaucratic system) (Seoul: Hanguk Yonguso, 1961); and Yoon Tae-bom, "Hankuk kwallyo ŭi pup'ae" (Bureaucratic corruption in Korea), *Hankuk Haengchŏng hakbo* 28, no. 1 (1994): 169–186.

[9] For more detail on the Japanese period, see Stephan Haggard, David Kang, and Chung-in Moon, "Japanese Colonialism and Korean Development: A Critique," *World Development* 27, no. 6 (June 1997): 867–881. For those who see the Japanese influence as positive or even formative, see Atul Kohli, "Where Do High-Growth Political Economies Come From? The Japanese Lineage of Korea's 'Developmental State,'" *World Development* 22, no. 9 (September 1994): 1269–1293.

Table 3.1. *Cabinet Turnover in Korea under Rhee and Park (average tenure in months in parentheses)*

	Syngman Rhee	Park Chung-hee
Foreign Affairs	6 (23.5)	11 (20.0)
Finance	9 (15.6)	16 (13.8)
Health	6 (23.5)	10 (22.1)
Education	6 (23.5)	14 (15.7)
Communication	8 (17.6)	14 (15.7)
National Defense	7 (20.1)	10 (22.1)
Transportation	8 (17.6)	12 (18.4)
Justice	9 (15.6)	13 (17.0)
Prime Minister	8 (17.6)	8 (27.6)
Commerce and Industry	10 (14.1)	10 (22.1)
Agriculture and Forestry	16 (8.8)	14 (15.7)
Home Affairs	20 (7.0)	14 (15.7)
Construction	—	15 (14.7)

Source: Compiled from the Ministry of Governmental Affairs, various publications.

1. Cabinet Composition

Scholars have often criticized the "revolving door" aspect of Rhee's political appointments. Table 3.1 shows the average tenure of cabinet ministers under both Rhee and Park. What is most striking is the absence of a clear trend. Although the ministers of foreign affairs, finance, health, education, and communication served *longer* average terms under Rhee than did their counterparts under Park, the ministers of home affairs, commerce and industry, and agriculture and forestry had markedly shorter average tenures under Rhee than under Park.

2. Examination Procedures

Another aspect of the developmental state that has received attention is the use of civil service examinations for entry into the higher civil service in Korea. Again, the differences between Rhee and Park are not clear. Table 3.2 provides the data for the exams from 1949 to 1979. The most important exam for my purposes is the Public Administration Exam, or *haengsi*. During Rhee's rule, from 1949 to 1960, an average of 22 aspirants passed each exam. The competition ranged from a low of 9 aspirants per

Table 3.2. *Higher Civil Service Exam, 1949–1979*

Year	Absolute Number Accepted	Attempts per Success
1949	5	100
1951	38	9
1952	16	14
1953	24	22
	9	75
1954	13	74
1955	58	29
1956	11	214
1957	7	315
1958	27	65
1959	36	47
1960	20	154
1961	72	21
1962	38	42
1963	40	37
1964	24	62
1965	28	25
1966	50	22
1967	24	73
1968	45	32
1969	55	36
1970	38	43
	27	70
1971	188	18
1972	41	94
	47	71
1973	96	43
	116	36
1974	47	92
	68	59
1975	100	44
	101	44
1976	73	93
1977	55	92
	131	38
1978	250	31
1979	248	41

Source: Ministry of Governmental Affairs.

each successful exam taker in 1951 (probably due to the disruption of the war), to a high of 315 aspirants per each successful exam taker in 1957. Under Park we also see a trend: the first decade of his rule, 1961–1970, the numbers are only slightly higher than Rhee's. In this period, an average of 36.9 aspirants passed each exam, and the difficulty ranged from a low of 22 aspirants per each successful exam taker in 1966 to a high of 73 aspirants per each successful exam taker in 1967.

In 1971, however, there is a jump upward in the number of successful exam takers. In 1971 alone, 188 aspirants passed the *haengsi*, or more than half of the entire number of aspirants who had passed the exam in the preceding decade. From 1971 to 1979, an average of 111.5 aspirants passed each exam, whereas the difficulty remained similar – a low of 18:1 in 1971 and a high of 93:1 in 1976.

In explaining these outcomes, the small number of initially successful applicants is not surprising. As I have argued elsewhere, in the late 1940s there was an absolute lack of educated and qualified Korean aspirants for the civil service. This fact is reflected not only in the smaller numbers of successful examinees but also in the higher numbers of *teukche*, or special appointments.[10] A number of Koreans who had served under the Japanese retained government posts, but the American occupation and independence also created the political opportunity for a flood of new entrants.

This lack of qualified aspirants is also reflected in the lower educational achievement of the Rhee bureaucracy and the inevitably higher numbers of external promotions: by 1960 even the first of those bureaucrats recruited at the *samugwan*, or Grade III level, had had only twelve years within which to rise through the various ministries. Park Chung-hee's regime benefited from the growing number of educated Koreans, as well as from the chance to promote more bureaucrats through internal means. To conclude that Syngman Rhee's personnel policies were consciously clientelistic is unfair; Rhee faced a number of constraints on reforming the bureaucracy that Park did not face. At the same time, the evidence does not reveal that Park Chung-hee was interested in reform.

The Bureau of the Budget within the Ministry of Finance, headed from 1958 to 1961 by Lee Hahn Been, was an island of innovation. As a division chief, Lee attended a UN workshop in Bangkok in 1955. On his return, he urged the adoption of a series of reforms of the budgetary process, including budget reclassification, performance budgeting, and

---

[10] Haggard, Kang, and Moon, "Japanese Colonialism and Korean Development."

commercial accounting for state-owned enterprises – all reforms that would have centralized the reach of the Budget Bureau over the activities of other ministries. Because of its importance to the stabilization effort, the Budget Bureau maintained particularly close links with the Americans through the Combined Economic Board (CEB); its focus on fiscal rationalization probably appealed to the Americans more than did the planning efforts of the Ministry of Reconstruction (MOR). As in the MOR, Lee recruited college graduates and those completing American training programs. This cadre also fed into the Economic Planning Board when it was established in 1961.

3. Internal Promotion

Tables 3.3 and 3.4 also include interesting data regarding the internal promotion of the Rhee bureaucracy. Here as well, the data are mixed. Table 3.3 shows the pattern of recruitment under Syngman Rhee. Grades III-B through II are the "heart" of the bureaucracy – Grade III-B is a *samugwan*, or section chief, Grade III-A is a *sŏkigwan*, or director, and Grades II-A/B are *isakwan* and *puisakwan*, director general and assistant director general, respectively. What is interesting is that by 1960 fully 78 percent of the Grade II (director general) civil servants had been promoted from

Table 3.3. *Pattern of Recruitment and Promotion of Higher Civil Servants (in percentages)*

Process of Recruitment and Promotion	Positions of Incumbents as of January 1960		
	Grade III-B	Grade III-A	Grade II
Grade II			
Originally recruited at Grade II			21.1
Promoted from below			78.9
Grade III-A			
Originally recruited at Grade III-A		20.4	43.7
Promoted from below		79.6	35
Grade III-B			
Originally recruited at Grade III-B	19.4	28.8	26.2
Promoted from below	80.6	50.7	8.8

Source: Bark Dong-Suh, *Hanjuk kwallyo chedo ŭi yŏksa chŏk kaepal* (The historical development of the Korean bureaucratic system) (Seoul: Hanguk Yŏnkuso, 1961), p. 206.

70

Table 3.4. *Pattern of Recruitment and Promotion of Higher Civil Servants under Rhee and Park (in percentages)*

| | 1948–1960 | | | | 1977–1979 | | |
Grade	*haengsi*	special	internal	Grade	*haengsi*	special	internal
I		63.9	36.1	I		34.5	65.5
II		52.9	47.1	II-A		6.8	93.2
				II-B		6.5	93.5
III-A		39.8	60.2	III-A		8.1	91.9
III-B	4.1	30.6	65.3	III-B	20.6	10.8	68.5

Source: Ministry of Government Affairs. Quoted in Byung-kook Kim, "Bringing and Managing Socioeconomic Change" (Ph.D. diss., Harvard University, 1988), p. 101.

within the bureaucracy, and almost 9 percent of those bureau directors had risen from below the rank of Grade II-B. Additionally, almost 80 percent of Grade III-A civil servants had been promoted from below, as had 80 percent of Grade III-B civil servants.

Table 3.4 compares Rhee and Park in their recruitment and promotion of higher civil servants. For the highest levels, the numbers are almost reversed: under Rhee roughly 64 percent of Grade I civil servants were special appointments, whereas under Park roughly 65 percent of Grade I appointments were internal promotions. At the entry level (Grade III-B) under Rhee, only 4 percent of appointments were through the *haengsi* exam, whereas over 20 percent of Park's entry level appointments were through the exam. Again, however, it must be remembered that in the typical Korean bureaucratic career path, advancing from Grade III-B to Grade III-A takes about ten years. Another decade winnows out the membership at Grade II and leaves a few that rise to Grade I. Thus under Rhee it would have been impossible for internal promotions to have filled much of the bureaucracy by 1960, whereas Park benefited from the thirteen years preceding him. This is not to say that the only differences between Rhee and Park were structural, but rather to point out that such differences did exist and clearly created constraints on Rhee that did not exist for Park.

Graduates of four-year colleges accounted for 29.9 percent of all bureau directors in the Korean bureaucracy in 1960; at the Ministry of Reconstruction, by contrast, all bureau directors had completed college. The Ministry of Reconstruction, the Ministry of Finance, and the banks were also the major beneficiaries of the U.S. program in public administration that exposed government officials to training overseas. Of 225 Koreans in the program through 1961, 39 came from the Ministry of Reconstruction, 59 from the Ministry of Finance, and 41 from the banking community.[11]

Other evidence of differences between Rhee and Park is also unclear. In Korea the bureaucracy's internal promotion system was based more on seniority than it was on merit; it is simply impossible to find a forty-year-old Grade II civil servant, for example. Ministers do not rotate through ministries and gain varied expertise; rather, they rise through only one ministry their entire career. As each entering class rises through the bureaucratic ranks, its members slowly begin to fall off for various reasons. After ten years or so they can expect to rise to Grade III-A level, and after another decade to Grade II. By the time a member of a class is eligible for a political post at the vice-ministerial level, the ranks have thinned. When one class member is successful in rising to the political appointment, the rest of the class then exit the bureaucracy and retire to other posts. They will not remain after one of their cohort has risen very high.

Amakudari, or "descent from heaven," occurs in Korea. In terms of insulation, this is the opposite of what the "autonomous state" theory would predict. The existence of *amakudari* is one major way in which business can influence policy decisions. By tying a bureaucrat's present performance to the prospect of future employment, particularistic interests can hope to affect policy choices and decisions.

4. Monitoring and Enforcing Bureaucratic Compliance under Rhee and Park

One difference between Rhee and Park concerns the method by which these rulers monitored and enforced bureaucratic compliance with the top political leadership's goals. There is a large literature on how political principals control bureaucratic agents. In particular, Matthew McCubbins and

[11] Under Park, the reverse brain drain truly began. The first wave of Koreans to study in the United States in the 1950s began to return to Korea in the 1960s, many going on to play key roles in the bureaucracy under Park. See Cho, "Hankuk kunsa chŏngbuha ŭi issŏsŏ ŭi tu kaji kwanhan pigyo yŏnku" (A comparative study of two adminstrative reforms under the Korean military government); Bark, *Hanjuk kwallyo chedo ŭi yŏksa chŏk kaepal* (The historical development of the Korean bureaucratic system); and Ahn Byung-yung, "Chŏnhwaki hankuk kwallyoche ŭi kaltŭng kwa palchŏn panghyang" (Development and discord in bureaucratic transitions), *Gyegan Sasang* (Autumn 1990): 63–104.

Thomas Schwartz have identified two generic strategies: police patrols and fire alarms.[12] "Police patrols" are regular, routine information-gathering exercises whereby the principal learns from the agent about various activities that have taken place, whereas "fire alarms" involve the principal's waiting until someone pulls the plug and says out loud that there is a problem. For Rhee, oversight involved the use of fire alarms, and his leadership style was hands-off until certain actions had been taken. Park, in contrast, made extensive use of "police patrol" systems, regularly meeting with bureaucrats and making instant decisions about what to do.

Did Rhee take an active interest in the bureaucracy? Although most reports show that Rhee had either little interest in or knowledge of the economy, he did have clear goals, and he communicated those to his bureaucrats. Song In-sang (reconstruction minister under Rhee) told me that "Rhee gave me three rules, and then he left me alone: First, keep trade with Japan as small as possible. Second, defend the exchange rate. Finally, never, *ever* sign anything in English until Rhee had read it first. My English was not very good at that time!"[13] Under the Rhee regime the bureaucrats were generally left to themselves unless there was a crisis, at which point Rhee would intervene. The relevant question is whether the bureaucracy responded to its political superior's wishes, or whether the political "principal" was unable to control his agent. On this count, the Rhee bureaucracy appears to have enjoyed little agency slack.

There was little agency slack under Park, although his method of control was different. The evidence shows that, far from creating an independent and neutral bureaucracy, Park conducted regular police patrols of the various bureaus. This included the monthly trade promotion meetings, "on the spot" guidance, and episodic purges. In 1965, the first National Export Promotion Meeting was held. Chaired by the president himself, these meetings included the economic ministers, the chief executives of the export associations, and the presidents of several of the largest enterprises. The moderator of the session was usually an economic minister, who would begin with a briefing on the general progress on achieving targets before turning to the problems facing specific industries. It is doubtful that these highly scripted meetings, chaired by an imposing and authoritarian president, really conformed to the model of a two-way

---

[12] Matthew McCubbins and Thomas Schwartz, "Congressional Oversight Overlooked: Police Patrols versus Fire Alarms," *American Journal of Political Science* 28 (1984): 165–179.

[13] Author's interview, October 17, 1996.

flow of information. Nonetheless, it is true that the centralized political structure permitted the president to act directly on problems that individual industries were facing, often by simply issuing directives on the spot.[14]

Such monitoring and enforcement created a bureaucracy that responded quite readily to regime interests. Both major and minor policy decisions were reached at the highest levels and then justified by the various ministries. Even though Park supported and protected the economic technocrats in his government from other branches of government and from certain social pressures, it is a mistake to see the technocrats as independent from the executive.

Thus, Park was more interventionist than Rhee, and his bureaucracy clearly paid close attention to the wishes of political superiors. Syngman Rhee was building a civil service, governmental institutions, and party politics from scratch. Much of the confusion during the 1950s resulted precisely from the inevitable shakeout process that accompanies any major institutional innovation. War, social dislocations, and a lack of qualified bureaucrats all compounded the constraints under which Rhee operated. In contrast, Park was able to capitalize on Rhee's efforts. However, both leaders were in control of their bureaucrats, and both leaders were able to use bureaucrats to implement their policy preferences. Agency slack was low under both leaders.

II. Clientelism and Reform in the Philippines

Comparing Korea with the Philippines reveals as much about the developmental state as does comparing Korea's rulers themselves. The dearth of comprehensive data is itself an indicator of the more lax approach to public administration in the Philippines. Although under democracy the Philippine bureaucracy had been riddled with patronage, under Marcos the bureaucracy experienced heightened autonomy and small-scale reform. The difficulty was that, regardless of reforms, Marcos's political goals did not include utilizing the bureaucracy for development. Instead, Marcos used technocrats to impress international and U.S. agencies into

---

[14] Tun-jen Cheng, Stephan Haggard, and David Kang, "Institutions and Economic Development in East Asia: Taiwan and Korea," UNCTAD series *Special Studies in Economic Development* (1996).

continuing to provide financial support, and Marcos and his cronies then siphoned off the proceeds for their own aggrandizement.

The Filipino bureaucracy is modeled on that of the United States, with movement in and out of the bureaucracy. Appointments are made by the executive, competitive examinations are putatively required for entry into the higher levels of the bureaucracy, and the Congress retains the right to approve Cabinet appointments. Under the Philippine Constitution of 1946 the president could make appointments to eleven major departments: Foreign Affairs, Finance, Justice, Agriculture and Natural Resources, Public Works and Communications, Education, Labor, National Defense, Health, Commerce and Industry, and General Services. Some agencies are not assigned to a regular department (for example, Civil Defense and Social Welfare). By 1988 the number of major departments had increased to nineteen, including Transportation, Tourism, Energy, Human Settlements, Youth and Sports Development, Public Information, Social Services, and Agrarian Reform.

The Philippines has been attempting to reform its bureaucracy for almost a century. One of the causes of discontent among Filipinos under Spanish rule was the inefficient and corrupt administrative system. When the Americans took power in the Philippines, the Philippines Commission passed "An Act for the Establishment of an Efficient and Honest Civil Service in the Philippines" in 1900.[15] The act mandated an examination system of recruitment for every position under that of bureau director, promotion by merit, prohibitions against discrimination by race or creed, and prohibitions against receiving political contributions. Forty-six years later, Article XI of the postwar constitution again stipulated that appointments to the civil service be by competitive examination, with promotions based on merit alone. Yet this has not happened. Bureaucrats in the Philippines have had neither the extensive capacity nor the autonomy to create and promote independent development agendas. The Philippines in many ways remains a classic "patronage" system. As Paul Hutchcroft writes:

The oligarchy took advantage of its independent base of power, and came to exercise powerful – yet particularistic – control over elements of the state apparatus

---

[15] Act No. 5, September 19, 1900. Cited in Raul P. De Guzman, Alex B. Brillantes Jr., and Arturo G. Pacho, "The Bureaucracy," in *Government and Politics of the Philippines*, edited by Raul P. De Guzman and Mila A. Reforma (Oxford: Oxford University Press, 1988), p. 183.

through a spoils system. While the oligarchy swamped the legislature, it showed little interest in directly assuming bureaucratic posts. Despite growth in the bureaucracy, a bureaucratic elite never emerged.[16]

1. The Democratic Era: Patronage Plus

The Philippine bureaucracy has traditionally been riddled with corruption, nepotism, and patronage appointments. David Wurfel writes that "by the early years of independence the pattern had been set; bureau directors and division chiefs received appropriations from the legislature in exchange for appointing friends, relatives, and needy constituents of congressmen."[17] And so it went: although putatively entrance to the bureaucracy was on an examination system, by 1964, 80 percent of national employees had not taken the exam, and at the level of administrative officers and above, 57 percent had not taken the exam.[18] This system of patronage drastically undercut the formal ties within the bureaucracy. Patrons and clients owed their allegiance and their jobs first to each other, and thus bureaucracies were splintered by the factional and clientelistic nature of the spoils system.

During the democratic era in the Philippines (1946–1972), the bureaucracy was continually decentralized, in a way that prevented the bureaucrats from accumulating expertise or power over time. In addition, the Philippines also experienced episodic attempts to reform the bureaucracy and purge corruption from the system. In 1950 the Quirino administration created the Bell Commission, staffed with U.S. experts, which presented a number of proposals for reform of the bureaucracy, including better training and higher salaries for bureaucrats and meritocratic appointment based on examinations.

The two-party system that emerged in the Philippines introduced partisan considerations into the spoils system. The National and Liberal

[16] Paul Hutchcroft, "Booty Capitalism: Government-Business Relations in the Philippines," in *Business and Government in Industrializing East and Southeast Asia*, edited by Andrew MacIntyre (Sydney: Allen and Unwin, and Ithaca: Cornell University Press, 1994). See also Benedict Anderson, "Cacique Democracy and the Philippines: Origins and Dreams," *New Left Review* 169 (May/June 1988): 3–33.
[17] David Wurfel, *Filipino Politics: Development and Decay* (Ithaca: Cornell University Press, 1988), p. 79.
[18] Gregorio Francisco, "Career Development of Filipino Higher Civil Servants," in Jose Abueva and Raul De Guzman, *Foundations and Dynamics of Filipino Government and Politics* (Manila: Bookmark, 1969), p. 403.

parties competed with each other and with the president for patronage posts in the bureaucracy. The situation became so chaotic that in 1959, the president and the Congress worked out a "50–50" agreement, whereby half the bureaucratic posts would be filled by presidential appointees and half by appointees of the House of Representatives.[19] Any more striking evidence of societal penetration and bureaucratic incoherence than this would be hard to find. The pressure on bureaucratic structures for patronage appointments is also seen in the size of the public sector. In the 1960s and 1970s, public sector investment averaged 2 percent of GNP, compared with 5.1 percent in Korea.[20] Despite the low level of capitalization, however, the public sector was the largest single employer in the country in 1969, with 531,000 employees. In 1962 the government accounted for 83.3 percent of employment in the organized segment of the services sector, once again reflecting the need of politicians to find patronage posts for their supporters.[21]

Table 3.5 shows the growth of the Philippine bureaucracy over time. The most interesting aspect of this data is the increase of personnel in "Corporations," state-owned enterprises created by fiat and basically used as vehicles for more patronage appointments and hiring. Similarly, although the size of the bureaucracy grew only marginally from 1961 to 1971, by the end of the 1970s, it had increased almost 200 percent.

2. Education and Exams

Despite political interference in its bureaucracy, it would be a mistake to view the Philippines as a nation devoid of qualified technocrats. Both education and the civil service have traditionally been held in high regard in the Philippines, and competition for public jobs is fierce. Lamented one academic in 1962: "The pressure upon public employment is in no way eased by a system of education that gives emphasis to white-collar training which, while giving a high social status to the graduate, often

---

[19] For more on the "50–50" agreement, see Gregorio A. Francisco Jr. and Raul P. De Guzman, "The 50–50 Agreement," in *Patterns in Decision Making: Case Studies in Philippine Public Administration*, edited by Raul P. de Guzman (Manila: Graduate School of Public Administration, University of the Philippines, 1963), pp. 93–102.

[20] Amando Doronila, *The State, Economic Transformation, and Political Change in the Philippines, 1946–1972* (Singapore: Oxford University Press, 1992), p. 142.

[21] Doronila, *State, Economic Transformation, and Political Change*, p. 144.

Table 3.5. *Growth of the Philippine Bureaucracy*

Year	National Government	Corporations	Provincial Governments	Total[a]
1961	182,436	—	16,383	361,312
1964	201,401	—	19,812	415,103
1968	224,651	—	18,832	481,320
1971	224,448	—	21,556	530,985
1973	218,091	—	24,020	569,985
1975	164,221	41,250	22,433	533,284
1977	369,817	80,913	71,091	992,798
1979	521,664	106,462	42,585	1,064,620

[a] This number includes personnel in municipal and city governments and universities.

Source: Adapted from Raul P. de Guzman, Alex B. Brillantes Jr., and Arturo G. Pacho, "The Bureaucracy," in *Government and Politics of the Philippines*, edited by Raul de Guzman and Mila A. Reforma (Oxford: Oxford University Press, 1988), p. 187.

disqualifies him from venturing into an individual economic enterprise or getting employment in modern industry."[22]

Table 3.6 shows the educational attainment of a sample of Filipino higher civil servants in 1960. Most surprising is the high level of education. Table 3.7 shows the methods by which civil servants were employed. Compared with recruitment in Korea during the same period, in the Philippines, although there is clearly less reliance on examination measures, exam procedures were not totally absent.

Entrance via exam to the Philippine bureaucracy could be bypassed either by receiving "special training" that qualified individuals for public service or by rising through the ranks from lower to higher civil service, or through pure patronage. A liberal interpretation of the need for "primarily confidential" or "highly technical" positions allowed numerous persons who were political protégés of various politicians to enter the bureaucracy and circumvent the examination system.[23]

---

[22] Carlos P. Ramos, "Public Administration in the Philippines," quoted in *Public Administration in South and Southeast Asia*, edited by S. S. Hsueh (Oxford: International Institute of Administrative Sciences, 1962), p. 148.

[23] See Francisco, "Career Development of Filipino Higher Civil Servants."

Table 3.6. *Educational Attainment of Filipino Higher Civil Servants (sample, 1960)*

Level of Education	Civil Servants (%)
Less than bachelor's degree	4.8
Bachelor's degree or equivalent[a]	69.0
Graduate work, no degree	7.1
Graduate degree[b]	19.1

Note: N = 127

[a] Includes degrees in law and medicine.

[b] This includes only master's degrees and doctorates. Including the law and medical degrees raises this number to 68%.

Source: Gregorio Francisco, "Higher Civil Servants in the Philippines" (Ph.D. diss., University of Minnesota, 1960), p. 155.

Table 3.7. *Recruitment of Filipino Higher Civil Servants (sample, 1960)*

Procedure	Younger[a]	Older
Oral interviews	48.1	34.7
Civil service examination	18.6	32.6
Civil service examination with oral interviews	7.4	5.1
Formal application	7.4	3.1
Special training	7.4	6.1
Recommendation by superior	0.0	4.1
Non–civil service examinations	3.7	3.1
Others	7.4	11.2

Note: N = 127

[a] "Younger" denotes those below age 40, "older" those age 40 and above.

Source: Gregorio Francisco, "Higher Civil Servants in the Philippines" (Ph.D. diss., University of Minnesota, 1960), p. 225.

Access to a U.S. education and familiarity with the West were greater in the Philippines than in Korea. Because of decades-long American colonial administration, the Philippines was both better prepared to use English than Korea and had deeper ties with the United States. As Richard

Doner has written of the early 1970s, "[The Philippines'] auto efforts were led by an experienced and highly regarded group of technocrats."[24]

3. Marcos and Martial Law

After declaring martial law in 1972, Marcos was able to centralize all the other aspects of the Philippine state under his control. Through disbanding the legislature and his adroit political maneuvering Marcos achieved a good measure of autonomy from previously influential interests. Although it initially appeared that Marcos was pursuing a radically new approach to politics, in many ways the Marcos era merely intensified the traditional practices of the Philippine political economy.[25]

The Board of Investments (BOI) was formed in 1966, a critical bureaucratic change that was intended to create a pilot development agency. Over the years the BOI suggested a number of ambitious projects and attempted to provide a coherent development focus for the administration. Although initially the BOI was successful in guiding investment and finance, as the 1970s wore on its plans were generally ignored by the presidential palace. Under Marcos, budget appropriations also were subject to highly interventionist and selective control, and after 1972 the budget was hidden from all but the highest levels of the administration, allowing Marcos to effectively conceal fiscal transfers. "Fiscal officers in particular agencies knew when budgeted funds had not been received, but even they had no clear indication as to where the funds had gone."[26] The financial system was similarly politicized. The Central Bank under Marcos misused funds, which hurt investment in all areas: "[T]he most egregious example of this was the Central Bank's use of overnight borrowings to cover external payments shortfalls. Coordination among agencies responsible for industrial policy, finance, and long-term planning was almost nonexistent. The Board of Investments came into frequent conflict with the Philippine National Bank's preferential lending and the liberal views of the National Economic Development Authority."[27]

---

[24] Richard Doner, *Driving a Bargain: Automobile Industrialization and Japanese Firms in South-east Asia* (Berkeley: University of California Press, 1991), pp. 158–159.

[25] De Guzman, Brillantes, and Pacho write: "The trend during martial law was towards centralization. The concentration of power, decision-making, and control over substantive and administrative matters, especially under martial law, have led to delays in the implementation of development programs and projects" ("The Bureaucracy," p. 195).

[26] Wurfel, *Filipino Politics*, p. 139.   [27] Doner, *Driving a Bargain*, p. 245.

Table 3.8. *A Sample of American-Educated Technocrats in the Marcos Administration*

Name	Degree and University	Position under Marcos
Cesar Virata	MBA, Wharton MS, Penn	Prime minister
Vicente Valdepenas	Ph.D., Cornell	Minister for economic planning
Jaime Laya	Ph.D., Stanford	Budget minister, central bank governor
Vicente Paterno	MBA, Harvard	Chairman, BOI (1970–1979), Minister of industry (1974–1979)
Alex Melchior	Annapolis	Minister of public works
Roberto Ocampo	MBA, Michigan	Presidential economic staff
Placido Mapa Jr.	Ph.D., Harvard	Minister for economic planning
Roberto Ongpin	MBA, Harvard	Minister of trade and industry
Gerardo Sicat	Ph.D., MIT	Minister for economic planning
Arturo Tanco Jr.	Ph.D., Harvard	Minister of Agriculture
Manuel Alba	MBA, Minnesota Ph.D., Northwestern	Budget Minister

Source: Author's interviews, and Manuel Montes, "Financing Development: The 'Democratic' Versus the 'Corporatist' Approach in the Philippines," in Setsuko Yukawa, *The Political Economy of Fiscal Policy*, edited by Miguel Urrutia, Shinichi Ichimura, and Setsuko Yukawa (Tokyo: United Nations University, 1989), p. 97.

Marcos did stock the bureaucracy with many well-educated and ambitious technocrats. For example, Vicente Paterno and Roberto Ongpin, steeped in Western management styles and developmental ideology, wanted to open up markets and focus on industry. Many American-educated individuals worked in the bureaucracy at all levels. Table 3.8 shows a sample. Indeed, as Paterno himself commented, "Initially Marcos was a wonderful president. From 1972 to about 1978 we had strong technocrats in the Cabinet. Marcos generally left us to our jobs, and he didn't actively begin interfering in my work until about 1978. But there was a real sense of excitement in those early years."[28]

The great irony is that under Marcos state capacity increased, and the overall quality and coherence of the bureaucracy improved, although at the same time political decisions overrode the technocrats' attempts to implement coherent economic policy. Indeed, Marcos appears to have fully

---

[28] Author's interview, September 8, 1999.

intended to ignore the technocrats that he hired.[29] Although important for international reasons (retaining legitimacy in the eyes of the World Bank and the United States), as a domestic source of innovation or reform the technocrats were insignificant. In bargaining with the International Monetary Fund (IMF) and the World Bank, Marcos would let the technocrats come to some resolution with the agencies. But although putatively giving power to technocrats, Marcos in fact ignored their advice and disbursed dispensations to his cronies, making a mockery of the bureaucratic policies. Raul Fabella writes that "technocrats were given the prerogative to formulate and rhetorize the public agenda in the form of economic and development plans which formed the basis for foreign loans. The political leadership then allowed the unconstrained introduction of exceptions that made a complete mockery of the spirit and letter of the plans."[30] The IMF sponsored a tariff reduction program, which "was undermined in part because specific corporations were exempted through presidential decree; similarly, efforts to increase the country's tax effort were hindered in part by tax incentives granted to Marcos associates."[31] In another example of his interference, Marcos accepted an inflated and crony-supported bid on a nuclear power plant by Westinghouse.[32]

As we have seen, the bureaucracy did not suffer from a lack of trained or dedicated personnel. Particularly after declaring martial law, Marcos was able to consistently increase bureaucratic authority and discretion in relation to social pressures. Paterno noted that "I had a rule: none of my civil servants were allowed to leave until they got a job offering twice their current salary. Since we averaged 25 percent turnover, this is a good testament to the regard that the private sector held for my staff."[33] However,

[29] Romeo B. Ocampo, "Technocrats and Planning: Sketch and Exploration," *Philippine Journal of Public Administration* 15, no. 1 (January 1971). Manuel Montes writes, "[Martial law] witnessed an increase in the importance of 'technocrats' in the government bureaucracy" (Montes, "Financing Development: The 'Democratic' versus the 'Corporatist' Approach in the Philippines," in *The Political Economy of Fiscal Policy*, edited by Miguel Urrotia, Shinichi Ichimura, and Setsuko Yukawa (Tokyo: The United Nations University, 1989), p. 96.
[30] Raul V. Fabella, "Trade and Industry Reforms in the Philippines: Process and Performance," in *Philippine Macroeconomic Perspective: Developments and Policies*, edited by Manuel Montes and Hideyoshi Sakai (Tokyo: Institute of Developing Economies, 1989), p. 197.
[31] Paul Hutchcroft, "Oligarchs and Cronies in the Philippine State: The Politics of Patrimonial Plunder," *World Politics* 43 (April 1991): 433.
[32] Doner, *Driving a Bargain*, p. 168.
[33] Author's interview, September 8, 1999.

the bureaucrats saw their advice and programs increasingly ignored or overridden, and by the late 1970s Marcos's political power became the key to the rent-seeking state.

4. State Strength and the Marcos Regime

How strong was the Philippine state? A focus on the ability of leaders to implement their goals through a responsive bureaucracy reveals that Marcos was able to strengthen the internal organization of the state to a fair extent. Concomitant with the definition that I gave in Chapter 1, Paul Hutchcroft argues that the Philippine state under Marcos experienced heightened state capacity but that "those technocrats themselves were not *autonomous* in relation to regime interests."[34] This is what we would expect to see in a coherent state. David Wurfel argues that in the early years of martial law the state had "autonomy from the dominant class, and had the capability to make and implement policy, and only later did the state serve the interests of the superpatron and his closest clients."[35] Finally, Benedict Anderson writes:

From one point of view, Don Ferdinand can be seen as the Master Cacique or Master Warlord, in that he pushed the destructive logic of the old order to its natural conclusion. In place of dozens of privatized "security guards," a single privatized National Constabulary; in place of personal armies, a personal Army; instead of pliable local judges, a client Supreme Court; instead of myriad pocket and rotten boroughs, a pocket or rotten country, managed by cronies, hitmen, and flunkies.[36]

Even before Marcos, the Philippine judiciary was considered to be little more than a rubber stamp for powerful oligarchs. But Marcos succeeded in pushing that idea to its logical conclusion, by cowing the judiciary and forcing judicial approval for the most undemocratic and unconstitutional of acts.[37] As Carl Lande argues, "Marcos's skill in using the law and the constitutional amendment process to destroy the rule of law . . . served to disarm those of his opponents . . . who could find no legal means of

[34] Hutchcroft, "Oligarchs and Cronies," p. 440. Emphasis in original.
[35] Wurfel, *Filipino Politics*, p. 334.
[36] Anderson, "Cacique Democracy and the Philippines," pp. 3–33. Cited in Hutchcroft, "Oligarchs and Cronies," p. 442.
[37] Rolando del Carmen, "Constitutionality and Judicial Politics," in *Marcos and Martial Law in the Philippines*, edited by David A. Rosenberg (Ithaca: Cornell University Press, 1979).

blocking him."[38] This situation once again highlights the problems facing weakly institutionalized countries. Power resides not in a paper constitution, but in the ability of domestic actors to engage in checks and balances upon each other. Over time, the rule of law may come to be the dominant means of protection, but until then rulers have virtually free rein for their policies and actions. This kind of legal cover allowed Marcos to engage in the most selective and deliberate of acts, such as his expropriation and transfer of capital to his cronies.

There are interesting twists to the stylized notion that in the Philippines the state was weak. Under Marcos the traditionally powerful families were generally weak relative to the state. By attempting to break the power of the traditional landed oligarchs, Marcos engaged in a process of narrowing the elites who had access to state resources. The transfer of authority from the old legislature, which engaged in patronage, to technocrats allied with Marcos, diminished the rent-seeking capacity of the old elites. However, this new technocratic bureaucracy had no mass base of support. In this sense the Marcos regime was far more independent of civil society in the Philippines than had been the democratic legislature and executive. Autonomy from civil society does not necessarily mean capacity or coherence, however. Political and economic decisions were not made by a disinterested technocratic elite that then presented Marcos with options; rather, Marcos overrode the bureaucracy and dispensed favors to that small band of elites that still held favor with him.

Under Marcos decision making became further centralized in the presidential palace. By disbanding the Congress, Marcos removed one major source of incoherence and patronage. Yet Marcos's vision was not one of development, and the external pressures from the World Bank tended to support Marcos's decisions.[39] As Richard Doner points out: "the critical locus of decision-making was the presidential palace, not the technocrats and economic bureaucracy."[40] The technocrats had no indigenous support base that would allow them to press forward with their ideas for reforming the Filipino economy. Instead, cronies close to Marcos were able to circumvent almost any policy implemented by the bureaucrats.

[38] Carl Lande, "Authoritarian Rule in the Philippines," *Pacific Affairs* 55 (1982): 82.
[39] For a critical account of the World Bank's relationship with Marcos, see Walden Bello, David Kinley, and Elaine Elinson, *Development Debacle: The World Bank and the Philippines* (San Francisco: Institute for Food and Development Policy, 1982).
[40] Doner, *Driving a Bargain*, p. 171.

III. What Was Different in Korea? Credible Commitments and the Bifurcation of the State under Park

The difference between Park Chung-hee and Ferdinand Marcos was that Park was able to combine the twin goals of retaining power and pursuing economic development. A conventional wisdom exists that the military officers who descended upon the South Korean bureaucracy after the coup d'état in 1961 provided a more principled focus on economic development, a rational and goal-oriented perspective, in contrast to the corrupt and inefficient civil servants, and possessed organizational skills honed during the war.[41] This is so accepted an article of faith that the assumptions underlying it are rarely questioned: why would military officers, trained in the arts of war, have any better idea than the civilian bureaucracy about how to manage an entire national economy? It is also not clear why military officers who had retired from the military would be less inclined to use their position for corruption. Indeed, Park compensated for the military's scant economic expertise by keeping his military cronies out of important fiscal bureaus. This strategy was evident to domestic capitalists and allowed Park a measure of freedom in his dealings with both the military and the capitalists.

Park carefully orchestrated bureaucratic appointments to allow for both patronage *and* reform. Cronyism was far from overwhelming and was differentiated by various ministries. This allowed Park to achieve domestic control by buying off supporters and also to create pockets of efficiency that were oriented toward promoting defense and development. Appointments of military officials decreased over time. Initially, Park Chung-hee needed military support in all sectors of the bureaucracy as a means of consolidating and keeping control. Yet he gradually phased out the military's influence in some areas, thereby creating efficient bureaucracies.

Table 3.9 shows the initial composition of the Cabinet under Park Chung-hee. In May 1961, following the coup, 100 percent of the Cabinet posts were held by military cronies. Yet by 1963 that percentage had dropped to 33 percent. Similarly, Tables 3.10 and 3.11 show military officials as ministers and assemblymen, respectively. Once again, the percentages drop precipitously for ministers, although the percentage of assemblymen has fluctuated over time.

[41] Huer, *Marching Orders*, pp. 80–81.

Table 3.9. *Shifting Composition of the Cabinet under Military Rule*

	May–June 1961	July 1961–1962	1963
Prime Minister	*Chang Toyong	*Song Yochan	Kim Hyonchol
Economic Planning Board	—	Kim Yutaek	Won Yongsok
Foreign	*Kim Hongil	*Choi Tokshin	Kim Yongshik
Home	*Han Shin	*Han Shin	*Pak Kyongwon
Finance	*Paek Sonjin	Chon Pyongguy	Whang Chongyul
Justice	*Ko Wonjung	*Ko Wonjung	Min Bokki
Defense	*Chang Toyong	*Pak Pyongwon	*Kim Songun
Education	*Mun Hisok	*Mun Hisok	Yi Chong-u
Agriculture	*Chang Kyongsun	*Chang Kyongsun	*Yu Pyonghon
Commerce	*Chong Naehyok	*Chong Naehyok	Pak Chunghun
Construction	*Pak Kisok	(under EPB)	*Cho Songgun
Health and Social	*Chang Toksung	*Chong Hisop	*Chong Hisop
Transportation	*Kim Kwangok	*Pak Chunshik	Kim Yunki
Communication	*Pae Tokjin	*Pae Tokjin	Kim Changhun
Public Information	*Shim Hungson	O Chaegyong	Yim Songhi
Cabinet Secretariat	*Kim Pyongsam	Kim Pyongsam	*Yi Sokje
Without Portfolio	—	—	*Cho Shihyong
Military as percentage of total	100	80	33.3

Note: Asterisk denotes previous military career.

Source: "History of Military Revolution in Korea," part I, pp. 341–342, cited in Hahn-been Lee, *Time, Change, and Administration* (Honolulu: East-West Center, 1968), p. 168.

Table 3.10. *Former Military Officers as Ministers or Vice-Ministers (percentage)*

	1964–1972	1973–1979	1980–1986
Ministers	42.4[a]	31.7	24.5
	73[b]	45	37
Vice-ministers	15.9	16.5	21.9
	23	20	30
Board directors	47.4	35.7	34.8
	37	30	32

[a] Percentage among all ministers, VM, or Directors.
[b] Absolute number.

Source: Kim Kwang-woong, *Hankuk ŭi Kwallyo chedo yŏnku* (Research on the Korean bureaucracy) (Seoul: Taeyong Munhwasa, 1991), pp. 13–15.

Table 3.11. *Former Military Officers among National Assemblymen and Committee Chairmen*

	Sessions					
	1963–1967	1967–1971	1971–1972	1973–1978	1978–1979	1981–1985
Assemblymen	17.7[a]	21.1	17.2	22.4	16	9.4
	31[b]	37	35	49	37	26
Chairmen	41.7	37.5	38.5	34.6	46.2	50
	10	9	5	9	6	13

[a] Percentage.
[b] Absolute number.

Source: Kim Kwang-woong, *Hankuk úi kwallyo chedo yŏnku* (Research on the Korean bureaucracy) (Seoul: Taeyong Munhwasa, 1991), pp. 10–11.

Most interesting is Table 3.12 with its ministry-by-ministry breakdown of the origins of ministers and vice-ministers. The "fiscal" ministries (EPB, Finance, MTI) had relatively little military infiltration. Yet ministries not directly related to development were staffed heavily with ex-military officials. The Ministry of Construction, regarded as one of the most corrupt ministries in Korea, saw a large number of military appointments, eight out of a possible twenty-five. In South Korea public works contracts and construction in general have been poorly controlled. Recent events, such as the collapse of a bridge over the Han River and of the Sampoong Department Store, and an explosion at a subway construction site, are evidence of the lax enforcement of standards. Tables 3.13 and 3.14 show the most critical breakdown, the Ministry of Trade and Industry and the Economic Planning Board. In these cases the military influence is still muted.

The point of this section has been to show that the military and patronage appointments under Park Chung-hee, although prevalent and necessary for political control, were also selectively implemented. Park was able to create a bifurcated bureaucracy, directing patronage appointments to domestic "service" ministries while maintaining the professionalism of the "fiscal" ministries.

In addition, Park Chung-hee was extremely assiduous in creating what one former bureaucrat called a "three-levels-deep" political network in all the ministries: "Don't forget that Park was also using a criterion of skill; if you didn't perform, he always had an assistant Vice-Minister and

Table 3.12. *Career Backgrounds of Vice-Ministers and Higher, 1963–1983*

Bureau	Total Number	Number with Prior Career in Military
Prime minister	11	3
Economic Planning Board (EPB)		
M	13	1
VM	13	0
Presidential secretary		
Chief secretary	8	2
Economic secretary	9	0
Finance		
M	14	0
VM	18	0
Trade and Industry (MTI)		
M	11	2
VM	9	0
Agriculture and Forestry		
M	15	0
VM	11	0
Energy and Resources		
M	7	1
VM	3	0
Construction		
M	15	6
VM	10	2
Transportation		
M	16	11
VM	13	2
Defense		
M	9	9
VM	9	6
Home Affairs		
M	13	9
VM	13	3
KCIA		
Director	9	7

Note: M: Minister; VM: Vice-Minister.

Sources: Byung-kook Kim, "Bringing and Managing Socioeconomic Change," p. 119, and Ministry of Governmental Affairs.

Table 3.13. *Ministry of Trade and Industry Assistant Vice-Ministers and Office Directors and Their Prior Careers (1961–1980)*

Years	Prior Military Career	Prior Other Career	Total
1961–1965	2	3	5
1966–1970	2	3	5
1971–1975	0	5	5
1975–1980	0	2	2
TOTAL	4	13	17

Source: Compiled from Byung-kook Kim, "Bringing and Managing Socioeconomic Change" (Ph.D. diss., Harvard University, 1988), p. 112.

Table 3.14. *Economic Planning Board Assistant Vice-Ministers and Office Directors and Their Prior Careers (1961–1980)*

Year	Prior Military Career	Other Prior Career	Total
1961–1965	1	2	3
1966–1970	0	1	1
1971–1975	0	0	0
1976–1980	0	3	3
TOTAL	1	6	7

Source: Compiled from Byung-kook Kim, "Bringing and Managing Socioeconomic Change" (Ph.D. diss., Harvard University, 1988), p. 112.

a Planning Coordination Officer in the wings, waiting for their chance. So it wasn't just patronage, it was effective competition for Park's favor that induced such responsiveness."[42] Cronies who had become dangerous or had lost favor were sent to ambassadorial posts in second- or third-rate countries, far from the action.

In fact, Park's networks comprised a set of concentric circles around him. For political purposes, the most important posts were the Seoul Defense Command (*Sudokyŏngpisa*) and the heads of the CIA and the National Defense Security Command (*poansa*, which Chun Doo Hwan

---

[42] Author's interview with a bureaucrat who wished to remain unidentified, February 16, 1993.

would later command). The headquarters of the Seoul Defense is located next to Kyungbookgung Palace, and the commander was one of the few generals who had instant and direct access to Park. This was a military regime, existing under the shadow of war with North Korea. Thus for Park, managing the civil service was only one aspect of the larger political problem of maintaining his rule while leading the country in the direction he wished.

IV. Park's Major Policy Shifts

Korean technocrats, as would be any other bureaucrats, were at the mercy of their political superiors. Korea is not an example of a disinterested executive tying its own hands and letting the professionals do their work. Although in comparison with the Philippines the Korean state was relatively insulated from social demands, the Korean bureaucracy was not some monolithic and technocratic elite guiding development. Most of the evidence points to the bureaus in Korea as being the implementors of political decisions over policy, and not the primogenitors of such policies. As this section shows, the bureaucracy was often bypassed as Park made abrupt decisions about economic policy.

Aside from individual businessmen, the most influential organization from the business sector to have a systematic influence on Park's policies was the Federation of Korean Industries (FKI). Founded by those leading businessmen who had been arrested in 1961 for illicit accumulation of wealth, the FKI operates as a sort of club for the richest and most influential of the big capitalists and limits its membership to an elite stratum of entrepreneurs. After their release from jail, the members of the FKI submitted a plan to the Supreme Council on National Unification identifying fourteen key industrial plants – cement, steel, fertilizer, etc. – in which they were interested in investing. Notably, these plants, with their capitalization requirements six times the penalties imposed by the Park regime, were all essentially import-substituting plants. The FKI was formed under pressure from the government. One of the FKI's initial actions was to travel overseas and invite foreign capital to invest in Korea. Each FKI member was designated a particular field for investment.[43]

---

[43] Federation of Korean Industry, *Chŏnkyŏngnyŏn Samsipnyŏnsa* (A thirty-year history of the FKI) (Seoul: FKI, 1992).

The influence of the FKI makes it clear that the Korean bureaucracy's role was to justify and implement economic choices made for political reasons. In an interview, Hahn-been Lee told me that "of course the political leadership made all the major decisions about projects. We were there to provide a rationale for the decisions the regime had already made, and then to implement them. The approval guidelines were there to help, but were not strictly enforced."[44]

The FKI lobbied successfully for the construction of an integrated industrial complex at Ulsan in 1962 and for the export industrial complex at Kuro that was an early predecessor of the export-processing zones.[45] As Lee Young-hwan has written, "During the implementation of the First Five-Year Plan, on January 10, 1962, FKI submitted the 'Integrated Plan for the Foundation of Industry' to the government, which became the basis of the enormously successful Ulsan Industrial Complex."[46] Thus the original investment decisions in the early 1960s were a result of business-ruler relations, not the EPB's determining what would happen.

The key private sector interest was in finance, particularly in gaining access to foreign exchange. Lee Byung-chull noted that the FKI "engaged in various lobbying activities involving the government's guaranteeing of foreign loans and simplifying legal and administrative procedures on foreign loans."[47] Because Korean businessmen in the early 1960s did not have experience in obtaining foreign capital, the FKI – in conjunction with the government – took on the role of selecting and overseeing firms that wished to borrow abroad. With FKI approval, firms were more likely to obtain approval from the state.

And yet it is questionable whether the FKI actually represented sectors and industries (such as steel or shipbuilding) or in fact represented the families that owned the various *chaebol*.[48] Although the definitive work on the *chaebol* has yet to appear, the familial – perhaps clannish – nature of

[44] Author's interview, October 22, 1996.
[45] Federation of Korean Industry, *Chŏnkyŏngnyŏn Samsipnyŏnsa*, pp. 35–49.
[46] Lee Young-hwan, "Hankuk ŭi kyŏngje tanch'e wa chŏngch'aek kyŏlchŏng kujo" (Corporatist development and the structure of policy making in Korea), in *Hankuk kiŏpŭl segyehwa chŏllyak* (Strategies to globalize Korean industry), edited by Lee Young-hwan (Seoul: Chulpansa, 1995), p. 304.
[47] Lee Byung-chull, *Ho-am chachon* (Ho-Am's autobiography) (Seoul: Jungang Ilbo, 1986), p. 134.
[48] Kang Chol-gyu, Choi Jong-pyo, and Jang Jisang, *Chaebŏl: sŏngjang ŭi chuyŏk inka t'amyŏk ŭi hwasin inka* (Chaebol: Pivotal role in growth or paragon of greed?) (Seoul: Gyonje Jongui Chonsiminyonhap, 1991).

the Korean *chaebol* is often overlooked.[49] A former director in the Ministry of Commerce and Industry in the late 1970s told me that when one of the *chaebol* chairmen called, "he was transferred directly to the Minister, bypassing any of the bureaucratic layers. Then a decision at the top level would be reached, and we would get new directions from our boss depending on the result."[50] This influence of personal relationships and relative ineffectiveness of the formal organizations highlights a contradiction in the Korean political economy.

Politics was paramount within the bureaucracy as well, and Park responded more to political exigencies than to technocratic suggestions. A significant example comes from the decision to pursue an industrialization plan for chemicals and heavy industry in the early 1970s. As the 1960s progressed, and Park began to seriously consider the imperative to develop indigenous heavy industries, he turned first to both the EPB and the Ministry of Commerce and Industry (MCI) for their expertise. The EPB advocated a "civilian-initiated" rather than "government-supplied" course of action. In this plan, the government would pursue two long-term, slowly implemented policies: the government would gradually change the focus of development from light to heavy industries and, simultaneously, would withdraw from the center of economic planning and development.

Institutionally, the EPB was mandated with broad oversight of the entire economy. This contrasts with the more specific ministries (Finance, Construction), which had sectoral constituents and supporters. According to the EPB, the government had for too long interfered with the basic functioning of markets in Korea, and the best method of overcoming the *samchungko* ("three large problems": recession, inflation, and balance-of-payments problems) was to get the government out of the economy. By the late 1960s a fragile consensus was beginning to emerge in the EPB toward that end. The EPB chairman at that time, Kim Hak-Ryol, said that "the Economic Planning Board will increasingly make the creative efforts of the private corporations the key [to growth]."[51] In 1970 the prime minister, Paek Doo-Jin, was quoted as saying that "The EPB emphatically explained the necessity of the civilian-initiated mode."[52] The

[49] The best is probably that of Eunmee Kim, *Big Business, Strong State: Collusion and Conflict in South Korean Development, 1960–1990* (Albany, NY: SUNY Press, 1997).
[50] Author's interview, September 16, 1995.
[51] *Seoul Kyongje Sinmun*, January 21, 1970.
[52] *Seoul Kyongje Sinmun*, December 21, 1970.

EPB had chosen to slowly remove the state from the economy and, at the same time, slowly increase the emphasis on heavy and chemical industries. The time frame for this completion was set at five to ten years, the idea being that slow but steady moves toward a private sector economy would ensure the smoothest transition.[53] An editorial in a leading economic newspaper, the *Seoul Kyongje Sinmun*, echoes this private sector approach:

[Prime Minister Paek] declared that the government from now on would gradually change to a civilian-initiated mode, owing mainly to the fact that the government can no longer carry the burden of the government-supplied approach . . . We cannot but say that it is great progress that the government has emphasized the private sector.[54]

Park ignored these proposals, however, as they did not address the overall crisis facing the ruling elite. In the late 1960s, Park Chung-hee faced domestic unrest, unbalanced economic development, possible U.S. military withdrawal, and an active North Korean threat. Economic proposals focusing purely on the industrial structure of Korea could not satisfy these other political exigencies. Thus Park's governing exigencies differed dramatically from a technocrat's economic logic.

Unwilling to implement the reforms advocated by the EPB, Park created an ad hoc Second Economic Secretariat under the direction of Oh Won-chul. Oh, a chemical engineer from Seoul National, had served in the MCI for a decade before coming to the Blue House.[55] This secretariat became known as the Oh Group, and it advocated massive investment in heavy and chemical industries. Arguing that the macroeconomic models used by the EPB were outmoded, the Oh Group developed an *illampyo*, or a "master catalogue," with which to guide development. This plan, entitled "The Study on the Reorganization of the Industrial Structure," called for an international focus on the heavy and chemical industries for reasons of national security. The plan also emphasized the central role that government planning should occupy in the assumption of this project. Focusing on heavy and chemical industries as *such'ulhwa* (export orientation) and

---

[53] Author's interview with Kim Kwang-soo, former EPB official, September 21, 1995.
[54] *Seoul Kyongje Sinmun*, February 23, 1971.
[55] Inwon Choue, "The Politics of Industrial Restructuring: South Korea's Turn Toward Export-led Heavy and Chemical Industrialization, 1961–1974" (Ph.D. diss., University of Pennsylvania, 1988), p. 295.

kukchehwa (internationalization), the plan envisioned a "public corporation" under state control.[56]

The Oh Group quickly gained favor with Park, and its offices were headquartered in the Blue House. As Choue Inwon described the plan, "according to [Wonchul Oh], effective and viable HC industries could be built only if the size of each HC industry was geared to unlimited world markets. Given the exigency of national security as well as the economic problems, the HC project could not be promoted by giving too much freedom to individual firms."[57] Defense needs and economic considerations were given weights of 20 percent and 80 percent, respectively, in decisions regarding the projects. Therefore, "industrial sites were located close to the southern end of the Peninsula for defense considerations, and the shipyard of Daewoo Shipbuilding was made the largest in the world so that it could be used for repairing U.S. aircraft carriers."[58] In July 1972 the *Seoul Kyongje Sinmun* reported that the government had planned to unify formerly diversified export industries, and in September 1972 the targets of the Third Five-Year Plan were scaled upward.[59] Thus, by late 1972 the EPB had clearly failed in its attempt to promote the private sector as the leading group in the Third Plan, and the Oh Group's ideas of massive government intervention prevailed.[60]

V. Conclusion

There is little evidence that Park Chung-hee treated bureaucrats differently than had Rhee or Marcos. In all three cases, power remained firmly

---

[56] Choue, "The Politics of Industrial Restructuring," p. 297.

[57] Choue, "The Politics of Industrial Restructuring," p. 298.

[58] Jung-ho Yoo,"The Industrial Policy of the 1970s and the Evolution of the Manufacturing Sector in Korea" (Seoul: KDI Working Paper No. 90-17, October 1990), p. 19. Much of the material collected has been from interviews with Kim Ki-hwan, special economic advisor to Chun Doo-hwan, and Ahn Young-ok, president of Taewoo Chemicals from 1970 to 1975. See also Lee Gye-Sik, "pokchi kukka ŭi chŏnkae wa chaewŏn chotal chŏngch'aek" (The development and financial policies of the public welfare state) (Seoul: KDI Working Paper No. 91-25, 1991).

[59] *Seoul Kyongje Sinmun*, July 3, 1972, and September 25, 1972.

[60] For a more detailed discussion of how political interests overrode the technocrats' suggestions in South Korea, see Yong Gwan, "kwallyo chŏk kwŏlli chuŭi ŭi t'aedo wa chunghwahak kongŏp chŏngch'aek" (The emergence of the bureaucratic authoritarianism and policies of the heavy chemical industries), in Han Sang-jin, ed., *Hankuk sahoe pyŏndong kwa kukka yŏkhwal e kwanhan yŏnku* (Studies on the changes in Korean society and the role of the state), edited by Han Sang-jin (Seoul: Hyundai Saho Yonguso, 1985).

in the hands of the executive and was not delegated to meritocratic technocrats. By the period of martial law, the bureaucracy in both countries
had become autonomous from societal interests, but not from regime
interests.

Bureaucratic arrangements in the two countries were largely similar and
do not explain much about their policy processes or economic outcomes.
Even though Park supported and protected the economic technocrats in
his government from certain social pressures, it is a mistake to see the
technocrats as independent of the executive. Short-term political objec-
tives of the executive prevailed over, and ultimately circumvented, the
bureaucracy, bypassing existing bureaucratic structures by creating new
ones directly responsible to the president. This chapter has shown that
in Korea and the Philippines the bureaucracy was not the central locus
of policy-making activity. The following chapters will show in greater
detail the politics of policy making. Although the Korean state managed
to provide developmental assistance in a manner more coherent and
orderly than in the Philippines, it was a result not of better institutions
but of the political leadership and its relations with the business class.

4

Mutual Hostages in Korea

I don't want any position. . . . I did not want even to be the leader of the revolutionary government, let alone that of the Third Republic. As for rank, my position was only the third. I wished only to be an errand-boy in the rear.

– Park Chung-hee

The year 1995 saw the emergence of a corruption scandal in Korea that resulted in convictions of three of the nation's former presidents, jail sentences for numerous businessmen, and the early retirement of a number of military officers.[1] Although it was revealed during their trials that Chun Doo-hwan and Roh Tae-woo had amassed over one billion dollars, many suspected that the actual amount was far higher. Indeed, woven into the story of Korea's economic success is an underside of systematic influence peddling and money politics, and both reflect substantial continuity in the institutional foundations of pre- and post-1987 South Korean politics. The 1995 scandals raise a number of questions, including, Why has corruption occurred so regularly in both Korea and the Philippines? Why has it taken the form it has?

In this chapter we turn our attention from the institutions of governance to the larger institutional environment. The series of institutional

---

[1] For good overviews of the trials, see Joh Yong-jun, "6 kong ch'ŏngsan No Tae-u kwiyang" (The liquidation of the Sixth Republic and the exile of Roh Tae-woo), *Donga Ilbosa* (News plus) (November 2, 1995): 12–14; Ahn Byoung-yong, "pichagŭm kwa taekwŏn yokŭi chuakhan janch'i" (The disgusting feast of illicit funds and presidential hunger for power), *Shindonga* (December 1995): 112; Kim Yong-suh, "No Tae-u kusokgwa YS ŭi sŏntaek" (The detention of Roh Tae-woo and Kim Young-sam's choices), *Sisa Wolgan* (December 1995): 56–65; and Shim Jae-hoon and Andrew Sherry, "Cutting the Knot," *Far Eastern Economic Review* (November 30, 1995): 66–72. On the 1979 coup and the Kwangju uprising, see Il Kim, "Miguk, Kwangju Haksal 'Bangcho/Sŭngin' Hettda" (The United States gave approval and assistance for the Kwangju incident), *Shisa Jonol* (March 7, 1996): 26–33.

changes made under the Park Chung-hee regime (1961–1979) is often used as the starting point of Korea's high-growth era. Yet the Park regime was hardly depoliticized, and in fact money politics was pervasive. Not only was corruption extensive, but political connections overrode economic criteria and allowed for overcapacity and bailouts of indebted and poorly managed firms. The process was simple: business and political elites exchanged bribes for political favors. Politicians used these political funds to buy votes and also to satisfy their basic greed. Businessmen used the rents from cheap capital to expand their companies as rapidly as possible, thus ensuring the businessmen's continued political and economic importance. Development and money politics proceeded hand in hand.

The Korea that will emerge in this chapter is one in which a rough balance between state and business forced accommodation, or "constrained collusion," by both parties. Yet to argue that Korean money politics was not as extensive as that in the Philippines does not make corruption peripheral to the story. And to argue that some form of constraint operated on Korean business does not mean that the state dominated business or imposed stringent controls. This chapter begins to make the descriptive argument (continued in Chapter 5) that, far from being different, Korea and the Philippines have experienced similar levels and patterns of money politics. Money permeates the normal politics of elections, economic policy making, taxation, and the day-to-day running of the country in both Korea and the Philippines. Like in the Philippines under Marcos, a significant level of corruption existed in Korea before, during, and after Park Chung-hee.

The discussion of Korean corruption brings us back to the theory laid out in Chapter 1. The existence of a small number of coherent political and economic elites limited the costs of rent-seeking games and made the social cost of corruption smaller than it was in the Philippines. However, the exchange was political, and although the Korean state may have wanted to exchange subsidies for performance, political considerations were often more important than merit. The constant bailouts of indebted firms, over-invoicing as firms padded their balance sheets, and the endemic over-capacity of the *chaebol* are evidence that the state was unsuccessful in imposing standards. All things being equal, Park wanted more- rather than less-efficient businessmen. But all things were not equal, and this chapter tells the political story that lay behind the developmental state.

The first section focuses on politicians and the demand for political funds, and the second section discusses businessmen and the supply of funds in return for favors. Together these sections show that ostensibly "objective" indicators were subject to manipulation, that performance standards were not enforced in any meaningful manner, and that bigger was better for political, not economic, reasons. The third section shows that personal connections and a mutual-hostage situation structured the pattern of money politics and constrained collusion. The final section shows that even events heralded as watersheds of the developmental state – in this case the Illicit Wealth Accumulation Act of 1961 – were motivated by politics and had little to do with eliminating corruption.

I. Politicians: The Demand for Political Funds

Money politics in Korea derived from the need to win elections and retain power. Even authoritarian leaders with a range of coercive and cooperative means of suasion at their disposal will look over their shoulders at who might be gaining on them. Indeed, whereas a democratically elected politician knows how long he will be in office and when he will face the next challenge, authoritarian leaders are fundamentally insecure because they could face a challenge at any time. Although it may appear in retrospect that Korea's rulers were stable and secure, Park barely won reelection in 1971 and was forced to declare martial law to retain power.[2]

Park Chung-hee's rule from 1961 to 1979 saw both dramatic economic growth and extensive money politics. Park's rise to power after the May 16, 1961, coup d'etat saw the creation of the Democratic Republican Party (DRP). Created by Kim Jong-pil, Park's nephew-in-law and head of the Korean CIA (KCIA), the party was imposed from above in October 1963.[3] The party was highly centralized, and its single chain of command governed its finances from the center to the district level. But like Rhee's Liberal Party before Park, the DRP evaporated after Park Chung-hee died in 1979, as power shifted to a new center of gravity.

After the military coup in May 1961, Park had made vague promises to turn the country over to civilian and democratic leadership "when the

[2] For more on the *Yushin* constitution, see Go Song-guk, "1970 nyŏndae chŏngch'i pyŏndonge kwanhan yŏnku" (Research on political changes in the 1970s), in *Hankuk chabon chuŭi wa kukka* (Korean capital and the state), edited by Choi Jang-jip (Seoul: Hanwul, 1985).
[3] See Gregory Henderson, *The Politics of the Vortex* (Cambridge, MA: Harvard University Press, 1968), p. 306; and Alexander Joungwon Kim, *Divided Korea: The Politics of Development, 1945–1972* (Cambridge, MA: Harvard University Press 1975), p. 236.

98

time was right." For two years Korea was run by the "Supreme Council for National Reconstruction (SCNR)," which pursued vigorous purges of politicians, civil servants, and businessmen. In late 1962, Park Chung-hee reversed course, saying that the time was not ripe for democratic elections. James Killen, U.S. AID director to Korea, began withholding portions of U.S. aid in March 1962 in an attempt to push the South Korean government under Park to undertake economic and political reform. President Kennedy personally protested to Park, and the State Department withheld $25 million in economic aid to "underscore the determination to bring constitutional government to Korea."[4] Korea's economic situation in 1962 was grave, as the country faced inflation, balance of payments crises, and surging interest rates. Park initially attempted to win funding from Europe and private international sources, but he was unsuccessful. Forced to rely on the United States to stabilize the economic situation, Park acquiesced in 1963 to U.S. demands and held elections.

Retaining power requires political organization, and that means political funding. Although Park was no great fan of democracy, he was forced to work behind a democratic facade. Despite the enormous resources of the state that could be used to further political goals, and despite blatant attempts to rig the vote, Park was never guaranteed a victory. Park and the DRP organized society through a number of means. Thus Park created a planning committee (the *tangchŏng hyŏphoe*, "party-government consultative body"), situated in the presidential mansion, that was more powerful than the formal Cabinet.

The largest organization outside of the DRP was the People's Movement for National Reconstruction (*Kukto kŏnsol tan*). Units were established down to the village level throughout Korea, and at one point the organization was reported to have 3.9 million members.[5] Not only did the DRP require a large staff and budget, it also bought votes through the traditional *huwŏnhoe* (personal vote) system: for example, by throwing parties, creating hiking clubs, and attending weddings and holidays. Although the DRP won the southern and rural districts, the opposition tended to win in the cities, a phenomenon that came to be known as *yŏchŏn-yado* (the ruling party is strong in the countryside, [and] the opposition is strong in the cities).

[4] From Stephan Haggard and Chung-in Moon, "Korea's Political Economy" (unpublished MS).
[5] Kwan Bong Kim, *The Korea-Japan Treaty Crisis and the Instability of the Korean Political System* (New York: Praeger, 1971), p. 158.

Money was important also because many of the provisions in the new constitution (approved by nationwide referendum on December 17, 1962) made party politics highly centralized. These measures were taken to restrict the chances of the opposition's actually winning any elections, but they had the consequence of raising the cost of politics. Independent politicians were barred from entering the National Assembly; hence a party organization was necessary to nominate candidates. Thus, whoever controlled the party could control politics, leading to even more concentration of power within the party. In addition, the Political Party Law further restricted party activities. Voluntary political activities such as campaigning were forbidden – only registered members of a party could campaign. Parties were prohibited from soliciting or accepting donations except from registered party members, and advertising was restricted to outlets such as radio – door-to-door canvassing was not allowed. This meant that money became even more important for those in pursuit of office, and it gave an enormous advantage to the ruling party, which controlled access to radio stations and permits for rallies.[6]

The election laws, imposed by the military junta, restricted political activities so severely that, as Alexander Kim notes, "[N]o party could be effective unless it had many wealthy members, or unless it could secure secret, illegal donations – something the ruling party could do, but which an opposition party would find immensely difficult."[7] Park's coalition base consisted of an extensive and expensive party apparatus that organized and controlled society as well as of side payments to his constituents in the form of direct vote buying.

According to the financial report of the Central Election Management Committee, the annual costs of running the DRP in the 1960s were as high as 5.7 billion *won* (or $43 million at an exchange rate of 130 *won* to a U.S. dollar). The DRP secretariat alone was estimated to have thirteen hundred staff members, and the estimated cost of operating the secretariat was $700,000 per month.[8] During the 1963 election, the DRP was estimated to have spent 76.9 percent of total campaign spending.[9] During the 1967 elections an estimated $40 million was spent buying votes.[10]

---

[6] Alexander Kim, *Divided Korea*, p. 244.   [7] Alexander Kim, *Divided Korea*, p. 245.
[8] Alexander Kim, *Divided Korea*, p. 237.
[9] Park Kyung-suk, "Taet'ongnyŏng kukhoe wiwŏn sŏngo chagŭm" (Campaign funds for presidential and assembly elections), *Shindonga* (May 1967): esp. pp. 204–207.
[10] Kim Jin-bae and Park Chang-rae, "Ch'agwan" (Foreign loans), *Shindonga* (December 1968): 88.

Lee Duck-soo, a civil servant with experience under three regimes (Rhee, Chang, and Park), noted that "with the benefit of hindsight, there was very little corruption in the Rhee regime, compared to later governments. The Liberal Party wasn't involved in payoffs and political fund-raising nearly to the extent that later governments were."[11] When queried about a direct Rhee-Park comparison, Lee noted that "Park had more money to play with than Rhee, because the economy was bigger. Of course Park was involved in political fund-raising. He'd give out $100,000 at a time to people who had done good work for him."[12]

Politics also had a repressive side that required funding. Chief among the tools used to keep domestic order was the KCIA (*Ankipu*), organized on June 10, 1961. By 1964 the KCIA had 370,000 employees – remarkable in a country that then consisted of 20 million people.[13] The comparison with the 1950s is striking: under Rhee the size of the police force had decreased from 63,427 policemen in 1953 to 33,000 in 1957.[14] The KCIA engaged in numerous activities, most designed to quell domestic dissent. Indeed:

The impression that Park's domain was infested with his intelligence agents permeated every nook and cranny of society. A sense of immediacy of his government pervaded the whole country. Bureaucrats, politicians, judges, military men, diplomats, businessmen, journalists, professors and scholars – not to mention his minions and sycophants – all performed for a one-man audience, "the personage on high." When it was necessary to refer to him in private conversation, even his critics resorted to hushed euphemisms.[15]

Mark Clifford reports that seventeen antigovernment students were kidnapped from West Germany in 1967.[16] Kim Dae-jung, the leader of the opposition party, was kidnapped from a Tokyo hotel room and barely escaped with his life after intensive U.S. pressure, and the former head of the KCIA, Kim Hyung-wook, disappeared in Paris in 1979 after

[11] Author's interview, October 2, 1996. [12] Author's interview, October 2, 1996.
[13] Alexander Kim, *Divided Korea*, p. 234.
[14] Chung-in Moon and Sang-young Rhyu, "Overdeveloped State and the Political Economy of Development in the 1950s: A Reinterpretation," Paper presented at the conference "Toward an Industrial Society in Korea," University of British Columbia, December 13, 1996, p. 7.
[15] Kim Suk Jo and Edward J. Baker, *The Politics of Transition: Korea after Park* (unpublished MS, East Asian Legal Studies, Harvard Law School, 1980), quoted in Mark Clifford, *Troubled Tiger: Businessmen, Bureaucrats, and Generals in South Korea* (M. E. Sharpe, 1994), p. 83.
[16] Clifford, *Troubled Tiger*, p. 81.

testifying before the U.S. Congress, presumed murdered by the Park regime. Other tools of political control included the Security Service (*Kyunghowon*), the Counter-Espionage Operations Command (*Bangch' opdae*), and the Military Intelligence Agency (*Boan-sa*).

To fund their operations, political elites took massive donations from the *chaebol*. Under Park Chung-hee this financial system of exchanging policy for bribes became quasi institutionalized. Leading members of the DRP were in charge of political fund-raising, the two most important persons being Kim Sung-Kon and Kim Jin-man.[17] These members of Park's inner circle had clear fund-raising duties: one dealt with personal connections, another with the parties, and others with big business. The allocation of bank loans, foreign loans, import licenses, and other policy decisions were based on a political funds system that required donations from the capitalists. During the 1960s, the expected kickback became normalized at between 10 and 20 percent of the loan.[18]

Businessmen often called "voluntary" donations *chun chose*, or "quasi taxes."[19] For example, the *Saemaul Undong* was a 1970s political organization whose ostensible aim was to improve the quality of rural life but that was also used as a home for embezzlement, nepotism, and cronyism. Hyundai donated 7.4 billion *won* to the cause from 1971–1975, Samsung 7.8 billion, LG 6.7 billion, and Daewoo 4.85 billion (Table 4.1). Even if the *chaebol* donations were used for the intended humanitarian purpose, such giving was certainly part of the larger web of money politics. The fact remained that if businessmen did not provide politicians with sufficient funds when asked, their loans got called by the Bank of Korea, or they suffered a tax audit, or their subsidy application was denied.[20] The best example of this is the Kukje group's refusal to make "voluntary" donations to the Ilhae Foundation, and Chun Doo-hwan's subsequent dismemberment of the company. In 1985 the Kukje group, with 38,000 employees, was the seventh-largest *chaebol* in Korea, and like all *chaebol*, was highly leveraged with significant loans from the government.

[17] Lee Young-suk, "sŏngŏ chagŭm kwa chaebŏl" (Election funds and chaebols), *Wolgan Chosun* (November 1987): 222–239.

[18] Jung-en Woo, *Race to the Swift* (New York: Columbia University Press, 1991), p. 108.

[19] Although much of these quasi taxes were accountable and not direct corruption, they were part of the government-business relationship and hence are important to understanding the political process.

[20] David C. Kang, "South Korean and Taiwanese Development and the New Institutional Economics," *International Organization* 49, no. 3 (1995): 560–561.

Table 4.1. *Details of Selected* Chaebol *Contributions and Political Funds (billion* won)

Rank in Sales, 1992	Saemaul Undong (Park, Chun)	Sae sedae YukyÒn ghoe (Park)	Sae sedae Simchang Foundation (Park)	Ilhae Foundation (Chun)	DJP Funds (Chun)	Total	Rank in Giving
1. Hyundai	7.4	2.5	3.0	5.15	.52	18.57	1
2. Samsung	7.8	2.0	1.0	4.5	.9	16.2	2
3. LG	6.7	.5	.3	3.0	1.3	11.8	3
4. Daewoo	4.85	.3	.8	4.0	.7	10.65	4
5. SK	5.8	1.0		2.8	1.0	10.6	5
6. Ssangyong	2.7			1.5	.8	5.0	12
7. Hanjin	4.5	.7	1.0	2.2	.6	9.0	7
8. Korea Explosives	1.1	.4	.8	1.5	.4	4.2	13
9. Hyosung	.8	.2	.2	.9	.2	2.3	20
10. Dongkuk	2.1		2.2	1.45	.6	6.35	10
11. Kia	3.6			.7	1.0	5.3	11
12. Doosan	1.1			.9		2.0	21
13. Lotte	3.9	.02	.87	2.0	.2	6.99	8
14. Kolong	0.75			.7	.4	1.85	22
15. Donga	1.0	1.0		1.3		3.3	17
16. Hanil	5.7	.6	1.8	.9	1.3	10.3	6
17. Daelim	3.3	.5		1.3	1.5	6.6	9
18. Kumho	1.9	.05		1.0	1.2	4.15	14
19. Dongbu	2.6	.1		.3	.4	3.4	16
20. Sammi	1.7	.3			.6	2.6	19
21. Poongsan	2.5			.8	.4	3.7	15
22. Hanbo	2.2	.03			.7	2.93	18
TOTAL	74.0	10.2	11.97	36.9	14.72	147.79	

Source: Han Heung-soo and Ahn Byung-hoon, "Hankuk ŭi pihap pŏpchŏk chŭngch'i chagŭm ŭi yuhyŏng kwa siltae" (Patterns and realities of illegal political funds in Korea), *Tong Suh Yonku* (East and West studies) 7 (1994): 207.

However, Kukje's president, Yang Chung-mo, seriously offended President Chun Doo-hwan by refusing to contribute significant sums to quasi-governmental organizations such as the Ilhae Foundation[21] and the *Saemaul Undong* (New Village Movement). As a result, the state refused to

---

[21] This research foundation, created by Chun Doo-hwan, was named for Chun's pseudonym, "sun and sea."

loan money to Kukje and refused to honor its checks. Within weeks, Kukje could not service its debt and had to declare bankruptcy.[22]

During the period leading up to the first presidential election in 1963, it was reported that the DRP received up to $66 million from Japanese sources.[23] To put this in context, South Korea's entire GNP in 1965 was $2.9 billion and its per capita GNP $106. Political elites received almost $10 million in commission fees for arranging Japanese imports, and $38 million in kickbacks from industrialists for the "Three Whites Scandal," in which sugar, flour, and cement companies made illegal profits. Other stories of malfeasance abound. The Walker Hill hotel complex, the *pachinko* machines illegally imported by Kim Jong-pil, and the reselling of imported cars were all sources of funding for Park's political machine.

Distributive coalitional politics was one major reason for the prevalence of political funds. However, political funds had another major "use" – satisfying basic greed. Not surprisingly, the size of the *chaebol* correlated with close personal relations, and *inmaek* and *honmaek* (personal relations and marriage relations) also figured significantly in the flow of political funds. Most of Korea's major businessmen have marriage ties with the country's major political figures, and all elites assiduously cultivate their personal relationships.

In addition to using political funds to retain power, those close to Park were able to benefit personally. One participant in the May 1961 coup was Kim Hyung-wook, a former military classmate of Park's. He headed the KCIA from March 1963 until October 1969 and was a member of the National Assembly. He later testified before the U.S. Congress about Park's regime. Mark Clifford quotes one congressional investigator's impressions of Kim:

> In all the many hours of interviewing Kim Hyung-wook, I came to the conclusion that this man was a caricature of a gangster. . . . Considering that he was one of the two or three most powerful people in the country for six or seven years, one has to conclude that either Park Chung hee was an idiot or he was condoning outrageous criminal behavior. Whether Park was putting money in his pocket or not, he knew he was heading a criminal enterprise.[24]

After Park's death, half a million dollars was found in his personal safe. His cronies also had benefited: Kim Jong-pil was reported to have amassed

---

[22] Clifford, *Troubled Tiger*, pp. 208–212; and *Wall Street Journal*, February 2, 1985, p. 32(W).
[23] Alexander Kim, *Divided Korea*, p. 253.
[24] Ed Baker, congressional staff, quoted in Clifford, *Troubled Tiger*, p. 89.

property and businesses worth more than $50 million at 1979 prices; this windfall included a 5,000-acre ranch, a tangerine orchard, a 2,100-head dairy farm in Chungchong-do, a newspaper company in Seoul, and over $36 million in real estate. Kim Jong-pil also reportedly had $7 million in thirty-four secret bank accounts, a 1.1 kilogram gold sword, a "huge collection" of antiques and jewelry, and $2.5 million in "cooperation fees" from companies.[25]

Kim Jong-pil's acquisition methods included diverting political contributions to his personal accounts. From 1961 until 1980 he received almost constant "donations" from businesses and individuals in return for export licenses, preferential loans, and other policy favors.[26] Kim invested in an orange farm on Cheju Island in 1968; when there was public outcry in 1974 over his arm twisting to obtain special favors and dispensations, he created a phantom foundation and "donated" the property to it, but he retained control of the farm's operations. In 1968, Kim also purchased from the government at a very low price a huge land area in So-san County, South Chungchong Province, and invested in livestock using an interest-free loan from the "D" Construction Company.

Lee Hu-rak, who had been the presidential chief of staff at the Blue House from 1964 to 1969, accumulated $40 million. As chief of staff, Lee received bribes from forty-one businesses and individuals totaling more than 2.9 billion *won*, including 50 million *won* from the president of "S" Automobile Company, a Mr. K., for his role in securing for the company favorable treatment in taking over an automobile factory. Lee established educational foundations in Ulsan, his hometown, and kept control of their finances, effectively avoiding paying taxes while enjoying flattering public relations.

Oh Won-Chul, the architect of the Heavy and Chemical Industrialization Plan (HCIP), accumulated wealth of at least $4.5 million. In 1976, Oh took a bribe of 2.2 million *won* from a Mr. K., president of "S" Electric, for helping the firm to obtain (manufacturing) machinery and

[25] "Kwŏllyŏkhyŏng ch'ukchaesa kyŏlgwa" (The investigation and disposition of corrupt officials), announcement by the Martial Law Enforcement Headquarters, June 18, 1980 (entire text included in *Chosun Ilbo*, June 19, 1980); "Kwŏllyŏkhyŏng puchŏng ch'ukjedŭl" (Corrupt officials), *Chosun Ilbo*, June 19, 1980; *Donga Yongam 1981*, "Jongchi" (Politics) (Seoul: Donga Ilbosa, 1981), pp. 105–119 and 804–819; and Shim Jae-hoon, "Seoul's Crackdown on Corruption," *Far Eastern Economic Review* (July 4, 1980): 54.

[26] Oh Hyo-jin, "JP, Taumŭn imcha ch'aryeya: Chonghwadae mildam" (JP, your turn is next: Secret conversations at the Blue House), *Wolgan Chosun* (December 1986): 42.

continuing to facilitate its procurement. Oh also took bribes of more than 100 million *won* from industrial firms.[27]

Former army chief of staff Lee Se Ho had $18.5 million, much of it from embezzling government funds. Former deputy speaker of the National Assembly Kim Jin-man had $17 million in assets, Kim Jong-pil's brother Kim Jong Nak had $15 million, presidential bodyguard "Pistol" Park Chong-kyu had $12.8 million, former prime ministerial aide Lee Pyong-Hi had $4 million – the list goes on.[28] However, there existed a downside to close personal relations with Park, as well as a positive side. Those who fell afoul of Park were in exposed positions, and Park was not afraid to use his power to destroy anyone who angered him. In his congressional testimony, Kim Hyung-wook noted that

> Mr. Park imposed severe pressures and sanctions on businessmen who did not give him their undivided loyalty. In many cases, charges were fabricated and these individuals were sent to jail. In addition to imprisonment, the businesses of these individuals were often confiscated. Some of the business companies that were destroyed or taken over were Yonhap Steel Co., Shinjin Automobile Co., Chungang Industries and Builders, Tongkwang Business, Koryo Shipbuilding Co., Kwang Myong Printing Co., Koryo Food Co., Kyungnam Business Co., Tachan Transportation Co., and the Cheju Bank.[29]

Thus Park engaged in money politics to retain power and to disorganize and limit the opposition. At the same time, individual political elites were able to benefit dramatically. Given the small number of elites, this web of interlocking ties was cemented by personal and marriage relations.

II. Businessmen: The Supply of Bribes in Exchange for Rents

The demand for political funds was met by a supply of political donations from businessmen seeking government favors. As noted previously, my argument complements Alice Amsden's that the state exchanged subsidies

---

[27] "Kwŏllyŏkhyŏng ch'ukchaesa kyŏlgwa" (The investigation and disposition of corrupt officials), announcement by the Martial Law Enforcement Headquarters, June 18, 1980 (entire text included in *Chosun Ilbo*, June 19, 1980).

[28] Shim Jae-hoon, "Seoul's Crackdown on Corruption," p. 54.

[29] U.S. Congress, House of Representatives, *Investigation of Korean-American Relations: Hearing before the Subcommittee on International Organizations of the Committee on International Relations*, 95th Congress, Part I, June 22, 1977, p. 11.

for performance.[30] The difference is that I provide a political story that explains the patterns of exchange. I also show that the process based on money politics is heavily biased and not nearly as efficient as Amsden maintains. Despite almost constant attempts by the EPB to limit their expansion, big, well-connected firms were able to use personal relations both to keep the flow of rents and to avoid sanction. After discussing the logic of this exchange, I show how the exchange worked in practice, focusing on overexpansion and indebtedness.

1. The Logic of the Exchange

In the context of an authoritarian regime that is selectively handing out favors in return for bribes, size is an advantage. A capitalist who had already acquired a license to invest in a project was at a great advantage in acquiring additional credit from the government. Because only a small number of capitalists had shown their ability to produce in the past, they stood out.

Bureaucrats have an innate tendency to avoid risky decisions and to rely on past performance as an indicator of future success, and so "the rich got richer." The few large firms were considered to be better investment risks, regardless of the actual quality of the business plan they had submitted to the government. In addition, most decisions were made at the highest governmental levels. Thus, because they had "back-door" access through personal connections that suggested precisely what officials at the top of the regime desired, some *chaebol* were able to submit applications specifically designed to fit the regime's political and economic goals. This became a reinforcing cycle, in which bigger was better, the rich got richer, and political connections were critical in getting favorable decisions.

Political and social strength came from size: profitability was not nearly as important to businessmen as survival and growth. Most Korean firms have had lax accounting procedures, and siphoning off funds was very easy to do. In addition, much of the conspicuous consumption by elites was for social purposes. Having a limousine, a driver, and money for entertaining was the means to political and social success. As long as the firm was not bankrupt, there was always a way to get discretionary cash. Thus, a number of factors, both economic and political, led to the enormous indebtedness of the *chaebol* in Korea and the focus on rapid expansion.

---

[30] Amsden, *Asia's Next Giant* (Cambridge: Cambridge University Press, 1989).

Byung-yoon Park noted:

If a high-ranking bureaucrat made a decision to support a less well-known small applicant, rather than an established *chaebol*, there followed invariably public suspicion: "Even large *chaebol* couldn't get it. How could a small unknown man get such support? There must have been a hidden reason or bribery."[31]

Also, bureaucrats are attempting to advance up their own career paths, and their progress was highly monitored by Park Chung-hee and the political leadership. Of course, the best way to advance is to be successful, and spreading out scarce government-allocated capital to many small firms was not as impressive as was picking proven winners. Monitoring and enforcement too were much easier with fewer firms. In addition, the larger *chaebol* were more likely to give the bureaucrat a job upon retirement from the government. All of these factors combined to make it politically wiser for bureaucrats to reward large size and to approve projects based on track record, personal connections, and historical background rather than on the pure merit of the proposal.

There were rewards for bureaucrats who helped this process. A bureaucrat who had worked in the EPB from 1963 to 1970 and risen to the level of *sogigwan* (director) recalled, with a mixture of pride and regret:

In 1966 we lived near Taehangno, in a little apartment. Many of my colleagues lived in much nicer houses, because they would accept the "donations" that were offered. One day around my birthday we got a cake delivered to our house, and inside was a packet full of money. I immediately knew who it was from, and I returned it the next day. My family would've been better off if I'd been like the others, but this way I slept at night.[32]

Because bigger was better and led more easily to rewards, and because personal connections and size were joined in a mutually reinforcing virtuous cycle, many firms either massaged or fabricated outright their export data during the period of high growth. Although it is true that firms in Korea did export a large percentage of their production, those numbers were frequently inflated. In addition, most applications for government support did not require the type of financial accounting and transparency that is expected in the West; in Korea, past performance and past use of

---

[31] Interview quoted in Kim Seok-ki, "Business Concentration and Government Policy: A Study of the Phenomenon of Business Groups in Korea, 1945–1985" (Ph.D. diss., Harvard University, 1987), p. 110.
[32] EPB bureaucrat from 1963 to 1970; author's interview, February 16, 1993.

government aid were used in selecting those companies that might succeed in the future. Thus any numbers about the Korean economy should be evaluated with care. A businessman who worked out of the chairman's office of one of Korea's largest *chaebol* told me that the numbers they reported to the Bank of Korea, to the World Bank, and to major publications such as *Fortune* were all highly inflated. "Of course we made them [the trade figures] up. I would wait for the chairman to let me know what the numbers were supposed to be and then find a way to make it so."[33]

2. How the Process Worked in Practice

Given the tendency to reward size, larger and more well-connected firms could more easily resist political pressure. In practice, two aspects of this pattern were critical. First, firms expanded as quickly as possible. Second, firms borrowed as much capital as they could, becoming heavily indebted. Given the Korean state's total control over the financial sector in the 1960s and 1970s, businesses were naturally interested in gaining access to the enormous rents that accrued to a *chaebol* if it received a low-interest-rate loan. The state's inability to limit borrowing, however, led to endemic expansion and overcapacity. Firms rushed to expand, whether or not it was economically feasible. The result was that in most major sectors of the economy there was excess capacity as well as overlapping and duplication of efforts as each *chaebol* tried to be the biggest.

The car industry is a good example. Despite numerous attempts to rationalize the automobile industry and force domestic firms to concentrate on core competencies, Korea throughout the 1970s had more capacity and more players than the EPB considered economically feasible. In 1969, Hyundai Motors operated at 49 percent of capacity and in 1972 at only 25.8 percent of capacity. The rest of the industry was no better. Even in 1979, after the rationalization efforts had accelerated, total Korean passenger car production was operating at 48.6 percent of capacity (Table 4.2).

Yet observers of the automobile industry have noted that continuous attempts by the government to impose a unitary automobile producer in Korea (beginning with the 1963 "unitarization plan") have been singularly unsuccessful, owing to the ability of the local capitalists to resist

---

[33] Author's interview with a member of the chairman's secretariat of a major *chaebol*, March 14, 1993.

Table 4.2. *Passenger Car Production/Capacity in 1979*
(percentage)

	Production/Capacity
Hyundai	61.8
Saehan/Daewoo	24.6
Kia	55.4
TOTAL	48.6

Source: Korea Development Bank, *Industry in Korea* (Seoul: Korea Development Bank, 1980), pp. 114–115.

government intervention. An effort by Kim Jong-pil, then head of the KCIA, to assemble Nissan vehicles collapsed in 1963 in part due to protests from Korean parts manufacturers that imports of Nissan parts would eradicate the home market. When Park Chung-hee attempted to consolidate the industry around Shinjin Company to assemble Toyotas, he failed as well. Park Byung-yoon argued that industry saw the government as ineffective and as "a weak organization that lacks the will and resources to implement its own policy. If the government had tried to enforce policies against the interests of industry, the government could not have done anything to make the business community comply with its program."[34]

Finally, between August and October of 1980, on an EPB initiative, the Korean government ordered the automobile industry to "merge by decree." The objective was to create financially sound companies that were more willing and better able to compete in export markets and to assemble foreign-designed cars in Korea. The plan was to merge Hyundai Motors with Daewoo's Saehan subsidiary to produce passenger cars, while

[34] B. Y. Park, "The Inside Story of the Automobile Industry," *Shindonga* (November 1979), quoted in Seok-jin Lew, "Bringing Capital Back In: A Case Study of South Korean Automobile Industrialization" (Ph.D. diss., Yale University, 1992), p. 176. For other analyses of the government-*chaebol* relationship, see Jong Byong-Gol and Yang Yung-sik, *Hankuk chaebŏl pumunŭi kyongje punsŏk* (An analysis of the economics of the Korean chaebol), (Seoul: Korea Development Institute, 1992); Kim Ju-hoon, Im Choi-song, Ok Song-chol, Han Guang-seok, Ha Woo-son, and Kim Dong-yol, "chuyo sanŏpŭi tonghyang, chŏnmang kua kwaje" (Trends in major industries: Perspectives and prescriptions) (Seoul: KDI Working Paper No. 91-03, June 1991); and Lee Gye-Sik, "Pokchikukka ŭi chŏnkae wa pokji chaewŏn chodal chŏngch'aek" (The development and financial policies of the public welfare state) (Seoul: KDI Working Paper No. 91–25, August 1991).

forcing Kia Industries out of the passenger car market. The government's plan failed.[35]

In fact, the influence of the automobile *chaebol* on Korean developmental plans has been so pervasive that one scholar has termed the state's policies "inconsistent and incoherent." Lew writes that "the lack of insulation in the policy-making process, from the business circle or the political circle, contributed to the oscillation and the incoherent character of automobile industrial policies. . . . Career bureaucrats did not exercise any decisive influence on the development of the South Korean automobile industry in the 1960s."[36]

As Byung-sun Choi writes: "Paradoxically, the fact that the government controlled credit allocation weakened, rather than strengthened, the force of the government's commitment to discontinue financing, because private investors knew that terminating financial assistance would be disastrous not only for themselves but probably more for the political regime. In sum, [the] Korean government's extraordinary measures to restructure excessive heavy industrial investment projects failed."[37] Essentially, the government had a noncredible threat: businessmen knew that the state could not credibly expropriate their wealth without severe disruptions to the entire economy.

Other industries were also able to successfully resist merger decrees.[38] Hyundai Power Company in the late 1970s was in deep trouble. Its capital-asset ratios were far below the values agreed on by the World Bank and the EPB.[39] And yet, because the process of creating a power plant had significant sunk costs, Hyundai was reluctant to abandon the power project. Daewoo and Samsung also produced power, and the government attempted to rationalize them in the late 1970s into one main group. But

[35] Lew, "Bringing Capital Back In," Ch. 5. See also Byung-sun Choi, "Institutionalizing a Liberal Economic Order in Korea" (Ph.D. diss., Harvard University, 1987), pp. 129–130.
[36] Lew, "Bringing Capital Back In," p. 145.
[37] Choi, "Institutionalizing a Liberal Economic Order in Korea," p. 132.
[38] Choi, "Institutionalizing a Liberal Economic Order in Korea," pp. 126–127, see also Kim Eun-mee, "From Dominance to Symbiosis," p. 238.
[39] By 1978, Hyundai Yanghaeng had invested $200 million in a huge integrated machinery plant and needed $200 million more to finish the project. Capital asset ratios were 8% by December 1978, far short of the target levels: 30% by 1979. See EPB, "Hyŏndae yanghaeng ch'angwŏn kongdan mit okp'o chosŏnsoe kwanhan taech'aek" (Measures regarding Hyundai International's Changwon plant and Okpo shipyard), in Korean Development Institute, *Kyongje anchŏnghwa sich'aek charyojip* (Collected Documents of Economic Stabilization Measures) (Seoul: KDI, 1981), pp. 1149–1173.

Table 4.3. *Year of Incorporation or Establishment of the Subsidiary Companies of the Ten Largest Chaebol in 1984*

	Total	Prior to 1950	1950–1959	1960–1969	1970–1979	1980–1984	Missing
Samsung	30	1	3	6	11	8	1
Hyundai	32	1	2	4	20	1	4
LG	24	1	2	5	10	3	3
Daewoo	24	0	0	0	21	3	0
Sunkyung	14	0	1	1	7	3	2
Ssangyong	14	2	1	3	6	2	0
Korea-Explosives	18	0	1	5	8	3	1
Kukje	18	1	0	0	13	0	4
Hanjin	12	1	0	5	6	0	0
Hyosung	20	1	2	5	12	0	0
TOTAL	206	8	12	34	114	23	15
Percentage		4	6	18	60	12	

Source: Minho Kuk, "The Governmental Role in the Making of *chaebol* in the Industrial Development of South Korea," *Asian Perspective* 19, no. 1 (Summer 1995): 116.

the EPB's proposal failed. "The government's proposal was not accepted by the rival business groups, although the former group had made some progress toward a merger. The Hyundai group pleaded for various kinds of government support and privileges, almost all of which the government grudgingly granted. Nonetheless the merger attempt was unsuccessful in the end."[40]

The Korean government's control over capital made unbelievable any threat to cut off credit to the *chaebol*, because all the actors knew that doing so would hurt the regime as much as the *chaebol*. Indeed, whether or not there existed a market rationale for expansion of the firms' activities, there certainly existed a rent-seeking rationale, when combined with the proper political connections. The entire Heavy and Chemical Industries project was characterized by massive expansion and very little oversight. Far from limiting and controlling *chaebol* expansion, the Park era saw the opposite result. Table 4.3 shows the year of incorporation or establishment of subsidiary companies for the ten largest *chaebol* in 1984. Sixty percent

[40] Choi, "Institutionalizing a Liberal Economic Order in Korea," p. 128.

of the expansion of the *chaebol* occurred during the 1970s, resulting in overcapacity.

The incentive to become heavily indebted and to focus on expansion instead of efficiency had predictable results: firms borrowed whether they needed to or not. Many firms expanded far too quickly and without adequate planning or management expertise. But because there were so few *chaebol*, it was politically dangerous to allow them to fail. As a result, the Korean state *did* bail out weak companies and rewarded political relations but not necessarily economic success. Far from imposing performance standards, the Korean government was continually forced to rescue inefficient firms that had overextended themselves.

Perhaps the best example of inefficient but large and politically connected firms receiving government aid is the August 3, 1972, "Presidential Emergency Decree on Economic Stabilization and Development" (informally known as the "8-3," or *pal-sam*, Decree), when Park Chung-hee decided to freeze high-interest informal ("curb") market loans and replace them with long-term bank loans. By early 1972, many firms were facing economic difficulties and were highly indebted, and the FKI was meeting daily to deal with the problem of excessive indebtedness to the curb market.

The chairman of the FKI finally decided to ask the president directly for help. After two personal meetings in June between the FKI chairman and the president, Park Chung-hee told his chief of staff, Kim Chung-nyum, along with presidential secretary Kim Yong-hwan, to prepare an emergency decree.[41] Designed by Park Chung-hee to alleviate the curb market, the bailout disproportionately helped more heavily indebted firms. The decree essentially placed a moratorium on new loans, and old loans were rescheduled to be paid back over five years, after a three-year grace period. Special finance bonds worth up to two billion *won* were to be issued to alleviate the debt burdens of major corporations, and the government established the long-term Industry Rationalization Fund.[42]

This case is instructive for two reasons. First, the companies that had been the most poorly managed and hence were the most heavily indebted

---

[41] Lee Young-hwan, "Hankuk ŭi kyongje tanch'e wa chŏngch'aek kyŏlchŏng kujo" (Corporatist Development and the Structure of Policy Making in Korea), in *Hankuk kiŏpŭl segyehwa chŏllyak* (Strategies to globalize Korean industry), edited by Lee Young-hwan (Seoul: Chulpansa, 1995). See also *Kyunghyang Ilbo*, August 31, 1991.

[42] *Seoul Kyongje Sinmun*, August 3, 1972.

were also those that benefited the most from the 8-3 Decree. Second, the FKI was in fact able to appeal directly to the president and to have an influence.[43]

As far back as 1971 the United States was alerting the Koreans to the problems South Korea faced because of the personalistic manner in which the state-run Bank of Korea disbursed foreign aid and loans. At a meeting on March 30, 1971, between EPB officials and U.S. Treasury and State Department officials, the Americans stressed that "insolvent industries, caused by political favoritism in earlier years, represented a major problem. They stressed that foreign banks looked closely at the prevalence of favoritism towards basically unsound companies. [EPB vice-minister] Lee acknowledged the problem and indicated that President Park had directed that these companies be 'rationalized' in the near future through a process of changing principal investors and mergers where appropriate."[44] However, the firms were rarely rationalized in the manner that Lee had promised.[45]

Historically, the *chaebol* have always been heavily indebted. Rents accrued merely from the interest differential between state-sponsored loans and the real interest rate. Capital was so scarce in developing Korea that the curb market interest rate in 1964 was 61.4 percent per annum. The opposition party in the National Assembly concluded that of the ten largest creditors, eight were "disguised curb market loans."[46] In 1970 estimates of the size of the curb market exceeded 345 billion *won*, which was 80 percent of the money supply (M2 basis) and 34 percent of the outstanding domestic credit held by the banking sector.[47] Having access to low-interest government loans was thus a license to print money.

Park Byung-yoon points out that in 1964, 38 percent of total bank loans – 43 percent of the M1 money supply – was given to only nine *chaebol*, all of which had family members in powerful positions in the ruling party or

[43] Carter Eckert, "The South Korean Bourgeoisie: A Class in Search of Hegemony," in *State and Society in Contemporary Korea*, edited by Hagen Koo (Ithaca: Cornell University Press, 1993), p. 108.

[44] House, *Investigation of Korean-American Relations*, Part II, 1978, p. 189, n. 120.

[45] EPB, *Kyonje kihoekwŏn isipnyŏnsa* (Twenty-year history of the EPB), p. 88.

[46] Lee Sung-hyong, "Kukka kyekŭp mit chabon ch'ukchŏk: 8, 3 chochi'rŭl chungsimŭro" (State, class, and capital accumulation: The president's decree of 8-3-72), in Choi, *Hankuk Chabon juŭi wa kukka* (Korean capitalism and the state), pp. 273–274.

[47] Ministry of Finance, *Chaechŏng kŭmyung samsip yŏnsa* (Thirty-year history of fiscal and monetary policy) (Seoul: Ministry of Finance, 1978), p. 155.

Table 4.4. *Bank Loans Given to* Chaebol *as of August 1964 (million* won)

Chaebol Company	Amount of Loan	Total loan amount (%)
Panbon Bangjik (cotton spinning)	5,556	
Samho Bangjik (cotton spinning)	3,717	
Hwashin	3,153	
Kumsung Bangjik (former LG)	2,680	
Samsung Merchandizing	829	
Daehan Yanghoe (cement)	754	
Daehan Chebun (milling)	396	
Kukdong Gonsul (construction)	383	
Daehan Sanop (industry)	132	
TOTAL(A)	17,600	
Amount of bank bill issuing	21,400	82
Currency circulation	40,900	43
Total Amount of Loans Given by Banks	46,200	38

Source: Reorganized data from Park Byung-yoon, *Chaebŏl kwa chŏngch'i* (*Chaebol* and politics) (Seoul: Hankuk Yangso, 1982), p. 199.

in the bureaucracy (Table 4.4).[48] The quid pro quo was an expected "political donation" (i.e., a kickback).[49]

In addition, acquiring debt provided a number of economic benefits that raising capital by other means did not.[50] Debt is cheaper than equity, because there are generally tax write-offs for interest payments. With high inflation, as existed in the 1960s in Korea, the real interest rate actually can become negative, making debt a superior form of financing. In addition, taking on debt is more secure than equity: the businessman retains control of the company, and loans create lower transaction costs than does equity. Debt also allows more political pressure on banks, and with good political connections it was relatively easy for a firm to acquire debt from the government. Finally, larger political needs were a further influence: the Koreans were generally quite worried about the Japanese coming in

[48] Park Byung-yoon, *Chaebŏl kwa chŏngch'i*, p. 210.
[49] For more on the 1960s era, see Alexander Kim, *Divided Korea*, p. 243.
[50] See, for example, Oliver Williamson, "Corporate Finance and Corporate Governance," *Journal of Finance* 43 (1988): 567–591.

and buying up their entire country, but with debt there is less foreign control. So, as a means of restricting foreign influence, debt is far superior to equity financing or to foreign direct investment (FDI). Creating equity markets is also much harder than taking on debt: capital markets require a legal and institutional infrastructure that is far more nuanced and sophisticated than is the mere borrowing of money on the international market. With personal guarantees made by close political connections, debt also lowered the transaction costs of monitoring and enforcing agreements. Moreover, debt gave politicians a measure of control over the *chaebol*; raising capital through issuing equity would have severed that connection.

The argument that the Korean state engaged in the exchange of favors in return for imposing performance standards and restraining *chaebol* growth is not supported by the data. The bureaucracy was marginal, political connections were central, and little oversight was undertaken. Money politics was extensive, allowing political leaders to finance their parties and retain power. Large firms benefited at the expense of small firms, and the resulting overcapacity and high indebtedness has been an endemic feature of Korea's political economy well into the 1990s.

III. Mutual Hostages

What kept the Korean pattern from devolving into a Philippine pattern of chaos (described in the next chapter) was a mutual hostage situation in which neither political nor economic elites could take excessive advantage of the other. This balance of power allowed elites to collude but also limited the chances for excessive rent seeking that might swamp economic growth. The bargain they struck was collusive – not cooperative – and both groups took as much advantage of the other as possible. But the process never spun out of control because the two groups were vulnerable to each other. In Korea the bank was the state, and the few large *chaebol* were all highly leveraged.

In the Park regime, government intervention into the economy was constrained by the business sector in a number of ways that reduced both rent seeking on the part of the entrepreneurs and transaction costs for the politicians and bureaucrats involved in monitoring the policy process. Whereas the "strong state" has been the focus of much of the literature, the surprising strength of the business sector has received less attention. State control over the financial sector had enormous consequences for the organization and conduct of business in Korea.[51] The state could, in fact, control business through its control over the flow of finance. Korean companies were highly leveraged, and therefore they were vulnerable to state control. Paradoxically, this weakness became a source of their strength relative to the state. The Park regime – intentionally or not – actively encouraged the centralization and enhancement of economic power in the *chaebol*. From Park's initial decision in 1961 to pardon the "Illicit Wealth Accumulators" to the bailout of highly leveraged firms in August 1972, to the 1976 decision to promote "General Trading Companies,"[52] the state made continuous policy moves to encourage the rise of the *chaebol*.

If the state has control over various policy instruments, can control or manipulate the judiciary and the legislature, and can redesign at will the terms of any agreement it makes, the problem will be that no action that the state takes can be credible. The farsighted ruler who realizes that the state is at risk will take action to gain greater confidence from the business sector. One way the state can make a believable commitment to various policy initiatives is by fostering domestic sources of power in specific areas – power centers that would later prove to be tremendously costly to overturn. A "mutual hostage" situation exists whenever two actors have significant vulnerability relative to each other. This can arise from either an explicit or an implicit exchange of hostages. In either such exchange, each side has an incentive to continue the relationship and also to limit its taking advantage of the other party. Exchanging hostages as a generic strategy involves exposure to the potentially affected party.

Thus, by encouraging the formation of the large conglomerates that accounted for large percentages of the Korean economy, the state in effect became "mutual hostages" with the *chaebol* (Tables 4.5 and 4.6).

Table 4.5 shows the size of the largest conglomerates in the Korean economy. In 1975 the five largest conglomerates accounted for over 7 percent of the entire economy, with the twenty largest conglomerates

---

[51] Woo, *Race to the Swift*; Ha-joon Chang, "Organising Development: Comparing the National systems of Entrepreneurship in Sweden and South Korea," *The Journal of Development Studies* 30 (July 1994): 859–891; and Leroy Jones and Sakong Il, *Government, Business, and Entrepreneurship in Economic Development* (Cambridge, MA: Harvard University Press, 1980).

[52] On *Chonghap Sangsa* (GTCs), see Dong-song Cho, *The General Trading Company: Concept and Strategy* (Lexington, MA: Lexington Books, 1987), and Sung-Hwan Jo, "Promotion Measures for General Trading Companies," in *Economic Development in Korea: A Policy Perspective*, edited by Lee-Jay Cho and Yoon Hyung Kim (Honolulu: East-West Center, 1991).

Table 4.5. *Mutual Hostages, Part I:* Chaebol *Value
Added, 1973–1975 (percentage of nonagricultural GDP)*

Chaebol (Ranking)	1973	1974	1975
Top 5	5.1	5.6	7.1
Top 10	7.9	8.5	10.7
Top 20	10.9	11.8	14.7

Source: Leroy Jones and Sakong Il, *Government, Business, and
Entrepreneurship in Economic Development* (Cambridge, MA:
Harvard University Press, 1980), p. 268.

Table 4.6. *Mutual Hostages, Part II: Debt/Equity Ratio of
the Top Thirty Korean* Chaebol, *1971–1990 (percentage)*

1971–1980	1981–1985	1986–1990
365.9	374.7	295.8

Source: Bank of Korea, Statistics Division (Chosabu), "Uri nara
kiŏp ŭi puch'ae kujo punsok" (An analysis of the structure of
Korea's indebted companies), October 21, 1998.

comprising almost 15 percent of the economy. Such concentrated economic power meant that the state could not lightly attack these companies. Disrupting their business could have meant economic troubles, labor
unrest, and political instability. However, these companies were also
heavily indebted to the government. Table 4.6 shows that debt/equity
ratios in Korea have been historically extremely high. Because the banks
were nationalized at that time, excessive reliance on debt meant that the
chaebol were reliant on governmental support to finance their operations.

Perhaps the most cited example of the South Korean state's power over
chaebol arises from Park's expropriation of major business leaders' wealth
soon after his coup in 1961.[53] Expressing horror at the corrupt system he
had inherited, Park promulgated the *bujong chukje-an*, or "Illicit Wealth
Accumulation Act." Hundreds of businessmen either were arrested or had
their assets seized for illicit wealth accumulation under the Rhee admin-

[53] Karl Fields, "Strong States and Business Organization in Korea and Taiwan," in *Business
and the State in Developing Countries*, edited by Sylvia Maxfield and Ben Ross Schneider
(Ithaca: Cornell University Press, 1997), p. 136.

118

istration.[54] This incident has generally been used as a stylized fact to buttress the "strong state" thesis, showing that Park had tremendous leverage over capital. However, expropriation was only the initial stage of this incident. By examining the whole incident and by looking at the end results of the actual expropriation, a different story emerges – one that shows the power of capital relative to the state.

The evidence indicates that instead of "dominating" capital, Park worked closely with capitalists and promoted rather than censured them. The thirteen businessmen with the largest assessed fines were the only Koreans allowed to go abroad and solicit foreign loans, and upon their return they made a number of policy recommendations to the Park government, "including the establishment of an industrial port at Ulsan, a proposal that was immediately implemented."[55] Additionally, many of those businessmen who had been assessed fines instead negotiated to invest in the Five-Year Plan under Park and received government loans for that purpose. When the manufacturing plants were completed, these entrepreneurs decided to pay their fines in cash rather than in stock, thus retaining control of the very firms the ruling junta had hoped to nationalize.

In this way, even at the beginning of the Park regime, capitalists realized that they were not entirely vulnerable to the state but that both had a certain ability to sanction the other. By themselves, mutual hostages impose no efficiency criterion, however – such a situation merely restricts the possibility that one side can take advantage of the other side.

Virtually no one in Korea believed that Park engaged in purges to clean up society. Declaring politicians and other leaders to be corrupt, promulgating lists of men deemed unfit to hold office, and punishing alleged wrongdoers were legitimizing tactics used by Korean military dictators to justify coups d'état: Park did it in 1961 and again in 1972 (when he declared martial law preparatory to promulgating the Yushin constitution), and Chun imitated his predecessor in 1980. Although this allowed both leaders to present themselves as simple and pure soldiers intervening to

[54] Pak Pyongyun, *Chaebol kwa chŏnch'i* (*Chaebol* and politics) (Seoul: Hanguk Yongusa, 1982); and Stephan Haggard, Byung-kook Kim, and Chung-in Moon, "The Transition to Export-led Growth in South Korea: 1954–1966," *The Journal of Asian Studies* 50, no. 4 (November 1991): 850–873.

[55] Kim, "The Role of the State and Public Policy in the Development of the Newly-Industrializing Countries," p. 334. See also Yi Chong, *Pihwa Chesam Konghwaguk* (The Third Republic: The secret economic story of the Park Chung-hee era) (Seoul: Tonggwang Chulpansa, 1985), esp. pp. 112–201.

punish the corrupt and rescue the nation, the main thrust was legitimization of the new regimes and neutralization of their political opponents. Most Koreans thought that the purges were motivated by an attempt to divert public attention from larger political problems and that, even so, the purges targeted the small fry and never went after the big fish.[56]

Mutual hostages lower transaction costs in a number of ways. Business and the state both knew that each needed the other, and both also knew that few alternatives existed. The set of favored cronies was relatively small, and thus the costs of competing with each other were lower, because the prospects for opportunism and the need to protect investments was lower.[57] In addition, elites knew they were playing an iterated game, where actors would be around for a while, with both the opportunity for reciprocity and the fear of payback.

Each needing the other, neither able to fully gain the upper hand, state and *chaebol* were forced to work together. This view emphasizes the continuing collaboration between big business and the state, the state's reliance on the *chaebol* for political funds, and the inability of the state to push too strongly in directions that the *chaebol* did not wish to pursue. This is analogous to a prisoner's dilemma: in PD both sides would prefer to defect, but they are restrained from doing so by the ability of the other side to respond in kind, and hence a form of stability ensues.

Thus, mutual hostages constrained collusion between political and economic elites. Firms rushed to become larger both to justify their continued access to cheap financing and to make themselves so large that the government would have no choice but to bail them out – a situation known as "moral hazard." A flow of political payoffs to politicians cemented this pipeline of easy money. For politicians, the need for political funds to run elections and other political activities, as well as a natural proclivity toward greed, gave them no incentive to sanction companies unless the business managers were utterly incompetent.

---

[56] Personal communication with John Duncan, October 12, 1997. For similar skepticism, see A. T. Rafique Rahman, "Legal and Administrative Measures against Bureaucratic Corruption in Asia," in *Bureaucratic Corruption in Asia: Causes, Consequences, and Controls*, edited by Ledivina V. Carino (Quezon City: JMC Press, 1986), p. 122. For a detailed account that argues that Park's moves in 1961 were a cynical propaganda attempt to justify a coup, see David Satterwhite, "The Politics of Economic Development: Coup, State, and the Republic of Korea's First Five-Year Economic Development Plan (1962–1966)" (Ph.D. diss., University of Washington, 1994).

[57] On bribes, see Yoon Young-ho, "Chòng Tae-su wa komún ton" (Chung Tae-soo and black money), *Shindonga* (March 1997): 201.

IV. Conclusion

Behind the developmental state was a political story based on the exchange of bribes for rents. Policy making in Korea followed a political rationale. Close associates of Park received favors, as evidenced by the size and quantity of the loans given as far back as 1964. The bureaucracy served as an instrument of Park Chung-hee and was not an independent actor. Decisions concerning bailouts, loans, and the benefits of policy were heavily influenced by personal connections rather than economic merit. When the EPB or other governmental institutions attempted to rationalize sectors of the market, they often failed. Whether corruption is pursued for wealth or power, it still involves the accumulation and distribution of illicit funds. Park certainly oversaw a regime that was designed to limit the opposition, buy support, and enrich those cronies close to him.

What kept this process from spinning out of control was the importance – and hence the power – of the *chaebol*. The *chaebol* were "too big to fail," and despite Park's rhetoric to the contrary, Park's actions throughout the 1960s and 1970s focused on and benefited the *chaebol*. This situation – one of mutual hostages – allowed political and economic elites to coexist in an uneasy but mutually beneficial relationship. The next chapter will examine the Philippines in detail and will show that the autonomous and centralized Marcos regime did not face the same incentives and constraints from business as did Park's regime in Korea and instead turned to plundering society.

5

Bandwagoning Politics in the Philippines

"Why do you have to order an investigation (into corruption) Mr. President? If
you cannot permit abuses, you must at least tolerate them. What are we in power
for? We are not hypocrites. Why should we pretend to be saints when in reality
we are not?"

– Jose Avelino

When we turn our attention to the Philippines, the pattern of money
politics appears superficially to mirror that in Korea: weak parties devolve
into personal vote machines that trade pork for payoffs. In both countries,
political payoffs allow business influence over policy decisions. In both the
Philippines and Korea, access to the state was the avenue to economic
success. Yet there was a major difference between the two countries as well.
In the Philippines no balance existed between economic and political elites
– no mutual hostages existed. The overarching point of this chapter is that
the pattern of influence in the Philippines reflects significant bandwagoning, as political and economic elites surged toward power like iron filings
toward a magnet. During the democratic period, society held sway and
plundered the state. Under martial law, the balance of power shifted to a
coherent state elite led by Ferdinand Marcos. Yet the more autonomous
and centralized Marcos regime did not have the same incentives and constraints that Park's regime did in Korea and turned to plundering society.
The Philippine bureaucracy, although made more autonomous from social
pressure, was not insulated from regime interests. Thus, the Philippines
lurched back and forth as different groups gained and lost power.

The story of the Philippine political economy approximates much more
closely the standard rent-seeking models. The distribution of rights has
been inequitable, and although rights were redistributed through the
power of the state, no constraint or incentive pushed Philippine actors to

use those rights more productively than before. Greater social mobility than in Korea allowed a larger group of political and economic elites to engage in rent-seeking games, driving up the social costs. Under Marcos the state had the capacity, but not the intention, to impose efficiency standards on those who received redistributed property rights. Especially when we remember that politics trumps economics, and that Marcos – despite his taste for wealth – was a politician first and foremost, the political story again emerges as central to understanding the pattern of Philippine development. The Philippines differed from Korea in two fundamental ways that had serious consequences for development. First, no mutual-hostage situation existed to constrain the actors or force them to reach accommodation. Second, the Philippine international environment was far more peaceful than Korea's. Although we might hope that Marcos would have risen above his situation purely because of his personality, given the institutional and structural environment within which he operated we should not be surprised at the outcome. Exceptional leaders may occasionally rise above their circumstances, but in both Korea and the Philippines the story is predominantly one of rulers responding to their environment and pursuing their baser personal interests.

In this chapter I make one overarching argument – that Philippine politics was dominated by a pendulum of corruption that swung from society in the democratic era to the state under Marcos. This pendulum might swing to and fro, but it never reached an equilibrium where corruption was constrained or limited. This chapter comprises three sections. In the first section I discuss the democratic era and how society was able to plunder the state. In the second section I show how Marcos was able to divide and conquer the elites during the period of martial law. In the final section I compare corruption in Korea and the Philippines.

I. The Democratic Era (1946–1972)

As in Korea, in the Philippines political parties are fluid, loyalty is to the leader and not to an ideology, and votes are bought and sold on the open market. The Nacionalista and Liberal parties were virtually identical in their ideologies and policies. Both drew support from the same social and regional sources, being centrist parties backed by large landowners and involving extensive patron-client relationships. The Liberal Party began as a splinter group of the Nacionalistas when Manuel Roxas broke away in 1945. Interest groups cultivated both parties in the struggle over the congressional pork barrel that dominated national politics.[1] This lack of ideological or policy differentiation between the parties came about because the building blocks of Filipino politics were not material or ideational interests. Such interests were instead subsumed under the basic unit, which was the extended family and its relationship with other oligarchic families.

Carl Lande writes that "the typical Filipino politician has both a personal following and a personal system of alliances with numerous other politicians. . . . Almost always he is a member of a political party, though he may shift his affiliation from one party to another."[2] Ferdinand Marcos first ran for the legislature as a member of the Liberal Party, but he rose to the presidency in the Nacionalista Party.

From 1939 to 1972 the Philippine government was composed of a bicameral legislature and a president. The upper house, or Senate, has consisted of twenty-four senators elected at large over the entire nation to six-year terms. The lower house, or House of Representatives, was composed of 120 single-member districts (204 under the 1987 constitution, the number of seats stands at 221 in 2001), whose representatives were elected to four-year terms. From 1946 to 1972, the Philippines had two major parties, the Liberals and the Nacionalistas. Over that time, the two parties won roughly the same number of seats and held power the same number of times. Both parties held a majority in the House in three of the six congressional sessions from 1946 to 1969. Each party produced three presidents, Ferdinand Marcos being the only president to win reelection.

During the democratic era, the legislature was an important focus of both rent-seeking competition and political competition. Oligarchs obtained access to the state through electoral competition, and the victors then divided the spoils among themselves. Under authoritarianism, the focus shifted to the executive branch, and the centralized Marcos dictatorship became the source of political influence peddling. Emmanuel S. de Dios, calling the Philippines an "elite democracy," writes that "it is not simply that wealth was required to gain entry into the political elite. More pertinently, even prior to 1972, access to the political machinery was in

---

[1] Kit Machado, "Changing Aspects of Factionalism in Philippine Local Politics," *Asian Survey* 11, no. 12 (December 1971): 1182–1199, and Amando Doronila, "The Transformation of Patron-Client Relations and Its Political Consequences in Postwar Philippines," *Journal of Southeast Asian Studies* 16, no. 1 (March 1985): 99–116.

[2] Carl Lande, *Leaders, Factions, and Parties: The Structure of Philippine Politics*, Yale University, Southeast Asia Series, no. 6 (New Haven, 1964), p. 6.

fact a principal means of direct or indirect wealth-accumulation."[3] Because of the importance of electoral politics, patronage systems were particularly critical.

1. Parties and Elections

At the highest level, the political process in the Philippines during the democratic era is best described as a pendulum, with the Liberals and Nacionalistas trading political power and control over spoils. This process naturally attracted to the politicians in power, through the bandwagon effect, hangers-on and those hoping to participate in the looting of the state. Over time, their demands would become too crushing, and aspiring opposition politicians would begin to have the opportunity to lure oligarchs to their side in return for promises of greater spoils. Eventually the defection of supporters from the incumbent politicians would lead to a tipping of the balance, and a headlong rush would begin as toadies and flatterers flocked to the new, rising politicians.

Governing this broad game were a number of unstated rules and schoolyard norms. All actors expected that they would participate over the long run, so excessive predation and, in particular, vendettas against other powerful actors, were generally restrained. This process of bandwagon-defection led to swings in who nominally held office, but essentially, the powerful oligarchs did not suffer.[4] The bandwagon was solid: at the initial stages, everyone jumped on to receive the benefits that the new politician could provide. Over time, as the presence of more hangers-on began to dilute the benefits and make ruling unwieldy, aspiring opposition politicians began to gain defectors, who hoped to get more for themselves by defecting. And then the pendulum would swing back, and a new politician would take office.

This process offered to the opposition the role of "fiscalizer," a unique Filipinism that means one who keeps criticizing the party and providing

[3] Emmanuel de Dios, "A Political Economy of Philippine Policy-Making," in *Economic Policy-Making in the Asia-Pacific Region*, edited by John W. Langord and K. Lorne Brownsey (Halifax, Nova Scotia: Institute for Research on Public Policy, 1990), p. 111. See also Lande, *Leaders, Factions, and Parties*, esp. pp. 1–2.
[4] The phrase "bandwagon and defection" is taken from Mark R. Thompson, *The Anti-Marcos Struggle: Personalistic Rule and Democratic Transition in the Philippines* (Quezon City: New Day Publishers, 1996). This work is the best I have seen on the patterns of politics in the Philippines.

exposés of fiscal corruption. The "fiscalizer" acts as a social safety valve even though he may well have taken graft previously or may simply be waiting for his turn.[5] As Mark Thompson writes:

The party that controlled the presidency had much greater access to government-distributed pork-barrel. Many people thus defected from the opposition to the newly elected ruling party and helped it win local elections and usually a second presidential term. But the longer the party controlled the presidency, the greater the conflict over limited government resources became. Inevitably, some members of the party in power began to feel shortchanged. The opposition could then woo them into switching parties by promising a bigger piece of the political pie after the next presidential election. The opposition's victory started this cycle again.[6]

Once in power, politicians traded policy for cash or influence. Figure 5.1 shows the pattern of political support and influence during the democratic period.

The president, although powerful, was restrained by an activist Congress. Aspiring middle-class politicians ran for political office. The transaction consisted of trading votes, financial and political support, and bribes for major deals. The spoils could be bureaucratic posts, special legislation, sweetheart deals. Carl Lande writes: "What are the sources of their funds? Only two [candidates] were known to have substantial personal wealth. The rest had to depend heavily on campaign contributions from others. Ordinarily, political contributions come mainly from wealthy individuals with large economic interests."[7] The difference between public and private spheres in the Philippines became increasingly blurred under democracy. David Wurfel writes that congressmen spent "most of their time . . . running an employment agency" as they found bureaucratic jobs for clients.[8] As Table 5.1 shows, the government typically overspent during election years as a way of handing out goodies and pork to its supporters.

At the local level, politics consisted of "guns, goons, and gold," which describes a Philippine electoral process in which violence, private armies,

---

[5] I thank Victor Venida for pointing this out to me. The other favored role of the opposition is that of "conscience" of the government. This helps make the system acceptable to the masses.

[6] Thompson, *The Anti-Marcos Struggle*, p. 16.

[7] Carl H. Lande, *Post-Marcos Politics* (Singapore: Institute of Southeast Asian Studies, 1996), p. 109.

[8] David Wurfel, *Filipino Politics: Development and Decay* (Ithaca: Cornell University Press, 1988), p. 80.

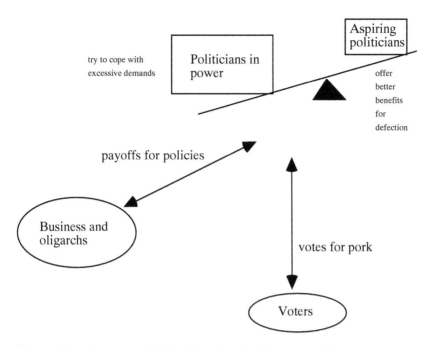

Figure 5.1. Structure of Political Funds in the Democratic Era

Table 5.1. *Government Net Receipts in Election and Nonelection Years, 1957–1968*

Year	President	Election Year	Net Receipts (million PP)
1957	Garcia	election	−123.4
1958	Garcia	nonelection	17.8
1959	Garcia	election	−60.7
1960	Garcia	nonelection	46.9
1961	Garcia	election	−159.2
1962	Macapagal	nonelection	88.8
1963	Macapagal	election	−110.0
1964	Macapagal	nonelection	75.3
1965	Macapagal	election	−208.2
1966	Marcos	nonelection	−86.7
1967	Marcos	election	−120.8
1968	Marcos	nonelection	−85.3

Source: Harvey Averch, John E. Koehler, and Frank H. Denton, *The Matrix of Policy in the Philippines* (Princeton: Princeton University Press, 1971), p. 101.

and bribes are the means to power. By the early 1950s the Nacionalistas and Liberals had penetrated to the outermost regions of the Philippines, where candidates were now selected by national convention. In each barrio was a party committee, and aspiring politicians returned the vote to the local branch of the national party. Brian Fegan notes that "representatives from the barrios met as a board of directors and chose candidates whose campaign expenses were supplemented by funds from the national party."[9] We should not overstate the democratic nature of local politics, however. These institutions merely reveal the dominance and coercive capacity of local major families and the ability of these families to control elections.

The concept of *utang na loob* (debt of gratitude) is important in the Philippines. It creates a bond between leader and follower, tying them together through reciprocal obligations. During elections, candidates hold parties and hand out hats and T-shirts. Local oligarchs with personal vote machines and landed oligarchs with cash and clout provide votes for national politicians. As Onofre Corpuz, more than thirty years ago, described Philippine politics: "The basic structure of Filipino parties has been determined by the social class of their members. Each party is made up of leaders who bring their respective followers with them. These followers owe a personal allegiance to the corresponding leaders, not to the party as an organization."[10] As in Korea, voters tend to be paid for their votes, and they expect lavish parties and clubs and trips from their local politicians. The major portion of a candidate's funds go to the local *lider* (local boss). If they are candidates for municipal or barrio office themselves, the *liders* keep some money and pass the rest on to their subordinates. An invitation to a feast is one centuries-old tradition in the Philippines by which potential leaders may gain support.

Occasional killings and political violence occur in Philippine politics, mostly at the local level. One of the rare instances of the use of violence at the national level involved the Marcos family. In 1935, Ferdinand Marcos assassinated his father's rival, Julio Nalundasan. Forty-eight years

---

[9] Brian Fegan, "Entrepreneurs in Votes and Violence: Three Generations of a Peasant Political Family," in *An Anarchy of Families: State and Family in the Philippines*, edited by Alfred McCoy (Manila: Ateneo de Manila University Press, 1994), p. 85.

[10] Onofre Corpuz, *The Philippines* (Englewood Cliffs, NJ: Prentice-Hall, 1965), p. 99.

later, Marcos had his henchmen assassinate Benigno Aquino. In general, however, political violence is not effective at the national level and remains the province of local political conflicts. Yet violence is nonetheless endemic. Alfred McCoy notes that "in 1965 . . . the Philippine homicide rate was about 35 per 100,000 persons – compared to just 25 for Colombia. . . . In Ilocos Sur, the murder rate ebbed to 1 or 2 in the months between elections and jumped to 30 during the November 1965 campaign."[11] As will be discussed in Chapter 6, political violence swelled during the 1980s and the turmoil of the late-Marcos era. In recent years, violence has considerably diminished.

In the Philippines, businessmen of Chinese origin face discrimination, and they have tended to compensate through bribes and influence peddling. It was not until 1974 that the naturalization process was liberalized. The previous, stringent requirements for naturalization had maintained the Chinese as aliens so that bureaucrats and politicians could take advantage of them. Many professions were closed to the Chinese because of their alien status, but they could enter business. Thus the ethnic Chinese gained a reputation as corrupters of bureaucrats and politicians. Campaign financing was the only way that they could enter the political process to protect their own economic interests.[12] Despite these barriers, race relations in the Philippines have been far more amicable than in other Southeast Asian countries. Whereas Malaysia and Indonesia have had recurrent rioting against and trouble in dealing with their ethnic Chinese citizens, the Philippines has for the most part been able to avoid serious problems.

The pattern of Philippine politics is built on the relatively stable building blocks of local vote machines. These machines offer their votes to aspiring politicians in return for favors, both legal and illegal. Because the known is worse than the unknown, power has careened wildly between parties.[13] The overall result, however, has been an excess of demands on the state and the inability of top politicians to formulate or implement coherent policies.

---

[11] Alfred McCoy, "An Anarchy of Families," in McCoy, *An Anarchy of Families*, p. 14.

[12] Wurfel, *Filipino Politics*, p. 58.

[13] See Gabriella Montinola, "Politicians, Parties, and the Persistence of Weak States: Lessons from the Philippines," paper delivered at the American Political Science Association annual meetings, Washington, DC, August 27–31, 1997.

2. Policy

Like South Korea, the Philippines contains large, diversified, family-based conglomerates. The landed oligarchic families that comprise the basic unit in the Philippines have traditionally been involved in agricultural-export ventures. As in South Korea, "foreign academics reading these long lists of names, broken by brief, inconclusive biographies, probably regard such a chronicle as insufficient for [a] broad, bold theory. For an informed Filipino audience, however, each family name – Soriano, Yulo, Lopez – is encoded with layers of meaning, and their mere recitation evokes convincing resonance of shared knowledge."[14] These powerful families have endured and survived over generations. Indeed, Filipinos talk of "the 100," the one hundred or so Philippine families that control most of the country's business.[15] As discussed in Chapter 2, each family diversified into many sectors, and each family would lobby separately. "The 100" could band together if necessary, but in general the families did not cooperate. "If you're in the 100 you're on your own," as one member told me.[16] "I don't want to be president, I want to own one."

As in South Korea, the large family-owned conglomerates in the Philippines dominate the economy. In 1980, 98 percent of all sectors had "four or fewer companies controlling 35 percent of sales."[17] In 1982 the combined net income of the top ten corporations was 130 percent of the total net income of the top one thousand companies, whereas those ten companies accounted for almost one-third of the gross revenues of the top one thousand corporations.[18] Indeed, among commercial banks, the

[14] Alfred McCoy, "Rent-Seeking Families and the State," in McCoy, *An Anarchy of Families*, p. 433.
[15] Edita Tan, "Interlocking Directorates, Commercial Banks, and Other Financial Institutions and Nonfinancial Corporations," discussion paper 9110 (September 1991), School of Economics, University of the Philippines, p. 12.
[16] Tony Gatmaitan, author's interview, February 22, 1998.
[17] John Doherty, "Who Controls the Philippine Economy?: Some Need Not Try as Hard as Others," in *Cronies and Enemies: The Current Philippine Scene*, edited by Belinda A. Aquino, Philippine Studies Series, no. 5 (Honolulu: University of Hawaii, Philippine Studies Program, 1982), pp. 12–33. Cited in McCoy, "Rent-Seeking Families and the State," in McCoy, *An Anarchy of Families*, p. 437.
[18] Manuel Montes, "Financing Development: The 'Democratic' Approach versus the 'Corporatist' Approach in the Philippines," in *The Political Economy of Fiscal Policy*, edited by Miguel Urrutia, Shinichi Ichimura, and Setsuko Yukawa (Tokyo: United Nations University, 1989), p. 95.

Table 5.2. *Assets of Commercial Banks, 1955–1990 (as percentage of total commercial bank assets)*

Bank	Family	Years of Operation	1955	1960	1965	1970	1975	1980	1985	1990
BPI	Zobel-Ayala	1851–present	5.3	4.4	3.3	3.7	4.2	6.1	5.7	9.1
FEBTC	Fernandez-Yulo	1960–present	—	1.3	1.6	2.0	3.5	4.0	4.4	8.5
Insular	Aboitiz	1961–1974	—	—	0.7	1.0	—	—	—	—
China	Yuchengco-Sycip	1920–present	7.8	7.5	4.2	4.1	3.1	2.4	1.4	2.4
Manila	Puyat	1961–present	—	—	1.5	1.9	2.7	2.3	2.8	n.a.
TOTAL			13.1	13.2	11.3	12.7	13.5	14.8	14.3	20.0

Source: Adapted from Paul Hutchcroft, "Predatory Oligarchy, Patrimonial State: The Politics of Private Domestic Commercial Banking in the Philippines" (Ph.D. diss., Yale University, 1993), p. 65.

concentration ratios tended to approximate those in Korea, with a few banks comprising large portions of the entire sector (Table 5.2).

However, in contrast to Korea, the actual number of relevant business families in the Philippines is far larger and more diffuse geographically, and more widely distributed across industries. This affects the competition for and the distribution of rents in a number of ways. First, greater economic and social mobility means that the competition for rents is both more costly and more diffuse. Second, the distribution of property rights is more tenuous because families have less influence on government and less power to resist. Finally, the mobility of families means less coherence in pressing demands on the state and an easier division by state actors.

These families have their own regional influence. In the southern region of Cebu, the Aboitiz and Osmena families hold sway, whereas the Cojuangco family is from the sugar-producing and rice-growing Tarlac region north of Manila. The Floirendo family hails from a banana concern in Davao, Mindanao, and the Lopez family began as a sugar exporter from the Negros and Panay regions. In the 1990s these families came to be known informally as Taipans if they were of Chinese descent and Tycoons if their origins were either Filipino or Spanish. However, these are 1990s categories. In the 1960s they were just called oligarchs. Prior to that they would have been known as *hacienderos*, or large landowners. From the late 1940s to the 1960s, the Philippines experienced impressive growth in manufacturing, recalled as the "golden age" in the Philippines.[19] Because of an overvalued currency, quotas, and high tariffs, many Filipino firms were able to expand quite dramatically. Yet the Philippines at this time also contained a high level of manufacturing expertise, with one report finding that in 1979 the Filipino supply of skilled workers and technicians equaled that of Singapore.[20]

However, transaction costs for Philippine business have been historically high. Beginning in the late 1950s, the traditional Filipino oligarchs began to diversify out of their primarily agricultural landed businesses into a wide range of other, mainly import-substituting, business ventures. In part this reflected a political calculation: if they had diversified business interests, the chance that the next administration would look unfavorably on them was lessened. This was also a way of protecting vulnerable property rights. Paul Hutchcroft writes that "a family can't depend on investments assisted by current friends in the Palace, because in the *next* administration those investments may be jeopardized by a lack of necessary connections in key government offices."[21] By diversifying out of pure agricultural exports, the landed families had by the 1960s become the dominant manufacturing class as well. This change had the added benefit of shielding families from widely fluctuating commodity prices, from devaluations of the peso, and from the political turmoil within the Philippines and between the Philippines and the United States.

Robert Baldwin estimated that industrial businessmen received profits of over 200 percent on commodities subject to quantitative restrictions.[22] Similar to the Korean system, a 10 percent kickback to politicians who intervened to help businessmen became the norm during the 1950s.[23]

[19] Walden Bello, David Kinley, and Elaine Elinson, *Development Debacle: The World Bank and the Philippines* (San Francisco: Institute for Food and Development Policy, 1982), p. 128.
[20] T. W. Allen, *The ASEAN Report* (Hong Kong: Asian Wall Street Journal, 1979), pp. 140–141. Cited in Richard Doner, "Domestic Coalitions and Japanese Auto Firms in Southeast Asia: A Comparative Bargaining Study" (Ph.D. diss., University of California at Berkeley, 1987), p. 129.
[21] Paul Hutchcroft, "Predatory Oligarchy, Patrimonial State: The Politics of Private Domestic Commercial Banking in the Philippines" (Ph.D. diss., Yale University, 1993), p. 65.
[22] Robert Baldwin, *Foreign Trade Regimes and Economic Development: The Philippines* (New York: NBER, 1975), p. 98.
[23] Montinola, "Politicians, Parties, and the Persistence of Weak States," p. 11.

Gleeck notes that in 1964, seven congressmen, five governors, and five city mayors were found to have been involved in smuggling imported cigarettes.[24]

As Hutchcroft writes: "As long as such rents can be obtained. . . . rent seekers find it more important to maintain their government connections than to concern themselves with the internal efficiencies and investments of their firms. Indeed, one study of the textile industry in the 1950s states that entrepreneurs 'considered effort at the Central Bank as important as [effort] at their plants.'"[25] Thus in the Philippines investment, lacking safeguards, was difficult to undertake. Similarly, transaction costs were high because much energy was diverted from developing efficient businesses and was channeled instead into securing political protection of one's economic interests.

The nature of Philippine government–business interaction raised transaction costs in other ways. Philippine business tends to be geographically more dispersed, limiting both the coordination and the collusion possible among the families themselves. In addition, given that interests are familial and cross-sectoral, it comes as no surprise that the business sector has been unable to coherently form demands and press the state for consistent policies. "Philippine business associations are notoriously weak and poorly institutionalized, and its members know that the way to make money is to gain privileged access to the government and then to 'exclude information from each other.'"[26] In contrast to Korea, where associations such as the Federation of Korean Industries or the Korean Chamber of Commerce were institutionalized and important for aggregating the interests of business, in the Philippines the Philippine Chamber of Commerce

---

[24] Lewis Gleeck, *Dissolving the Colonial Bond: American Ambassadors to the Philippines, 1946–1984* (Quezon City: New Day Publishers, 1988), p. 307.

[25] Hutchcroft, "Oligarchs and Cronies," p. 423. The study cited comes from Laurence Davis Stifel, *The Textile Industry: A Case Study of Industrial Development in the Philippines*, Data Paper Number 49 (Ithaca: Southeast Asia Program, Cornell University, 1963), p. 50. Thomas R. McHale wrote that "business is born, flourishes or fails, not so much in the market place as in the halls of the legislature or in the administrative offices of the government." Thomas R. McHale, "An Ecological Approach to Economic Development" (Ph.D. diss., Harvard University, 1959), quoted in Stifel.

[26] Hutchcroft, "Oligarchs and Cronies," p. 426. Hutchcroft cites an interview with Wilhelm G. Ortaliz, former director of the Bureau of Industrial Coordination, Ministry of Industry. Ortaliz described the preeminent business association, the Philippine Chamber of Commerce and Industries, as a "mere post office of diverse concerns, very personality oriented, and unable to formulate common positions on major issues."

and similar associations were notoriously incapable of providing a unified voice for Philippine business. Although there were homogenous interests among the Philippine elite over macroeconomic policy, the nature of political competition under both democracy and authoritarianism meant that the families were concerned about providing particularistic goods to themselves only, and that public goods were thus underprovided. This headlong rush to rent seeking has been accurately summed up by Manuel Montes:

> Consultations are dominated by the need to protect individual interests. . . . The private sector does not have a well-defined interest as a private sector. This protecting of individual interests also involves the need to have advance information of the government's intentions. . . . Access to information tends to be individual, based on kinship and other ties.[27]

Business associations may have been weak, but the large oligarchic families were not. Because the families were so powerful, business as an independent voice could not emerge. But individual families were very strong, so the state could not create coherent policy either.

The best work on family conglomerates is John Doherty's work on interlocking Philippine directorates.[28] Again, the contrast with Korea is instructive. In Korea the *chaebol*, although family owned, are controlled through an informal and personalistic process. The personal guarantee of the founder or chairman is critical in Korea, not the legal organization of the board of directors. In the Philippines, although families also are powerful, far more legalistic means of control and organization exist. In the Philippines, the board of directors and other institutional controls are important. Table 5.3 shows a sample of the interlocking directorates in 1979. These family corporations look strikingly like the Korean *chaebol*, with the exception of the bank in the center. That most major Philippine families had control of a bank meant that the state's ability to reward or punish actions was limited. Doherty writes: "interlocks means that decision making is restricted. The more interlocks there are in the banking, finance, and business sectors of a country the more significant the control exercised by this small group of corporate directors over the economy of that country. One way, therefore, to learn where control of the Philippine

---

[27] Montes, "Financing Development," p. 97.
[28] John Doherty, "A Preliminary Study of Interlocking Directorates among Financial, Commercial, Manufacturing, and Service Enterprises in the Philippines" (MS, Manila, 1979).

Table 5.3. *Family Ownership in the Philippines, 1979*

Ayala Group (24 companies)	Aboitiz Group (13 companies)
Bank of the Philippine Islands	Insular Bank of Asia and America
8 Petroleum and chemical companies	1 Heavy equipment company
2 Mining companies	1 Industrial gases company
2 Machinery companies	3 Automobile companies
2 Automobile companies	2 Pulp and paper companies
2 Textile companies	1 Tobacco company
1 Pulp and paper company	5 Shipping companies
3 Real estate companies	**Yuchengco-Sycip Group** (33 companies)
2 Hotel companies	China-Rizal Banking
2 Communications companies	5 Mining companies
Fernandez and Yulo Group (32 companies)	2 Heavy equipment companies
Far East Bank and Trust Company	1 Fertilizer company
3 Chemical companies	5 Automobile companies
6 Mining companies	6 Textile companies
2 Heavy equipment companies	7 Pulp and paper companies
3 Automobile companies	3 Pharmaceutical companies
5 Pulp and paper companies	2 Tobacco companies
3 Textile companies	2 Communications companies
1 Pharmaceutical company	**Puyat Group** (17 companies)
3 Shipping companies	Manila Banking
1 Tobacco company	1 Chemical company
1 Real estate company	5 Mining companies
2 Hotel companies	1 Explosives company
2 Communications companies	2 Automobile companies
	3 Textile companies
	1 Pulp and paper company
	3 Shipping companies
	1 Real estate company

Source: John Doherty, "A Preliminary Study of Interlocking Directorates among Financial, Commercial, Manufacturing, and Service Enterprises in the Philippines" (MS, Manila, 1979), pp. 98–99.

economy lies is to study such interlocking directorates."[29] The Ayala Group is a typical example of this process: a total of twenty-four companies across a range of sectors, from petroleum and chemical to mining and real estate.

[29] Doherty, "Interlocking Directorates," p. 3.

The large families tend to cluster their corporations around a central bank, which provides them with financing. For example, the Philippine Bank of Commerce was controlled by the Cojuangco family, and the Puyat family controlled the Manila Bank before it went bankrupt in 1987. In addition, interlocking seats on various boards give a small group of individuals control over a large number of corporations. In this manner, a family can create a diversified group, even if the family itself remains behind the scenes. This pattern arose in part because of the weakness of the state. Whereas in South Korea a family needed a corporate identity to protect itself, in the Philippines such an overt sign bred resentment. It was a politically safer strategy in the Philippines to remain in the background rather than out front – the opposite of the situation in Korea.

In 1979 only sixty of the one thousand largest corporations in the Philippines were publicly traded. The vast majority of the large firms were privately held by the various families, and thus large segments of the economy were controlled by the oligarchs with little public accountability.

In the democratic era politics in the Philippines was controlled by large oligarchic families and their crony politicians who overwhelmed the state with their particularistic demands.

II. Marcos and Martial Law (1972–1986)

If the democratic era featured a weak government overrun by interest groups, martial law saw the pendulum swing too far in the opposite direction, with Ferdinand Marcos being able to concentrate power in the presidential palace to a degree that gave him the opportunity to do virtually whatever he wished. Under the nominally democratic system the legislature had played a major role in securing access to and apportioning out rents. By disbanding the legislature, Marcos was able to take full control of all the state's functions. Rather than install in office a local congressman who could support the family's interests, a family now required support from Marcos himself.

Thus the pendulum had swung from a weak state and a strong society during the democratic era to a coherent state able to divide a weak society and prey upon it. One reason why Marcos could lord it over business was the disorganization of business. Although Philippine family conglomerates were well organized in some respects (they were diversified, many had their own banks, they were able to extract rents from the state), as a sector the families found it difficult to work together to further their interests with respect to the state. If Korean business interests did indeed have real power, then the difference in the Philippines becomes clearer. Unlike in Korea, there was no mutual-hostage situation in the Philippines. Another reason for Marcos's power is that, unlike Park, who was seeking to distinguish himself from Rhee, Marcos did not have the incentive to separate himself from his predecessors, and thus his situation was different.

In the early 1970s, Marcos, with the aid of martial law, declared the "New Society." He formed the Kilusang Bagong Lipunan, or KBL, as the "New Society Movement." The movement's goal was to increase concern for the poor, increase discipline and coherence in the government, and provide leadership for development. Although initially Marcos had declared "war" on the oligarchs and the old way of doing business, he was an astute politician; his playing of "divide and conquer" allowed him to take the initiative against the oligarchs who had ruled Philippine politics since before independence. "The agenda was ultimately set by business and political interests closer to the Palace."[30] Emmanuel de Dios writes: "The split in the Filipino elite had reached crisis proportions, owing mainly to this bid for political and financial hegemony by the Marcoses and Romualdezes . . . against the Lopezes, Osmeñas, Aquino-Cojuangcos, and Jacintos. It was these whom Marcos, adopting a populist rhetoric, referred to as 'oligarchs,' to legitimize the expropriation of their holdings and their political persecution."[31]

Perhaps the best indicator of the transformation that Marcos wrought in the power of the state and its capacity is the virtual elimination under martial law of local warlords. Fegan notes that "Marcos reduced the significance of private force by means of an arms roundup in 1972, a later transfer of municipal police command from local mayors to the central Philippine Constabulary, and the rapid reassignment of any PC officers who established cozy arrangements with local politicians and/or *mafiosi*."[32]

---

[30] De Dios, "A Political Economy of Philippine Policy-Making," p. 114.
[31] De Dios, "A Political Economy of Philippine Policy-Making," p. 112. See also Manuel Montes, "The Business Sector and Development Policy," in *National Development Policies and the Business Sector in the Philippines*, edited by Manuel Montes and Kenji Koike (Tokyo: Institute of Developing Economies, 1988).
[32] Fegan, "Entrepreneurs in Votes and Violence," p. 88.

With the help of the United States, Marcos restructured the military and the police to centralize control under his own command. According to Sterling Seagrave, "Under martial law, he [Marcos] was as firmly in control of Manila as the South Korean generals were in Seoul and the Chiang regime in Taipei."[33] As one politician who held a series of high positions under Marcos noted, "Marcos was a brilliant leader. And, at least initially, his rule under martial law had us all hoping that he had us on the right track: Marcos focused on infrastructure, improving the quality of life in the provinces, and other developmental projects."[34] For instance, the rural electrification project of the early 1970s brought electricity for the first time to the poorest provinces.

To maintain his rule, Marcos sought to divide and conquer his opponents (Figure 5.2). He attacked those oligarchs strong enough to be potential competitors, developed new oligarchs who were solely dependent upon him for their success, and left the majority of the oligarchs alone as long as they left him alone. As one anonymous politician stated, "Marcos' tactics were purposeful. First, grab the cash flow of heavy industries such as Mercalco [power generation]. If you have cash, you can pay anybody off. Second, divide and conquer. Third, obfuscate by creating a squid's screen of ad hominem attacks and distortions. Finally, deliberately create trouble so you can be the savior."[35]

1. The Players

Marcos created new oligarchs who were dependent solely on him for their success, and he also rewarded traditional elites who cooperated with him. Hawes writes that "the power of the state was used for individual political goals . . . and [in the sugar industry] the vast bulk of the surplus went to the personal and political needs of the First Family."[36] Thus the direction of corruption shifted from the bottom-up plundering of the state to the top-down plundering of society. Given the opportunity to impose his will on society and to choose economic policy that would benefit Filipino society, Marcos chose instead to take the gains for himself.

---

[33] Sterling Seagrave, *The Marcos Dynasty* (New York: Harper and Row, 1988), p. 317.
[34] Author's anonymous interview, September 10, 1999.
[35] Author's anonymous interview, September 10, 1999.
[36] Gary Hawes, *The Philippine State and the Marcos Regime: The Politics of Export* (Ithaca: Cornell University Press, 1987), p. 82.

138

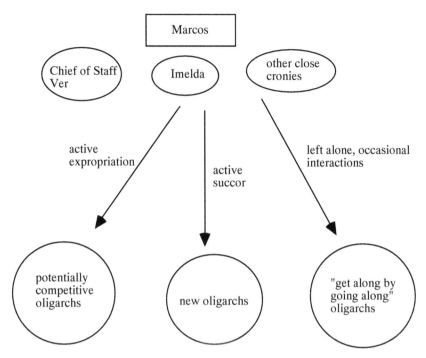

Figure 5.2. Structure of Political Funds under Marcos: Divide and Conquer

Marcos's cronies regularly received preferential treatment that gave them monopolies and windfall profits, while the bureaucracies ostensibly charged with overseeing development were bypassed or ignored. Herminio Disini (who married a cousin of First Lady Imelda Marcos and was one of the president's golfing partners) was able to corner 90 percent of the tobacco-filter market in the Philippines after paying only a 10 percent import tax while competitors were subject to a 100 percent tax.[37] Other traditional elites who cooperated with Marcos included the Eduardo Cojuangco and Ramon Cojuangco branches of the Cojuangco family, Roberto Benedicto, and the Jose Yulo family.[38]

---

[37] Robin Broad, *Unequal Alliance: The World Bank, the International Monetary Fund, and the Philippines* (Berkeley: University of California Press, 1988), p. 45.
[38] The third branch of the Cojuangco family – Jose Cojuangco – was Cory Aquino's branch and was thus persecuted.

However, instead of forcing firms to become competitive in the international economy, Marcos created a new set of rent-seeking capitalists. As Richard Doner argues:

These were businessmen, who, by virtue of close links to the Marcos family, grew so large as to control strategic portions of the economy . . . the Filipino private sector of the 1970s came to be dominated by a set of entrepreneurs who, while financially quite well off as a result of state subsidies, were poorly managed and largely oriented towards short-term profits.[39]

These capitalists included Cuenca in construction, Disini in textiles, Benedicto in sugar and shipping, and Silverio in automobiles.[40] But these gigantic business conglomerates were generally no more than "cash cows" for their crony owners. William Overholt points out:

The Marcos regime focused on nuclear power, steel, aluminum, copper, and other capital-intensive industries, known as the eleven major industrial projects . . . these huge projects, utterly unsuited for the nation's skills and comparative advantages, permitted equally huge foreign borrowings, and much of the foreign borrowing could be siphoned off to Swiss bank accounts.[41]

What remains clear is that Marcos supported those who were loyal to him. Sugar, coconuts, and grain all became monopolies under Marcos and were given to his cronies under the guise of rationalization. Similarly, the Philippine National Bank and the government frequently rescued these crony firms from bankruptcy. Also, Silverio's Delta Motors – a Toyota assembler – was exempted from a 1981 decree that changed the local content requirements on General Motors and Ford investments.[42] By the time Silverio's Delta Motors went bankrupt in 1984, the Philippine National Bank held 70 percent ownership in the firm and had loaned it one billion *pesos*.[43] Robert Benedicto, a former ambassador to Japan, gained a virtual monopoly over the sugar sector. Heading the government's

---

[39] Doner, "Domestic Coalitions and Japanese Auto Firms," p. 131.
[40] Benedicto was not a new oligarch, but an old, entrenched, and cooperative one.
[41] William H. Overholt, "The Rise and Fall of Ferdinand Marcos," *Asian Survey* 26, no. 11 (November 1986): 1143.
[42] Walden Bello, David Kinley, and Elaine Elinson, *Development Debacle: The World Bank in the Philippines* (San Francisco: Institute for Food and Development Policy, 1982), p. 189. By then, the Silverio family had fallen from grace, because Ricky Silverio, who courted Marcos's eldest daughter, Imee, was deemed unsuitable for a son-in-law.
[43] Cited in Doner, "Domestic Coalitions and Japanese Auto Firms," p. 148.

Philippine Sugar Commission (PHILSUCOM), Benedicto assumed control of sugar plantations that had been deemed "inefficient," and in 1978 he also created the Republic Planter's Bank, which gained control of crop loans.[44] In a similar vein, defense minister Juan Ponce Enrile and "Coconut King" Eduardo Cojuangco were able to monopolize the coconut industry. As described by Walden Bello et al.:

> Enrile was chairman of the board of Cojuangco's United Coconut Mills, or UNICOM. Enrile was also honorary chairman of COCOFED, while Cojuangco served as a director of the government regulatory board, the Philippine Coconut Authority (PCA). In the fall of 1979, Marcos stunned Manila business circles with a presidential decree ordering all coconut processing companies to sell out to or affiliate with UNICOM. This was the first phase of what the Enrile-Cojuangco conglomerate candidly and cynically described as "vertical integration" of the industry.[45]

2. The Competitors

Marcos actively attacked those oligarchs who were powerful enough to be potentially dangerous to his rule. After he imposed martial rule in 1972, Marcos expropriated the holdings of many of the traditional oligarchs, including their broadcasting and newspaper facilities, land, financial institutions, and public utilities, and deeded them to his cronies. Thus Marcos was able to use the state against the traditional political powers, and by centralizing authority under himself was able to set up a new class of political entrepreneurs, his "cronies."

The Lopez family posed the most significant potential threat to Marcos. From the Negros and Panay regions, the Lopez family began its career as sugar farmers and traders-exporters in the nineteenth century and made its fortune in the sugar boom of that era. From that beginning, Eugenio Lopez Sr. built a political and economic empire.[46] By the early 1970s the Lopez brothers, Eugenio and Fernando, owned a bus company, an airline, a shipping firm, Manila Electric Company (Meralco), the Philippine Commercial and Industrial Bank, the *Manila Chronicle* newspaper, the

---

[44] This story is from Bello et al., *Development Debacle*, p. 185.
[45] Bello et al., *Development Debacle*, p. 186.
[46] For details, see *Philippines, Inc.* (Manila: Business World, 1995), pp. 5–11.

Table 5.4. *The Lopez Group, 1972*

Manila Electric Company
Meralco Securities Company
Meralco Securities and Industrial Company
Philippines Electric Company
Philippine Engine and Construction Company
Philippine Petroleum Company
MSC-Computers
ABS-CBN
SCAN
Monserrat Broadcast
Nuvue Television
Philippine Telegraph and Telephone
Mountain Top Resort
Benpres Holdings
AFISCO
Lopez Incorporated
Lopez Foundation

Source: Jose V. Abueva, ed., *Eugenio H. Lopez, Sr.: Pioneering Entrepreneur and Business Leader* (Diliman, Quezon City: University of the Philippines, 1998, 1997), p. 22.

ABS-CBN television network, sugar mills, and numerous other ventures (Table 5.4). On September 22, 1972, Metrocom troops occupied ABS-CBN and commandeered the *Manila Chronicle*'s printing presses. Imelda Marcos's brother, Kokoy Romualdez, eventually purchased the Lopez presses, worth 50 million *pesos*, for just 500,000 *pesos*. Charging the Lopez family with not paying taxes, Marcos eventually appropriated their ABS-CBN television network for essentially no compensation at all, and in a more subtle manner, he also expropriated Meralco and other Lopez holdings.[47]

The Aquino family was another potentially dangerous competitor for Marcos. In 1958 the Aquino family had purchased 12,000 hectares of prime rice paddies in their home province and bought an American-owned sugar refinery. In 1978, Marcos commenced legal action against the property, offering the owners the repurchase price at 1958 prices and thus

[47] McCoy, "Rent-Seeking Families and the State," pp. 508–510.

clearing more than one billion *pesos* in the transaction.[48] Also, of course, Ninoy Aquino was enough of a threat to Marcos that when he returned from exile in the United States in 1983, he was assassinated as he stepped off the plane in Manila.

The Osmeña family was also a potential Marcos rival. The Osmeña family, from central Cebu Province, was a political dynasty going back to 1906, when Sergio Osmeña won the Cebu governorship. Metropolitan Cebu is the largest Philippine city after Manila, with over one million residents and a well-developed infrastructure. Control of Cebu easily translates into significant national power, and thus its politicians were a threat to Marcos. Sergio Osmeña Sr. was vice-president 1935–1944 and president 1944–1946. Sergio Osmeña's son, Sergio Jr., was a national senator, a contender for the vice-presidency in 1961, and a contender – against Marcos – for the presidency in 1969. Sergio Osmeña Jr. was injured in the Plaza Miranda bombing of 1971, and he left the Philippines for the United States, where he died in 1984. Sergio Jr.'s son and heir apparent, Sergio Osmeña III, was arrested for alleged sedition in 1972 together with Gerry Lopez, heir to the Lopez family fortune, and a cousin, Emilio Osmeña, was arrested and then exiled. Their wealth was also confiscated: the Hacienda Osmeña was appropriated under the land reform program in 1974, and the government also expropriated the family's Cebu Development Corporation, a land reclamation project worth millions of U.S. dollars.[49]

Vicente Tan, majority owner of Continental Bank and Philippine Trust Company (Philtrust), was arrested in 1974 for "economic sabotage." Marcos held him in jail until he agreed to sell control of the two banks that he owned.

3. The Survivors

Finally, there was the majority of the oligarchs – those who "got along by going along." These elites kept to their own business, and despite their personal feelings, did not protest against Marcos's heavy-handed tactics as long as he left them alone. The occasional acts of great courage, such as by Ninoy Aquino or José Diokno, should not be overlooked. However,

[48] Author's interview with Ambassador Sedfrey Ordonez, the Aquino family's lawyer during the martial law period, February 17, 1998.
[49] Resil Mojares, "The Dream Goes On and On," p. 316.

as Tony Gatmaitan (former president of Commercial Bank of Manila) put it, "the Philippine super-elite, like elites everywhere, are physical cowards."[50] Marcos tended to leave these oligarchs alone as long as they did not protest his rule or interfere with his other operations. Occasionally these groups would interact over some matter. Marcos convinced ex-president Macapagal to undertake to explain and justify the new constitution around the country. Enrique Zobel de Ayala was made ambassador to St. James, and his cousin was allowed to develop the family's vast property in Makati into the country's business and financial center.

By thus dividing and conquering, Marcos was able to create a strong state that took advantage of a disorganized business class. Yet Marcos, being part of the system, did not fundamentally transform Philippine society. Marcos's aims were limited, and he was not able to extend centralized control over the banks and the capitalists. Instead, he took the pattern of Philippine corruption to its "logical" end. The oligarchs were not destroyed; rather, new oligarchs were brought in, who rapidly tried to become like the old oligarchs. Land reform and landed interests were also not destroyed, they were just redirected in ways that benefited the ruling regime. The bandwagon process of the democratic era continued but in an institutionally more coherent manner. Everybody still needed – and desperately wanted – access to the presidential palace. As in Park Chung-hee's Korea, all major decisions in the Philippines were made at the top.

4. The Endgame

This system worked smoothly for a decade. Initially Marcos made great strides in implementing reforms, weakening local warlords in the provinces, and convincing foreign capital and international organizations such as the World Bank to invest in the Philippines. But in the early 1980s, the Marcos regime began to crumble under its own weight. As Marcos himself became bedridden through illness, his ability to lead diminished, and the cronies who were close to him began to squabble among themselves. Many of the oligarchs who had been content to allow Marcos a measure of discretion now became increasingly worried. In the early 1980s, the economy began a long slide, the insurgencies in the provinces grew, and unrest bubbled up not only from the poor but increasingly from

[50] Author's interview, February 18, 1998.

the elites in Makati as well. The last straw was the snap election of 1986 that led to "People Power" and Marcos's downfall at Edsa.

III. Philippine Bandwagoning and the Pendulum of Corruption

The pattern of crony relations is the Philippines has contributed to high transaction costs and resultant lower economic performance. Business groups competed with each other over the spoils of the state, with power shifting rapidly between groups. Property rights were not stable and elites were not stable. Business itself was unable to organize and as a result had no coherent voice with which to press the government for consistent policies, and more importantly business devoted many resources to competing among themselves for government favor. Although the Marcos era saw increased state strength, new cronies created by expropriating traditional oligarch's wealth further exacerbated the high transaction costs in the economy. As a typical case the Philippines is of a less-developed country where cronyism and personal relations lead to high transaction costs and resultant low-performing economy. This pattern of Philippine government-business relations has both similarities and differences with Korea.

1. Similarities

In Korea and the Philippines the broad patterns of money politics were similar: elites traded pork for votes, and policy for bribes. As a consequence, in both countries the state had trouble disciplining business and enforcing limits. Under martial law, both countries experienced an autonomous state. Under Park and Marcos, government intervention was highly selective, and decisions were made in the executive branch and not by the bureaucracy. In postindependence Korea and the Philippines, the imposition of similar democratic institutions on top of a society in turmoil led to a similar overall pattern of politics and corruption. This pattern had serious but predictable consequences, from constrained collusion between state and business to recurrent political crises, a weakened legislature, and an unstable party system. As such, there remains substantial continuity in both countries' deeper political patterns and institutions.

The institutional structures of Korea and the Philippines are remarkably similar. First, both are presidential systems that invest enormous power in the executive. The president's influence generally comes from the power that resides in the presidency. But the president also holds considerable power within the party as the party leader, and within the state as leader of the majority party. Relations between the ruler and the party thus become a classic principal-agent problem as to whether the party can constrain the ruler. Indeed, the presidential systems of Korea and the Philippines constitute a category that differs markedly from that of other Asian countries. For example, Japan has a parliamentary system in which a weak prime minister rules at the consent of the party, and the bureaucracy is relatively autonomous from regime interests.

The institutional framework of Korea and the Philippines drives similar patterns of politics and influence. First, the need to develop extensive networks of business-government support derives from nominal democratic institutions in both countries.[51] With episodic regularity, South Korea and the Philippines have been rocked by corruption scandals. Compared with Taiwan, where Kuomindang (KMT) dominance was accepted by the United States, in Korea and the Philippines leaders needed to develop and sustain political support.

Second, the institutional framework led to the need to finance parties and thus to the pivotal role of big business, which also had implications for economic policy. In Korea and the Philippines business has been more influential than in Taiwan because of the need of the political parties to court business in order to win elections. The erratic economic policy and extensive corruption can be seen as outcomes of this effort to build these bases of business support. Finally, in both Korea and the Philippines politics is notoriously criticized as being factional and personalistic.[52]

Given their similar institutional frameworks, we would expect to see similar patterns of politics and influence in Korea and the Philippines. Politics is not passive; it involves the active struggle to create coalitions, minimize enemies, and negotiate policies and positions. In this case, various political groups engage in illegal practices to persuade, buy, or coerce society to either acquiesce or support their rule. This requires great amounts of money and expertise. Political parties also utilize the standard practices for generating votes: they organize townships, hold parties,

---

[51] For a more complete explication of the comparison between Taiwan and South Korea, see Tun-jen Cheng, Stephan Haggard, and David Kang, "Institutions, Economic Policy, and Growth in Korea and Taiwan" (MS, UC San Diego, 1996).
[52] See Doronila, *The State, Economic Transformation, and Political Change in the Philippines*, p. 5.

sponsor hiking trips, and pay people to show up at rallies. The need to fund these activities has resulted in consistent pressure by political elites for donations from private business, a process that goes back to liberation in both countries.

Once one group has control of the state, it is in a position to exchange preferential access or policy decisions for favors from business groups. Policy decisions are made with an eye toward sustaining coalitions, persuading opposition members to change their stances, or heading off potential future problems. In this instance, because government policy has a direct impact on their success and profits, businessmen compete with each other in seeking to influence governmental policy.

In both Korea and the Philippines, close personal or family connections were central to political and economic life. In both countries this process involved intermarriage among elites and the assiduous cultivation of personal relationships. In both countries an introduction from a mutual acquaintance was critical in opening doors. Also, in both countries the elites tended to persist over a long time, and even though individual members of a family might suffer short-term problems, the family, and usually the individual, would eventually return to influence.

2. Differences

Corruption in the Philippines was different from that in Korea. Whereas in Korea the business sector had to become more organized because of the strength of the military regime, in the Philippines both the state and the oligarchs had less around which to cohere. Thus, during the democratic era, the powerful oligarchs were able to overrun the state, in a process that, although chaotic, had a certain predictability and order to it. The state reeled under the demands of the oligarchs, but as long as the oligarchs were receiving their share of the benefits, they had no incentive to implement genuine change in the system. This approximated a prisoner's dilemma, in which changing the rules might help the nation as a whole, but not the individuals with the power to actually change the system.

Under Marcos, the pendulum swung too far in the opposite direction. The state became far more coherent and was initially unified, with a clear set of predominant elites, including General Ver, Imelda Marcos, and ultimately Ferdinand Marcos himself. This is not to argue that there was no conflict; in fact, Malacañang Palace was notoriously divided, particularly between Imelda and Ver on one side, and Enrile on the other.[53] However, when compared with the cacophony of voices that existed during the democratic era, decisions were more centralized in the Marcos palace. The state was able to seize the initiative and divide the oligarchs, making the oligarchs react to state policies rather than letting them impose their demands on the state. The bureaucracy, although strengthened from within and more autonomous from societal interests, became subject to the tastes and whims of the regime. Unfortunately for the Filipino people, the power of the state was not put to effective goals, but rather to maximizing the corruption that Marcos could harvest.

Korea and the Philippines were also different with respect to expropriation. No Philippine leader, either authoritarian or democratic, has attempted – or been forced – to craft a credible commitment in which investment is encouraged. To do so the ruler would need to limit his discretionary power. Compare this with Chapter 4, where we saw that the Korean state, despite its bluster, rarely moved against the economic elite. When the state did attempt rationalization in Korea, as with the automotive industry, it generally failed. This rather counterintuitive situation underscores the importance not only of state capacity but also of the goals of the state. Marcos, lacking any external threat to his rule and wishing to keep his relations with the United States and the IMF warm, had every incentive to pursue this method of rent seeking to its extreme. The amount of graft that occurred under Marcos was truly staggering. Whether the estimates are $5 billion or $20 billion, the Marcos regime perfected the art of corruption. In Korea, by contrast, a much greater degree of uncertainty regarding American and North Korean intentions caused elites in the state to place a higher priority on efficiency and reform.

It is common among scholars to discuss the high level of institutionalization in Korea. Yet this book has shown that Korean elites routinely ignored institutions, whether it be the EPB, the legal and judicial system, or the electoral system. Ironically, and surprisingly, it could be argued that the Philippines rather than Korea was the more institutionalized country, if only because of the reliance by all Philippine actors on the judicial system. Even Ferdinand Marcos at the height of his power used the courts – lawsuits, summary judgments, and presidential directives – to organize

---

[53] For details of intrigue in the Marcos palace, see William Rempel, *Delusions of a Dictator: The Mind of Marcos as Revealed in His Secret Diaries* (Boston: Little, Brown, 1993); and Seagrave, *The Marcos Dynasty*.

his expropriation of assets and to deal with political and economic actors. This contrasts sharply with the Korean experience, where even today the courts are notoriously underutilized. As one influential lawyer put it, "the trouble with the Americans is that they taught us too much law."[54] It might be argued that Marcos's use of the courts was merely a sham and that in reality politics in the Philippines was as unstructured as in Korea. This would be a mistake, because the differences had real consequences for politics. In Korea institutions were so weak that ignoring them had no consequence for economic and political elites. In the Philippines, by contrast, leaders were forced to follow procedure. The outcomes may have been similar, but the paths were different.

In Korea, directors and boards and judicial suits and review were meaningless. There, bank loans, regulatory policies, and tax policy were accomplished through the personal guarantee of an influential person. In the Philippines, even under martial law, Marcos used the courts and the legal system to implement expropriation. It might be argued that use of the legal system in the Philippines was more form than substance, and to an extent this is true. Marcos was clearly abusing the legal system to profit from it. However, the point remains that being forced to seek "cover" through the legal system is consequential in politics. To blithely ignore laws and institutions is one thing; to have to work within a system – however mangled – is another. And it bodes well for the Philippines that the emphasis on the rule of law, although violated in spirit, remained intact. The important point is that no one cared enough about laws in Korea to make even a passing attempt to legitimize rule through the judicial system. Thus, qualitatively, it appears that corruption and rent seeking in Korea have more similarities than dissimilarities with the Philippines, although in the Philippines the actual amount of graft was probably slightly higher. It is also possible to utilize some rough quantitative measures.

We might begin by looking at the cost of elections. David Wurfel estimated that the equivalent of 13 percent of the national budget was spent on the Philippine election campaign of 1961 and that perhaps the equivalent of 25 percent of the national budget was spent on the 1969 campaign.[55] These numbers are equivalent to estimates of the cost of elections in Korea, where an estimated 16 percent of the government budget was spent on the 1992 campaign.

---

[54] Ambassador Sedfrey Ordonez, author's interview, February 17, 1998.
[55] David Wurfel, "The Philippines," *Journal of Politics* 25 (1963): 758.

IV. Conclusion

Both Korea and the Philippines have had endemic corruption that centered around the exchange of political funds for favorable economic policies. In both countries rulers pursued a political agenda aimed at retaining power by using corruption as one of many different tools at their disposal, and business interests sought government intervention when possible. It is true that similar institutional structures led to superficially similar patterns of political behavior and money influence in both countries. But institutions are not deterministic: Korea and the Philippines had different structures of social organization, and rulers and elites faced different constraints and incentives over the years. These difference shaped the patterns of corruption in both countries. Corruption in Korea, although endemic, was constrained by the collusion of a powerful business class and a coherent state. Both of these major actors were able to benefit from their close relationship with the other, but neither was ever able to gain the upper hand, and despite each group's constantly bemoaning its counterpart's utter lack of qualifications, they needed each other and relied upon each other. In contrast, corruption in the Philippines swung like a pendulum, as one group or another gained predominant power, and each group in turn would busily set about lining its own pockets, aware that in the next round its fortunes might well be reversed. As one group or another managed to become fleetingly dominant, others jumped on the bandwagon, only to jump off at the first sign of trouble. It was only with the fall of Marcos and the economic chaos of the mid-1980s that the Philippines showed signs of real change.

6

Democracy in the 1980s and the Financial
Crisis of 1997

"We got to the party late, so we didn't get as drunk."
                                    – Philippine businessman, September 1999
"We popped the champagne cork a little too soon."
                                    – Korean businessman, December 1997

The pattern of government-business relations discussed in previous chapters was not static, and in both Korea and the Philippines patterns led to changes in the composition and power of the actors themselves. Society as well in both countries stabilized, with a new generation of citizens that had grown up under neither war nor colonialism. A growing middle class, urbanization, and industrialization all altered the character of the government-business relationship.

The changed government-business relationship was expressed most clearly in the dramatic turn to democracy in both countries.[1] In little over a year, first the Philippines and then Korea saw the ouster of a widely unpopular chief executive and the return of democracy. However, a country's shift from authoritarian to democratic institutions will have different results depending on the relationship between state and business (Figure 6.1). In Korea, where both the state and business were strong, a shift to democratic institutions benefited business more than it did the state – the state was weakened by the imposition of democratic processes. Democratization did not change the generally high demand by the business sector for rents, but it did affect the supply. With more politicians competing on the supply side, fewer limits were placed on the behavior of

---

[1] Stephan Haggard and Robert Kaufman, *Transitions to Democracy* (Princeton: Princeton University Press, 1996).

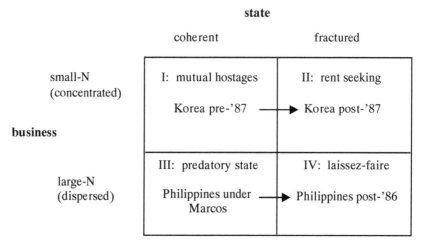

Figure 6.1. The Changing Relationship between Business and the State in the 1980s

the business sector. In the Philippines, where one group could already take advantage of the other, democracy was beneficial. The diffusion of state power to match an already diffuse business sector moved the country to a situation in which neither group could take advantage of the other.

By the mid-1990s, decades of rapid growth in Asia had spawned heady optimism across the region. Discussion of a "Pacific Century" became commonplace, with analysts predicting everything from a coming war between China and the United States to the emergence of Japan as the world's largest economy by the year 2005.[2] Against this backdrop, the abrupt advent of the Asian financial crisis of 1997 caught almost everyone by surprise. However, the crisis did not appear overnight – the seeds were sown long in advance of the summer of 1997. Rapid economic growth masked the roots of Asia's vulnerability, which were deeply embedded in historical structures and practices. To understand why Korea and not the Philippines was caught by the crisis, we need to explore how the democratic transitions of the mid-1980s transformed the historical pattern of government-business relations.

[2] See, for example, Richard Bernstein and Ross Munro, *The Coming Conflict with China* (New York: Alfred A. Knopf, 1997); and "Paradigm Paranoia: CIA Report Warns of Japanese Economic Domination," *Far Eastern Economic Review* (June 27, 1991): 15.

The implications of the Asian financial crisis are that in Korea, the *chaebol* ran amok, whereas in the Philippines a number of political and economic reforms began a decade before the crisis. In this chapter, I discuss how Korea and the Philippines changed during the 1980s, and how these changes affected government-business relations as portrayed in the model presented in Chapter 1. I then show how the model explains the Asian financial crisis of 1997.

I. Democratic Transitions in the 1980s

The mutual hostage situation that allowed rapid growth under Park Chung-hee continued with the coup d'etat by Chun Doo-hwan in 1979. The Chun regime was even more militaristic than the Park regime. However, although the Korean state continued to exert immense, centralized, and top-down authority, three decades of growth had caused changes in the makeup of business and society. The *chaebol* rapidly diversified into disparate sectors. An increasingly wealthy middle class, which for decades had been content to forgo political freedom in favor of economic gains, now came to the fore as a politically influential group. Other groups, such as labor and students, began to make their voices heard as well.

Promising to serve only one term as a means of legitimizing his rule, Chun worked himself into a corner. By spring 1987, Chun's attempts to anoint a successor and rule like Rasputin behind the scenes brought literally millions of citizens into the streets in protest.[3] In June 1987, Chun stepped down and allowed popular elections to be held. With the election of Roh Tae-woo, Korea had made a genuine transition to democracy.

The transition to democratic rule, although fitful, radically altered the relationship between state and business. Democratization severely weakened the power of the state to check the *chaebol*. This led to increased demands for political payoffs, as politicians began to genuinely compete for electoral support, and to the decreased ability of the state to resist or contain the demands of the business sector. The small number of massive Korean firms, unrestrained by any market forces because of their size, made increasingly risky decisions. Thus "too much" democracy in

---

[3] On the democratic transition, see James Cotton, "From Authoritarianism to Democracy in South Korea," *Political Studies* 37 (June 1989): 244–259.

combination with a still collusive business-government relationship resulted in increasingly ineffectual policy making.

In the Figure 6.1 model, Korea's position moved from mutual hostages (Cell I) to rent-seeking business (Cell II). Rapid growth changed the conditions under which the state and the *chaebol* interacted with each other. The *chaebol* were increasingly confident that they could manage their own affairs without interference from the state. The state increasingly wanted to reduce both the size and the influence of the *chaebol*, but each individual politician had a private incentive to retain collusive ties for purposes of fund raising.

The 1980s also saw profound changes in the Philippines. Under martial law, Marcos had taken predatory behavior to its logical extreme. Marcos was able to steal from society up to and past the point of rebellion, and by the mid-1980s no amount of patronage or pork could keep his fragile coalition of supporters together. Fourteen years of increasingly outlandish rule by Marcos and his cronies had left the country bankrupt, in economic and political chaos, and with rising separatist insurgencies in the provinces. The Philippine economy actually contracted during this period, with real GNP per capita at constant U.S. dollars (1987 prices) dropping from $678 in 1980 to only $631 in 1990. Over the period 1960–1996, whereas South Korea grew at an annual average rate of 8.82 percent, the Philippines grew at only 3.89 percent.[4] On the political front, in August 1983 the leading opposition leader to Marcos, Benigno Aquino, returned to Manila from exile and was assassinated as he stepped off the plane. Massive demonstrations followed, including for the first time one by the business community from Makati, Manila's financial district.

The situation of increasingly chaotic and tenuous rule by Marcos came to a head in 1986. Marcos held "snap" elections in February 1986, hoping to win a quick victory. However, Cory Aquino, widow of the assassinated opposition leader, returned to the Philippines to be swept into office as president. Marcos panicked and declared himself the winner, causing an emotional uprising known as the "People Power" that led to the overthrow the Marcos regime.[5] Deputy Chief of Staff Fidel Ramos and Minister of Defense Juan Ponce Enrile led a military uprising against Marcos. The

---

[4] Figures from World Bank, *World Development Indicators, 1997* (Washington, DC: World Bank, 1997).

[5] For a good overview of this time, see Stanley Karnow, *In Our Image* (New York: Random House, 1989).

rebels located themselves on military bases on the Epifanio de los Santos Avenue, popularly known as Edsa. As the days passed, hundreds of thousands of civilians filled Edsa in support of the anti-Marcos movement. Having lost the support of the Catholic Church and the United States, Marcos went into voluntary exile in Hawaii. Asia's first democracy had reappeared.

As president from 1986 to 1992, Cory Aquino began the painful process of restructuring and restoring politics and business. The economy was in shambles. Marcos's cronies either left the country or took a low profile, their businesses failing. Foreign banks were reluctant to lend to a country in such an unstable situation. Cory Aquino restored civil liberties and offered the communist insurgents a six-month cease-fire in return for surrendering their arms. A new constitution was promulgated that largely restored the constitution used before 1972. But the new regime was fragile – Cory Aquino, despite immense popularity, faced enormous obstacles. Deep divisions in the country led to personal grievances, and politics remained tenuous, as evidenced by a series of failed coup attempts. The much-anticipated land reform effort soon bogged down in political wrangling, and the government once again came to be seen as ineffective. Filipino politics splintered into a number of competing parties.

Perhaps Aquino's great accomplishment was that she survived and achieved a peaceful transfer of power. With only 23.6 percent of the total vote, Fidel Ramos was elected president on May 11, 1992. Widely perceived as a tough leader because of his military actions during the uprising at Edsa in 1986, Ramos continued and deepened the reforms begun under Aquino.

Although the Philippine communist movement had been virtually nonexistent in the early 1970s, deteriorating economic and political conditions in the country in the 1980s revived the Muslim and communist insurgencies. By 1986, James Nach of the U.S. Embassy estimated that the communists had between eight and ten thousand regular troops and perhaps a half-million supporters.[6] Whereas Aquino had been unable to end the internal insurrections that plagued the provinces of the Philippines, Fidel Ramos was able to negotiate a cease-fire with the insurgents in 1993. Although many of the issues of land reform and exploitation remained to be addressed, an end to the hostilities boded well for both the bargaining

[6] Karnow, *In Our Image*, p. 406.

power of the state and the stability of the country. Peace with the rebels meant that the threat of coup attempts and instability diminished greatly. Gregorio "Gringo" Honasan, rebel leader of several coup attempts, was even elected to the Senate in 1995, marking the integration of military rebels into mainstream politics. In September 1996 the largest Muslim separatist organization, the Moro National Liberation Front, or MNLF, signed a peace settlement in Mindanao. Although the separatist movements in the south have not completely disappeared, they are greatly reduced.

In terms of the model, the Philippines moved closer than ever before during the twentieth century to a weak-weak configuration (Cell IV). The economic and political chaos left by the ouster of Marcos heralded a changed set of circumstances. A long history of democratic institutions and traditions – however chaotic and unruly – was a base upon which the modern Philippines could build. The state, although weakened, was now run by democratically elected officials in what were widely considered to be, despite some violations, relatively clean and fair elections. As the Philippines slowly recovered from the excesses of the late-Marcos era, both state and business were less powerful and less coherent, creating an opportunity in the early 1990s for the country to begin a painful restructuring process. The pendulum appears to have stabilized.

The changes of the 1980s meant that both Korea and the Philippines were entering a new phase in their government-business relationships. As the decade of the 1990s dawned, Korea and the Philippines were feeling increasingly confident about their futures.

II. The Asian Financial Crisis of 1997

The most compelling example of the impact of democracy on money politics is the Asian financial crisis of 1997. The panic by international investors beginning in the summer of 1997 over the various Asian currencies caught almost every analyst and pundit by surprise. The Hanbo Steel Company's collapse, mentioned in Chapter 1, showed that the Korean economic system was teetering on a precipice and would need only a slight push to send it over the edge. That push came from attacks on Southeast Asian currencies during the summer of 1997. A confluence of negative regional trends led to the attack on the Korean *won* in November 1997. Had the Thai *baht* and the Hong Kong dollar not fallen in the summer of 1997, the Korean *won* would never have followed suit. But by the time the currency traders began to attack the Korean *won*, sending it from 780 *won*/dollar to almost 2,000 *won*/dollar by late 1997, the Korean system was under great strain. An IMF bailout plan of $57 billion, the IMF's largest ever, was concluded on December 3, 1997. In the widest terms, the total foreign debt held by various Korean companies at the end of September 1997 stood at $51 billion outstanding, with total effective debt being $170 billion.

Economies around the region tumbled into recession: in 1998 Malaysia's economy contracted 7.5 percent, Thailand's 9.4 percent, Korea's 5.8 percent, and Indonesia's 13.4 percent. Unemployment and interest rates in all the Asian countries surged. Stock markets from Bangkok to Seoul lost over half their value, and exchange rates deteriorated across the region. The social contract that had sustained Asian growth for over three decades came under pressure, leading to electoral reform and the end of outright Liberal Democratic Party (LDP) rule in Japan, the ouster of Suharto in Indonesia, and bank and company restructuring around the region. The panic of 1997 saw banking outflows from Asia turn into a cascade. Every Asian country except the Philippines experienced banking losses during the final quarter of 1997.[7] Korea lost $17 billion, Singapore $13.3 billion, and Thailand $8.4 billion. In contrast, the Philippines saw a gain of $204 million.[8] The Philippines managed to avoid the worst of the crisis and was one of the few bright spots in the region. Indeed, the Philippine economy contracted only 0.5 percent in 1998 and was poised for positive growth in 1999.[9]

How could Korea end up needing the largest bailout in the history of the IMF? And why did the Philippines avoid the worst of the crisis?

Two contending views have emerged as explanations for the Asian financial crisis. The first view places the burden on the international economy and emphasizes the influence of increasingly mobile global capital and of the financial contagion that can ricochet rapidly through deregulated markets.[10] Thus Steven Radalet and Jeffrey Sachs emphasize

---

[7] From East Asia Analytical Unit, *The Philippines: Beyond the Crisis* (Canberra: Australian Department of Foreign Affairs and Trade, 1998), p. 154.

[8] *CrossBorder Capital*, cited in Michael J. Howell, "Asia's 'Victorian' Financial Crisis" (mimeo, London, 1998), p. 8.

[9] Segundo E. Romero, "The Philippines in 1997," *Asian Survey* 38, no. 2 (February 1998): 200.

[10] See, for example, Robert Wade, "The Asian Debt-and-Development Crisis of 1997–•• Causes and Consequences," *World Development* (August 1998); and Steven Radalet and Jeffrey Sachs, "The Onset of the East Asian Financial Crisis" (NBER Working Paper 6680, August 1998).

the role of "financial panic on the part of the international community as an essential element of the Asian crisis."[11] The second view, as articulated by Paul Kragman, among others, focuses on the Asian countries themselves, emphasizing weaknesses in the financial sectors, poorly regulated economies, and political systems that reward corruption and cronyism.[12] This view stresses the role of "moral hazard" – government guarantees to banks that weakened the banks' incentive to effectively monitor their loans. Firms were allowed to borrow more than was prudent based on the assumption that for political reasons the government would not let the company or bank fail. As Corsetti, Pesenti, and Roubini argue, "[T]he *moral hazard* problem in Asia magnified the financial vulnerability of the region . . . at the corporate, financial, and international level."[13]

Both explanations contain an element of truth, but both also share two shortcomings. First, neither explanation is focused enough to explain variation across individual cases, and neither can explain the differential impact of the crisis on Korea and the Philippines. Second, neither explanation provides any historical context for how the Asian countries arrived at 1997. The explanation I provide here incorporates many of the ideas present in both these rival explanations. Krugman's focus on moral hazard fits nicely with my notion of mutual hostages. Crony capitalism and exposure to international finance also figure prominently in my explanation. But the explanation I provide is more deeply grounded in history, and it also explains individual cases. Clearly, the rapid increase of mobile international capital and a globalized economy were part of the reason that the crisis occurred. As a result, I focus not so much on changes or on the impact of the international economy, but on those distinctive aspects of Korea and the Philippines.

1. Korea

Korea was vulnerable to the Asian financial crisis for three reasons that derive directly from my model.[14] First, an increased demand for political

[11] Radalet and Sachs, "The Onset of the East Asian Financial Crisis," p. 2.
[12] See, for example, Paul Krugman, "What Happened to Asia?" (MS, MIT, 1998); and Alan Greenspan, "Remarks before the 34th Annual Conference on Bank Structure and Competition," Federal Reserve of Chicago, May 7, 1998.
[13] Giancarlo Corsetti, Paolo Pesenti, and Nouriel Roubini, "What Caused the Asian Currency and Financial Crisis? Part I: A Macroeconomic Overview" (MS, NYU, 1998), p. 2.
[14] There is also an international political economy (IPE) explanation, and I may be leaving out some exogenous factors. My sense was that the depreciation of the *yen* in 1995 placed

payoffs shifted the advantage to business. Second, Korea's legal and corporate institutions remained underdeveloped even in the 1990s. Finally, given increasingly mobile international capital, the overcapacity and over-diversification of the Korean conglomerates made them vulnerable to international speculative attacks.

1. Increased Demand for Political Payoffs. The scandals of the late Kim administration show that the transition to democratic rule in Korea has by no means reduced the ability of rent-seeking groups to exercise political influence; indeed, the demand for campaign funds has probably increased. One reason that Kim Dae-jung and Kim Young-sam are no different from previous political elites in their manner of and appetite for political fundraising is that the costs of winning elections and running a party are vast. Because of the way parties are organized, politicians need enormous amounts of money to stand for office.

Table 6.1 gives estimates for spending on elections from 1981 through 1997. Even though total officially reported expenses for the 1981 National Assembly was 31 billion *won*, estimates of actual spending were ten times higher. A popular phrase during the 11th National Assembly election (1981) under Chun was "*sipdang, kurak,*" which roughly translated means "expenditures of 1 billion *won* [$1.3 million in U.S. dollars] wins the seat, expenditures of 900 million *won* [$1.2 million] will lose."[15] Most striking is the vast expansion in spending after 1987. By the 14th National Assembly election (1992), the phrase had become "*isipdang, simnak,*" or "expenditures of 2 billion *won* wins the seat, expenditures of 1 billion *won* will lose."[16] In the 1992 presidential campaign, Kim Young-sam officially reported 28 billion *won* in expenses, although unofficial estimates of his actual expenses ran as high as one trillion *won*.

The total cost of National Assembly campaigns and the presidential campaign of 1992 was estimated at 5 trillion *won* ($5.1 billion), or the

---

far greater strain on Korean currency and trade balance than occurred in other countries. In addition, there was greater pressure on Korea to peg the *won* to maintain dollar-denominated debt at a manageable level, thus creating speculative opportunities absent in the Philippines.

[15] Park Jong-yol, "5 kong hwakuk chŏngch'i chagŭm" (Political funds in the Fifth Republic), *Shindonga* (January 1989): 290.

[16] Ku Bon-hong, "Hanguk sahoe esŏ pup'ae wa chagŭme kwanhan yŏnku: 6 kong hwakuk ŭl chungshimŭro" (Research on the sociology of Korean corruption and funds with a focus on the Sixth Republic) (Ph.D. diss., Yonsei University, 1999), p. 57.

Table 6.1. *Estimates of Election Spending, 1980–1997*

Election	Unofficial Estimate of Actual Expenses	Officially Reported Expenses
1981 NA (11th)	Total: 200–300 billion *won* ($266–400 million) 500 million – 1 billion *won* per candidate	31.7 billion *won* ($45.2 million)
1985 NA (12th)	Total: 200–300 billion *won* ($266–400 million)	n.a.
1987 presidential	Total: 443 billion *won* ($590 million) Roh: at least 200 billion *won* ($266 million) from Chun	13.9 billion *won* ($18.5 million)
1988 NA (13th)	Total: 400–500 billion *won* ($533–666 million) Government: 500 million – 1 billion *won* per candidate Opposition: 200–300 million *won* per candidate	n.a.
1992 presidential	Total: 2 trillion *won* ($2.7 billion) YS: 1 trillion *won* ($1.3 billion) JP: 30 billion *won* ($40 million)	YS: 28.4 billion *won* ($37.8 million)
1992 NA (14th)	Total: 1 trillion *won* ($1.3 billion)	n.a.
1996 NA (15th)	Total: >1 trillion *won* ($1.3 billion) 1–2 billion *won* per candidate	NKP: 6.45 billion *won* total ($8.5 million) Kukmin Hoeŭi (DJ): 6.43 billion *won* Jamillyŏn (JP): 6.29 billion *won*
1997 presidential	Total: 2 trillion *won* ($2.7 billion)	DJ: 26 billion *won* ($34.6 million)

Note: NA: National Assembly election; YS: Kim Young-Sam; DJ: Kim Dae-Jung; JP: Kim Jong-pil; NKP: New Korea Party. U.S. dollar amounts converted at exchange rate from that year. Figures are given in current *won*, not adjusted for inflation.

Sources: Ku Bon-hong, "Hanguk sahoe esŏpup'ae wa chagŭme kwanhan yŏnku: 6 kong hwakuk ŭl chungshimŭro" (Research on the sociology of Korean corruption and funds with a focus on the 6th Republic) (Ph.D. diss., Yonsei University, 1999), pp. 55–59; Park Jong-yol, "5 kong hwakuk chŏngch'i chagŭm" (Political funds in the 5th Republic), *Shindonga* (January 1989): pp. 280–300; Yoon Sung-yong, *Pichagŭm* (Secret funds) (Seoul: Jiyangsa, 1995), pp. 137–139; Lee Chang-won and Kim Hong-jin, "DJ pichagŭm 5-kae kiŏpesŏ 39 ŏk chegong" (DJ accepted 3.9 billion from 5 *chaebols*), *Chosun Ilbo*, February 20, 1998; Lee Jong-won, "97 Taesŏn: DJ pichagŭm" (The 1997 election: DJ's secret funds), *Jugan Chosun* (October 23, 1997): 26–34; and Kim Jonghoon, "Yŏya 4 tang chŏngch'i chagŭm 22,617 ŏk sottda" (The 4 parties raised 261 billion last year), *Donga Ilbo*, April 12, 1998.

160

equivalent of 16 percent of the government's annual budget. However, in twenty days of legal campaigning, National Assembly campaign expenditures were capped at 83 million *won* ($105,000). For the 1996 National Assembly campaign it was estimated that each candidate spent between one and two billion *won* during that period, not including expenditures made before the legal campaign. In addition, running an office over four years is estimated to cost $6 million – so a winner would need $7–8 million just to win and operate a normal Assembly seat.[17] Interestingly, all three major parties in the 1996 National Assembly elections reported official expenditures of 6.2 to 6.4 billion *won*, while estimates are of actual expenses at over one trillion *won*.

Normal party expenditures are also enormous. The Korean phrase "*oribal*" (duck feet) describes the situation: on the surface decorum is maintained while below the surface the parties scramble like mad to raise funds. In the 1970s, Park's Blue House disbursed approximately 10 billion *won* each year.[18] After democratization, each local district had expenses of 10 million *won* ($13,000) per month, meaning annual party expenditures in the early 1990s were approximately $39 million.[19] Over five years, Roh reportedly gave at least 180 billion *won* ($240 million) to his political party for normal operating expenses and disbursed 30 billion *won* ($40 million) to local constituencies four times per year while personally raising at least $800 million in secret funds.[20] In 1996 political parties officially reported raising 315 billion *won* ($420 million).[21] As one observer noted, "[I]f they admit to raising 315 billion *won*, we know the actual total must be far greater."[22] In comparison, in a country with six times the population and an economy fifteen times larger, the U.S. Republican Party's fund-raising goal in 2000 was $179 million.

[17] Park In-hwan, "1 chowŏn kongsa: Kim Young-sam, Kim Dae-Jung, Chung Juyoung sŏngo chakŭm" (The billion dollar deal: Campaign funds and Kim Young-sam, Kim Dae-jung, and Chung Ju-young), *Shingonda* (December 1992): 268–277.

[18] Han Heung-soo and Ahn Byung-hoon, "Hankuk ŭi pihap pŏpchŏk chŭngch'i chagŭm ŭi yuhyŏng kwa siltae" (Patterns and realities of illegal political funds in Korea), *Tong Suh Yonku* (East and West studies) 7 (1994): 205.

[19] Yoon Sung-yong, *Pichagŭm* (Secret funds) (Seoul: Jiyangsa, 1995), p. 138.

[20] Yoon, *Pichagŭm*, p. 138; and Ha Jong-dae, "No-ssi pichagŭm 8 ch'on ŏk nŏmnŭnda" (Roh's secret funds exceeded $800 million), *Shindonga* (March 1998): 230–251.

[21] Kim Jonghoon, "Yòya 4 tang chŏngch'i chagŭm 22,617 ŏk sottda" (The 4 parties raised 261 billion last year), *Donga Ilbo*, April 12, 1998.

[22] Kim, "Yòya 4 tang."

Table 6.2. *Estimates of Quasi Taxes, 1980–1987*

Year	Quasi Taxes (million won)	Quasi Taxes as percentage of total sales
1980	219.6	0.48
1981	345.9	0.55
1984	710.0	0.85
1985	683.9	0.77
1986	1,020.4	0.82
1987	988.3	0.74
TOTAL	3,968.1	

Sources: Kim Chun-gun, *Hankuk kiŏp ŭi chunjose ŭi kwanhan yŏnku* (Research on quasi taxes on Korean companies) (Seoul: Korea Economic Research Institute, 1988), p. 11; and Choi Dong-gyu, *Kiŏpŭi chun jose pudame kwanhan silchŏngchŏk yŏnku* (Concerning the burden of quasi taxes on companies) (Seoul: Korea Economic Research Institute, 1986), p. 11.

Table 6.3. *Estimates of Quasi Taxes for Ten Largest Chaebol, 1994–1998*

Company	Quasi Taxes (billion won)	Quasi Taxes as percentage of net profits
Samsung	1,217.3	25.0
Hyundai	702	37.2
LG	623.9	27.1
Daewoo	572.6	78.5
SK	375.6	18.7
Hanjin	268.6	n.a.
Hanhwa	152.6	>100.0
Kumho	135.1	>100.0
Ssangyong	114.9	n.a.
Lotte	74.1	n.a.
TOTAL	4,236.7	

Source: Kangwon Ilbo, August 18, 1999, p. 1.

Korea's political funds came from business. Tables 6.2 and 6.3 compare estimates for quasi taxes (*chun-chose*) paid by business for the periods 1980–1987 and 1994–1998, respectively. Although it is true that quasi taxes are largely accountable, they are still imposed in a coercive manner and are part of the overall government-business relationship. To not make "voluntary" donations is to run the risk of payback in the form of tax audits or rejected loan applications, for example. Total estimated quasi taxes for 1980–1987 were 3.9 billion *won*; the estimated total for 1994–1998 was 4.2 trillion *won*. Part of this increase is attributable to the increased size of both the economy and the largest *chaebol*, but neither the economy nor the *chaebol* expanded a thousandfold over the decade. Additionally, the figures for quasi taxes include neither entertainment expenses nor individual donations. According to the National Tax Administration, between 1988 and 1992 the top 30 *chaebol* spent approximately $1.4 billion for banquets and entertainment and only $215 million for research and development.[23]

Indeed, Hyundai founder Chung Ju-yong admitted, "I personally handed to the ruler about 1 billion *won* yearly during the 3rd Republic [Park], about 5 billion *won* yearly during the 5th Republic [Chun], and 10 billion *won* yearly in the 6th Republic [Roh]."[24] With the coming of democracy, Roh Tae-woo's regime had by 1988 instituted a system in which over 200 *tochang* ("stamps," or bureaucratic approvals) had to be obtained in order to undertake any project in South Korea. Thus even the smallest bureaucrat now had veto power, and the scale of the economy was much larger. As one businessman lamented to me: "By the late 1980s Roh and later YS [Kim Young-sam] had established so much 'democracy' that I needed over 100 envelopes [bribes] in order to build a factory last year. That never occurred under Park or Chun – they eliminated the middleman, and while you had to pay for access, you could do it at the top levels, and not worry so much about the bureaucracy."[25]

Under Kim Young-sam the trend continued. In 1999, the market-research firm Taylor Nelson Sofres PLC polled 1,250 middle-class, upper-income Korean decision makers, who were predominantly white-collar or self-employed urban men. Of the five categories considered – entertainment, law enforcement, government, business, and education – respondents said that only the education sector was less corrupt than it had been five years earlier. For business generally, 42 percent of respondents said

[23] Coalition for Social Justice/Citizen's Coalition for Economic Justice, *Uridŭlŭi pukkŭrŏn chahwasang* (Our shameful self-portrait) (Seoul: Umjiginun Chaek, 1993), p. 272.

[24] *Chosun Ilbo*, January 9, 1992, p. 3.

[25] In Korea, bribes and honoraria are traditionally passed in white envelopes. Interview, October 6, 1995.

Table 6.4. *Value Added to GNP by Korea's Four Largest Chaebol, 1986–1995 (%)*

	1986	1987	1988	1989	1990	1991	1992	1993	1994	1995
Hyundai	1.9	1.9	1.9	2.1	2.0	2.2	2.3	2.3	2.4	2.9
Samsung	1.2	1.3	1.6	2.2	2.0	1.8	1.9	2.0	2.4	3.1
LG	1.2	1.2	1.3	1.4	1.4	1.4	1.6	1.6	1.8	2.1
Daewoo	1.4	1.3	1.1	1.2	1.2	1.2	1.2	1.3	1.2	1.2
TOTAL	5.7	5.7	5.9	6.9	6.6	6.6	7.0	7.2	7.8	9.3

Source: Choi Sung-no, *1996 nyŏn 30 dae kiŏpchipdan* (An analysis of the 30 Korean conglomerates in 1996) (Seoul: Korea Economic Research Institute, 1997), p. 41.

the level of corruption was the same as before, and 32 percent said that it was worse.[26]

This exchange was not mere extortion, however – the *chaebol* continued to expand at the expense of small and medium-size industries. Although many assumed that globalization and liberalization reduce rent seeking and the power of the *chaebol*, the opposite might very well occur. Table 6.4 shows that although in 1986 the four largest *chaebol* added 5.7 percent to Korea's GNP, by 1995 their share had grown to 9.3 percent of value added to GNP.

Unless matched by stringent regulatory oversight to limit collusive practices and the exercise of market power, liberalization can provide new opportunities for large firms to buy favorable policy. Whereas measures to rein in the *chaebol* remain popular politically, because of government-business ties such policies were unsustainable even after 1997.

Three examples should illustrate my point. The first comes from the construction sector. During the rule of authoritarian regimes, the construction sector consisted of a small number of highly privileged firms, most of them affiliated with one of the major *chaebol*. And although this cartel allowed for significant corruption and bid rigging, the process remained constrained. Small firms without connections had virtually no chance of winning major government contracts or even of winning permits and approval for property development. With the advent of democracy, the government changed its practices to be more open and to allow smaller firms ("chungso kiŏp," or small and medium-size enterprises) to become

[26] *Wall Street Journal*, December 31, 1999.

realistic competitors. The result, however, was rampant corruption, shoddy workmanship, and an explosion of unqualified and underregulated firms that flooded the market. The result of this competitive bid process was a series of disasters, including the collapse of the Songsu Bridge in 1994, of the Shinhengju Bridge in 1992, and of the Sampoong Department Store.[27] It was only in May 2000 that the government formed an investigative unit to attempt to re-regulate the construction sector.[28]

The second example concerns direct political influence. Lee Kun-hui, the chairman of Samsung Group in the 1990s (and son of the founder), had long wanted Samsung to enter the automobile industry. Although the government had been unable to rationalize the industry in the late 1970s, it had been able to forestall Samsung's entering the market after that. By the early 1990s Samsung was again considering a move into the automotive sector. Despite vigorous family discussions questioning the wisdom of entering such a crowded and competitive sector, Lee ended up deciding to attempt the venture.[29] With Kim Young-sam running for president in 1992, Samsung declared that, if allowed, they would situate the plant outside of Pusan, which was also Kim Young-sam's hometown. This pledge, combined with other back-channel persuasion, won Samsung approval for the project early in Kim's tenure as president.[30] After investing more than $1 billion U.S. dollars, Samsung opened the plant, but managed to sell only 60,000 cars, mostly to Samsung employees.

The third example was mentioned in Chapter 1. Hanbo Steel Company had ambitious expansion plans in the late 1980s. A combination of bribes and political influence provided the support that allowed the company to continue to operate a badly mismanaged plant and receive over $6 billion in loans.[31] By the time of Hanbo's collapse in 1997, between 1.5 and 2 trillion *won* (over $1 billion) was unaccounted for in Hanbo's accounts.[32] At

---

[27] For details, see "kŏnsŏlŏp ŏpmu p'yŏllam" (Construction firms business operations handbook) (Seoul: Ministry of Construction and Transportation, November 1999), pp. iii–vii.

[28] *Hankuk Kyongje Sinmun*, May 24, 2000.

[29] Author's anonymous interview, February 19, 1997.

[30] "Four's a Crowd: Samsung Wants to Produce Cars but Faces Competition," *The Economist* (March 5, 1994): 72.

[31] "House of Debt: South Korea's Hanbo Group Reels from Corruption Allegations," *Far Eastern Economic Review* (March 14, 1991): 42–43.

[32] Yoon Young-ho, "Chŏng Tae-su wa kŏmŭn ton" (Chung Tae-soo and black money), *Shindonga* (March 1997): 201.

the first scheduled auction of Hanbo's assets, in June 1997, there was not a single bid. Under government pressure, POSCO steel company eventually offered $2 billion for Hanbo, declaring that it hoped it could return Hanbo to profitability by 2001. In the aftermath of the bankruptcy, president Kim Young-sam's son was jailed for accepting bribes from Hanbo, as were other lawmakers and bank officials.[33]

2. Weak Legal and Corporate Institutions. Not only did the opportunities for business to influence the government increase after democratization, but the importance of personal relations (*inmaek*) in corporate and legal institutions also increased. A historically weak legal environment – and the corresponding importance of personal ties – creates an environment in which a founder/chairman can control a vast array of subsidiaries with little or no formal title and can evade or influence government policy.

As described in Chapter 4, a typical Korean conglomerate is characterized by family ownership, control, and management. The founder's family generally takes over control of various subsidiaries or companies, with one family member ultimately being chosen by the founder to succeed him. The founder/chairman of the entire group is called *chongsu*, and the group is controlled by the chairman's office (sometimes called the planning and coordination office). The *chongsu* controls numerous subsidiaries with a high degree of diversification under his singular leadership. Control is both structural and personal. Structurally, the chairman wields power through cross-shareholding among the subsidiaries within a group through equity investment and through mutual loan guarantees among subsidiaries. Often, bank loans are given only on the personal guarantee of the *chongsu*, whose reputation and personal connections are the ultimate guarantor of repayment.

The *chongsu* is not accountable to any form of corporate control. Minority shareholders have historically had no rights, in Korea, and even now are only beginning to press for rights taken for granted in the United States.[34] In addition, corporate directors are almost always insiders chosen for their loyalty to the *chongsu* and do not serve any role in monitoring

[33] John Burton, "South Korean Steel Groups Make Half-Value Offer for Hanbo Works," *Financial Times*, July 30, 1997, p. 17.
[34] *Donga Ilbo*, March 27, 1998, p. 2.

corporate strategy.[35] Absolute corporate control by the *chongsu*, based on the concentrated ownership structure, results in incentive distortion and agency costs because they inevitably face a dilemma in maximizing the value of corporations versus their own private benefits of control.

Within this institutional environment, the rule of law in Korea has been fluid and seldom enforced. Until 1997, *chaebol* regulation consisted of a credit control system, the Monopoly Regulation and Fair Trade Act (MRFTA), and other policies. Direct cross-shareholdings between any two subsidiaries of each of the thirty largest conglomerates, designated annually by the Korean Fair Trade Commission (KTFC), were prohibited. The MRFTA also prescribed regulation of mutual debt payment guarantees among *chaebol* subsidiaries (the practice of subsidiary *A* underwriting subsidiary *B*'s liabilities to financial institutions).

Legislation by itself, however, is no guarantee of solid institutions, nor does it guarantee equal treatment under the law. Kim Jong-Seok notes that

Korean regulations are not just pervasive and large in numbers, but also highly judgmental and vague so that most of the decisions and interpretations of the regulations are left with the regulators themselves. . . . The subsequent opaque procedures, ambiguous rules, and unpredictable results create total instability for businesses in Korea. Under such regulatory circumstances, both regulators and regulatees know that the regulation cannot be enforced as written, and thus the regulatees have a strong incentive to lobby the regulators to circumvent enforcement.[36]

As an example of how loose Korean corporate governance has been, it was only in 1993 (for bank accounts) and 1995 (for real estate) that the system of "false names" was outlawed by the government. Previously, it was possible to register a false name (a grandmother, "Mr. Kim," etc.) and under that name own stock, engage in land speculation, and transfer money, thus avoiding taxes and circumventing regulations prohibiting land speculation and corporate shareholder limits. Indeed, when this system was outlawed by then-president Kim Young-sam, there was a horrific outcry from the business community. The Ministry of Finance estimated that in 1993 over one million false names were used by politicians

---

[35] Yoo Seong-Min, Korea Development Institute, "Corporate Restructuring in Korea: Policy Issues before and during the Crisis," in *Korea and the Asian Economic Crisis: One Year Later* (Georgetown University, 1999), p. 147.

[36] Jong-Seok Kim, "Korea's Regulatory Reform: A Critical Review," *Korea's Economy, 1996* (Washington, DC: Korea Economic Institute of America, 1996), p. 11.

and businessmen, corresponding to over 30 trillion *won* ($40 billion) in assets.[37] Although it was common knowledge that business and political elites used false names to circumvent legal restrictions – and common sense that false names should be prohibited – the practice had existed since the 1960s.

Another example of the power of informal connections instead of legal rules concerns intragroup transactions. Regulations on intragroup transactions were finally introduced in 1992, and then provisions were added to the MRFTA in 1996. However, in typical Korean fashion, these regulations were completely dormant until after the Asian financial crisis. It was only in 1998 that the KFTC embarked on the first round of in-depth investigations of the top five *chaebol*.

In this fluid institutional environment, personal ties between *chaebol* and politicians – always important – have become even more critical to business success. The transition to democracy did not change this need. Rather, the 1990s saw expanded opportunities for bribes, personal connections, and influence peddling.

3. Overcapacity and Overdiversification. Korean companies have historically relied on personal ties, debt-led expansion, and a "bigger is better" mentality. This is nothing new. What is new is the inability of the state to constrain the business sector. Business concentration has continued to increase, while cross-holding ownership remains a standard Korean business practice. Instead of being limited to their "core competencies," the *chaebol* increasingly overlapped in their efforts in the automotive, electronic, and financial sectors. Why did this happen? Because neither Kim Young-sam nor Roh before him coupled their executive orders with realistic incentives for the *chaebol* to comply. Banks would not invest in any firms aside from the *chaebol*, which were the only internationally competitive domestic firms. In addition, the rest of the government bureaucracy – which had been knee-deep in big business-government relations – was also not convinced that a policy of limiting the *chaebol* would be successful in any serious manner. Thus, because there has been no credible shift in government policy, traditional government-business practices have continued, awaiting the return to "business as usual."

A typical *chaebol* group is composed of several dozen separate companies operating in different business areas, ranging from furniture to

[37] Yang Gi-Dae et al., *Toduk konghwaguk* (Republic of thieves) (Seoul: Donga Ilbo, 1997).

fashion, semi-conductors to securities, and automobiles to construction. This system has acted as an insurance system for these companies. When one company is in trouble – perhaps because it is a new entrant or it is in the early stages of investment and market creation, or due to unforeseen shifts in the export prices, as in the recent collapse of semi-conductor prices – it could rely on other companies within the group – which are faring better – to bail it out. The need to create such a "self-help" backup network of support led to the expansion and consolidation of the *chaebol* system (also known as the "convoy system").

To expand their "insurance coverage," the *chaebol* groups have spread their tentacles into all possible, available, and promising fields of business activities. The overall consequence of the *chaebol* system is twofold. On the one hand, the resources of each *chaebol* group are spread thin. A successful company within a group is not given an opportunity to develop into a specialist enterprise within its own field of expertise through research and development and market entrenchment. Such a problem occurs because the profits obtained by this company are rechanneled to fund or support other companies within the group that are either having difficulties or starting new ventures. Furthermore, its assets are used as collateral for loans obtained by other members within the family. (This is known as a "cross-loan guarantee.") It may, therefore, be forced to shoulder the burden of debt repayment in some cases. Thus, companies within a group are financially vulnerable and face the possible failure to develop into stable, specialized business organizations.

On the other hand, any given field of the economy – or a promising new industry – becomes crowded by the indiscriminate entry of a number of companies of different *chaebol* groups. The result is competitive overlapping and excessive investment – and overall overcapacity (Table 6.5).

This convoy system has served the political purposes of growth and protection. Much of the pressure for "structural adjustment," therefore, stems from this practice rooted in the *chaebol* system. Table 6.6 shows the levels of indebtedness in the Korean economy in 1996. As explained in Chapter 4, Korean *chaebol* have always had enormous debt, and their practice of pursuing rapid expansion served them well for thirty years.

The Kia Group case of 1997 is just one demonstration of the common problem faced by all Korea *chaebol* groups. The Kia Group, the eighth largest business group in Korea, with twenty-eight individual companies, had a total debt of 9.54 trillion *won* with an overall debt-to-equity ratio of 523 percent. The capital required for Kia Group's expansion was obtained

Table 6.5. *Korean Auto Supply and Demand (in thousands)*

	1992	1993	1994	1995	1998
Supply					
Capacity (A)	2,660	2,835	3,069	3,351	4,040
Production (B)	1,725	2,046	2,306	2,610	3,150
A/B	0.648	0.722	0.751	0.779	0.780
Demand					
Domestic	1,267	1,432	1,550	1,547	1,800
Export	456	638	738	1,091	1,350

Source: Figures derived from Korea Economic Institute, 1996.

Table 6.6. *Debt/Equity Ratio of Korean Chaebol, 1996*

Group (Rank in Sales)	Debt (% of Equity)
Hyundai (1)	373.29
Samsung (2)	207.60
LG (3)	313.08
Daewoo (4)	334.35
Halla (12)	2,980.44
Sammi (23)	3,380.38
Hanil (29)	1,328.60
1–4th largest *chaebol* (avg.)	295.50
5–10th largest *chaebol* (avg.)	360.97
11–30th largest *chaebol* (avg.)	503.85

Source: Choi Sung-no, *1996 nyŏn 30daekiŏpchipdan* (An analysis of the 30 Korean conglomerates in 1996) (Seoul: Korea Economic Research Institute, 1997), p. 57.

mostly through loans from various financial institutions. As a result, Kia Motors, the flag-carrier of the group, with 7 billion *won* in net profit in 1996, had to bear the burden of keeping alive other members in the group, such as, Kia Steel, which had a loss of 89.5 billion *won* in 1996.

The bankruptcies of large *chaebol* do not end just with the groups' collapse. They produce a chain reaction among the suppliers and subcontractors, affecting thousands of smaller companies. The current difficulty in the Kia Group has forced some eighteen thousand "cooperating companies" – with a total workforce of five hundred fifty thousand – into irrecoverable trouble, many ending in bankruptcy.

Rapid expansion thus was politically useful. Bigger has always been better in the Korean context, both as a means of ensuring a continuous flow of funds to the companies and for the political purpose of protecting entrepreneurs from the vicissitudes of Korea's fluid political sphere.

Perhaps the most fundamental "cause" of the 1997 crisis was another set of political restraints on economic reform: the simple fact that the previous model worked well and had extensive support. There were thus few political incentives, beyond those emanating from American pressure, for the government to fundamentally change its policy course; as one would predict in such a setting, those economic reforms that were undertaken, such as the financial market and trade openings, were extremely gradual and designed to limit their direct impact on Korean firms, whereas other policy actions, such as support for small and medium-size firms, showed surprising continuity with Korea's past policy regime.[38]

2. The Philippines

Contrary to what one might have predicted, the Philippines came through the 1997 financial crisis relatively better than most of its Asian neighbors. Many of the Philippines' economic problems of the last few years arose not so much because of direct vulnerabilities but because of regional repercussions. As Roberto Ocampo, finance secretary under Ramos, noted, "Our currency didn't really come under attack. But we devalued because all the other countries were devaluing, and keeping our exchange rates at the previous rates would've demolished our trade and financial possibilities."[39]

1. The Philippines Was Absolutely Poorer. The most common explanation for the relatively benign impact of the crisis on the Philippines is that the Philippines had been so poor relative to the other Asian economies that it was not as heavily indebted and was thus not as vulnerable to capital flows as were the other developing nations. There is an element of truth

---

[38] Stephan Haggard and David Kang, "The Kim Young-sam Presidency in Comparative Perspective," in *Democratization and Globalization in Korea: Assessments and Prospects*, edited by Chung-in Moon and Jongryn Mo (Seoul: Yonsei University Press, 1999).
[39] Author's interview, September 12, 1999.

Table 6.7. *Debt-Equity of Philippine Companies, 1995*

Company (Rank in Sales)	Debt (% of Equity)
National Power Co. (1)	231.16
Meralco (2)	60.08
Petron (3)	99.17
Pilipinas Shell Petroleum (4)	127.93
San Miguel Co. (5)	57.08
Philippine National Bank (12)	815.11
IDS, Inc. (34)	4,925.43
Ayala Group (41)	35.99
5 largest companies (avg.)	156.60
10 largest companies (avg.)	157.20
50 largest companies (avg.)	263.33
50 largest (excluding banks)	128.29

Source: Derived from SEC, *Philippines Top 5,000 Corporations, 1995* (Manila: Securities and Exchange Commission, 1996), pp. 31–32.

to this statement. Table 6.7 shows the debt-equity ratios of the top fifty corporations in the Philippines in 1995. These numbers, while high, are significantly below those of Korea.

In addition, being poorer meant that the Philippines was already under IMF stewardship. In 1997 the Philippines was poised to move out from IMF jurisdiction just as the other ASEAN nations were seeking IMF bailouts. Long under the IMF's "Extended Fund Facility" (EFF), in 1997 the Philippines was close to meeting the requirements for exit from the EFF. Remaining hurdles were comprehensive tax reform and oil deregulation.[40] Given the problems of the 1980s, foreign capital had largely bypassed Manila in its exuberant rush to invest in Asia's economies. Thus the Philippines was poorer than its neighbors in 1997 and neither as desirable a location for foreign business nor as vulnerable to international capital flows.

2. Reforms and Restructuring Ahead of the Other Asian Countries. However, arguing that the Philippines was "too poor for the crisis" is at best a partial explanation, and it misses a number of reasons that derive

[40] Segundo E. Romero, "The Philippines in 1997," p. 200.

Change in FX, 1968–1998

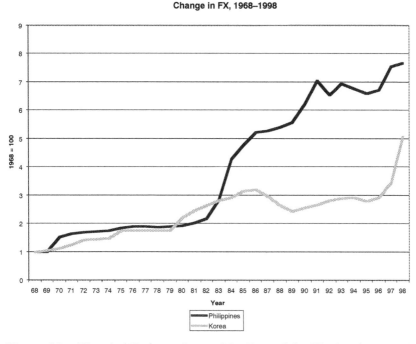

Figure 6.2. Historical Exchange Rates of the *Peso* and the *Won* (yearly average)
Source: Derived from the IMF, *International Financial Statistics Yearbook, 1998* (Washington, DC: IMF, 1999), pp. 540, 720

directly from Philippine experiences in the preceding decades. First and foremost, the painful experience of the late Marcos era had already prompted a number of financial and economic reforms in the Philippines. Also, the Philippines had experienced a foreign exchange crisis of its own during the 1980s. This experience had prompted financial and corporate reforms and had made Philippine businessmen wary of significant international exposure (Figure 6.2). In contrast, Korea's currency had remained relatively stable throughout that period.

The Philippines began an aggressive program of economic liberalization under Aquino, and although the program had its fits and starts, Fidel Ramos continued the measures. Decentralization, privatization, and long-term reforms in the post-Marcos era appear, in the short run, to be effectively breaking the ties of the powerful oligarchs. The program included eliminating monopolies, opening previously protected sectors to foreign investment, privatization of government corporate holdings, easing tariff

Table 6.8. *Philippine Economic Indicators, 1991–1997*

	1991	1993	1994	1995	1996	1997
GNP (U.S.$ billions)	63.7	67.0	68.6	70.3	71.9	73.1
GNP/capita (U.S.$)	608.0	599.0	616.0	631.0	660.0	682.0
GNP growth rate (real % change)	0.5	2.1	5.3	5.0	6.9	5.8
Tax revenue (% GDP)	15.1	15.7	16.1	16.3	16.6	16.5
Government budget (% GDP)	−22.1	−1.7	0.9	0.6	0.3	0.1
Foreign debt (% GNP)	65.7	62.0	56.4	49.6	48.1	53.1

Source: East Asia Analytical Unit, *The Philippines: Beyond the Crisis* (Canberra: Australian Department of Foreign Affairs and Trade, 1998), p. 48.

barriers, simplification of the tax system, and increased regulation of the financial sector.

With these reforms, the Philippine central government budget began to finally show a surplus in 1994, and it continued to operate in surplus for the next three years. Growth began to rapidly expand (Table 6.8). Inflation steadied, and with the introduction of stricter legislation, the banks began to become competitive with foreign banks.[41]

Even tax compliance and tax revenues began to increase in the Philippines, culminating in the comprehensive tax reform of 1997. By 1997 the Philippines was collecting taxes at a rate equivalent to that of other ASEAN nations.[42]

Ramos was persistent in his pursuit of economic reforms begun under Aquino, and he was able to work with the Congress and pass several major pieces of legislation, including the Comprehensive Tax Reform Act and laws involving accession to the World Trade Organization in December 1994, reforming the Central Bank, liberalizing the financial sector, making build-operate-transfer (BOT) projects more attractive, and liberalizing the foreign investment regime. In addition, Ramos attacked the issue of infrastructure.

3. Democratic Traditions and Flexibility. Lower debt-equity ratios in the Philippines were not merely a mark of caution by international lenders. One major contrast that we have noted in this book is that the Philippines,

---

[41] For more on the banking reform of the early 1990s, see Paul Hutchcroft, *Booty Capitalism: The Politics of Banking in the Philippines* (Ithaca: Cornell University Press, 1998).
[42] East Asia Analytical Unit, *The Philippines: Beyond the Crisis*, p. 77.

despite some troubles, has had a much longer experience than Korea with Western institutions and legal systems. As a result, Philippine companies tend to be more professionally run than Korean firms, with more decentralized control, with institutionalized management that does not come from the family, and with better oversight by their boards and auditors. Even family firms in the Philippines are not dominated by their families the way Korean companies are. It is no surprise that Asia's first multinational accounting firm – SGV – was Filipino. In contrast to Korea, the Philippines uses U.S. accounting methods, consolidated income statements, and Security and Exchange Commission filings.

In addition, the Philippine experience with democracy has also introduced a measure of flexibility in the country. The democratic tradition in the Philippines, however messy, has resulted in a vibrant set of institutions and groups that are more autonomous and more responsive than in many of the other Asian countries. As globalization and liberalization has spread, societies in all countries are being forced to react more quickly and creatively than ever before. Its experience with democracy has placed the Philippines in a favorable position. As one example, the quality of the Philippine workforce is widely considered to be among the best in Asia, and Philippine comfort with English and American legal practices positions the Philippines with a number of advantages in an increasingly globalized world (Table 6.9).

The traditional political practices of *lider* are beginning to give way to issue-based politicians. Political violence in the Philippines has receded, and rates of incidents and casualties have dropped to levels not seen since the 1960s (Table 6.10). Joseph Estrada's victory in the 1998 presidential election, with 40 percent of the vote, was the largest electoral mandate in modern Philippine history.

This is not to say that all bodes well for the Philippines. Excessive ownership concentration continues to prompt fears about the return of crony capitalism.[43] Approximately 60 to 90 percent of most publicly listed companies are owned by the top twenty stockholders, with the top five stockholders owning more than 50 percent of the publicly listed firms (Table 6.11). Yet due to the extensive family nature of the Philippines, only 22 percent of the top 1,000 corporations are publicly traded. Furthermore, cross-shareholding is extensive. Table 6.12 shows a sampling of the Philip-

---

[43] Kevin Hamlin, "Can a Movie Star Run the Philippines?" *Institutional Investor* (November 1998, international edition): 95.

Table 6.9. *Skilled Labor in Asia*

Country	Rating of Skilled Labor
India	2.0
Philippines	2.63
Australia	3.90
Taiwan	4.27
Japan	4.55
Vietnam	4.67
South Korea	4.72
Malaysia	4.83
Singapore	5.04
Thailand	5.08
Hong Kong	5.10
Indonesia	5.85

Note: 0 = best, 10 = worst.
Source: *Far Eastern Economic Review*, September 2, 1999, p. 10.

Table 6.10. *Political Violence in the Philippines, 1965–1998*

Year	Type of Election	Violent Incidents	Deaths
1998	Synchronized	188	42
1997	Barangay (local)	n.a.	4
1995	Congress	97	73
1994	Barangay	n.a.	26
1992	Synchronized	87	60
1989	Barangay	n.a.	30
1988	Provincial	127	98
1987	Congress	48	50
1986	President	296	153
1984	Congress	918	154
1982	Barangay	n.a.	14
1981	President	178	102
1980	Provincial	180	71
1978	Congress	9	n.a.
1971	Senate and provincial	534	905
1969	President and Congress	59	52
1967	Senate and provincial	192	78
1965	President and Congress	69	47

Source: John Linantud, "Whither Guns, Goons, and Gold? The Decline of Factional Election Violence in the Philippines," *Contemporary Southeast Asia* 20, no. 3 (December 1998): 301.

Table 6.11. *Ownership Concentration by Selected Industries, 1997*

Industry	Top 20 Stockholders	Top 5 Stockholders
Banks		
Bank of the Philippine Islands	90.7	75.9
Far East Bank and Trust	81.4	58.2
Metropolitan Bank and Trust	69.1	57.3
Philippine Commercial and	80.8	
Industrial Bank		63.3
Philippine National Bank	66.2	53.8
Rizal Commercial Bank	85.3	76.8
Union Bank of the Philippines	81.5	59.3
Communication		
ABS-CBN	84.6	79.9
Philippine Long Distance	75.4	66.0
Power and energy		
Manila Electric Corporation	68.2	46.2
Petron Corporation	82.8	80.8
Transportation		
Kepphil Shipyard	83.6	73.6
Asian Terminals, Inc.	78.8	47.8
Construction		
Alsons Cement	88.1	68.3
Mariwasa Manufacturing	99.1	83.9
Food and beverages		
Jollibee Foods	92.7	61.0
San Miguel Corporation	59.0	28.8
Manufacturing		
Atlas Fertilizer	81.3	72.5
Pryce Corporation	74.8	50.6
Property		
Ayala Land	66.3	63.9
C&P Homes	83.1	79.3
Filinvest Land	66.8	62.1
Megaworld Properties	90.5	82.2
Oil		
Sinophil Corporation	68.9	38.5
Oriental Petroleum	61.3	52.1

Source: Figures derived from Cheng Hoon Lim and Charles Woodruff, "Managing Corporate Distress in the Philippines: Some Policy Recommendations," IMF Working Paper 1998/138, p. 11; SEC, *Philippines Top 1,000 Corporations, 1997* (Manila: Securities and Exchange Commission, 1998); and company annual reports.

Table 6.12. *Share Holding of Selected Philippine Conglomerates*

Company	Ownership (%)
The Lopez Group, 1997	
ABS-CBN	70.99
Sky Vision Co./Sky Cable	20.0
Bayan Telephone	47.34
International Communications Company	99.7
Radio Communications of the Philippines	86.8
Eastern Visayasa Telephone Company	98.2
Butan City Telephone Company	72.8
Express Telco	46.6
Philippines Commercial and Industrial Bank	17.8
First Philippine Holdings	37.5
First Private Power Company	40.0
Barang Private Power Company	20.0
First Gas	51.0
Panay Power Company	50.0
Manila Electric (MERALCO)	16.9
Panay Electric Company	30.0
Philec	86.5
First Philippine Balfour Realty	60.0
First Philippine Industrial Company	60.0
First Philippine Industrial Park	70.0
First Philippine Infrastructure Development Company	50.0
Manila North Tollway	60.0
Rockwell Land Company	24.5
Maynilad Water Company	50.0
The Ayala Group, 1998	
Ayala Land, Inc.	72.5
Ayala Hotels	83.6
Program Realty and Development	60.0
Ayala Agricultural Development	100.0
AYC (Overseas)	100.0
Ayala Aviation	100.0
Ayala International Finance	100.0
Bank of the Philippine Islands	100.0
Ayala Life Insurance	79.0
FGU Insurance	100.0
Universal Reinsurance Company	74.1
Ayala-Bain Insurance	100.0
Globe Telecom	100.0
Pure Foods	92.6

Table 6.12. (*continued*)

Company	Ownership (%)
Purefood-Hormel	92.6
Integrated Microelectronics	76.1
EDINet Philippines	60.0
Ayala Systems Technology, Inc.	62.6
Honda Cars Philippines	100.0
Isuzu Philippines Company	100.0
Manila Water	100.0
The Aboitz Group, 1995	
Union Bank of the Philippines	27.0
Aboitz Transportation System	50.0
Consolidated Industrial Gases	30.0
Pilipinas Kao, Inc.	17.6
Visayan Electric	13.8
Tsueneishi Shipbuilding	20.0
Mindanao Container	35.0
City Savings Bank	29.9
JAIB, Inc.	49.0
Jardin-Aboitz Insurance	22.5
Hydro-Specialist	50.0
Metaphil	23.0
Cotabato Ice	99.5
Aboitz Manufacturing	100.0
Davao Light and Power	100.0
Aboitz Shipping	100.0
Aboitz Marketing	100.0
Power Development Corporation of the Philippines	100.0
Cebu Shipyard and Engineering	100.0
Amanu Realty and Development	100.0
Pillsbury-Mindanao Flour Milling	100.0

Sources: Jose V. Abueva, ed., *Eugenio H. Lopez, Sr.: Pioneering Entrepreneur and Business Leader* (Diliman, Quezon City: University of the Philippines, 1998, 1997), p. 315. Ayala Holding Company Annual Report, 1998. Aboitz Group Annual Report, 1995.

pine family conglomerates. Notable is both the extensive diversification of the groups and also the surprisingly large number of privately held firms.[44]

[44] Cheng Woon Lim and Charles Woodruff, "Managing Corporate Distress in the Philippines: Some Policy Recommendations" (IMF Working Paper 138, September 1998), p. 14.

As much as 30 percent of total bank loans outstanding ($10.7 billion in 1999) is accounted for by the top 100 corporate borrowers.

Land reform in the Philippines has still not been undertaken with any urgency, poverty and graft still dominate the headlines, and the belief that the powerful families of old still run the country is widespread. Much remains to be restructured in the government, the provinces remain far poorer than metro Manila, and rebels remain in their strongholds in the south. Even so, as Vinay Bhargava of the World Bank noted in late 1998, "The Philippines is correctly perceived as having weathered the crisis better than many of its neighbors."[45]

III. Conclusion

The patterns of money politics in Korea and the Philippines are not static, and the most influential institutional change in each country was the transition to democracy. This institutional shift altered previous patterns of government-business relations, with significant implications for both countries. In Korea, democracy weakened the power of the state and created incentives for politicians to provide even greater access to businessmen in return for political funds. Competing in genuine elections meant politicians had a greater need for campaign spending, and business was not slow to exploit this opportunity. In the Philippines, the democratic transition brought business and politicians into more of a balance, and although the Philippines continues to struggle, many of the worst excesses of rent seeking and corruption seem to have been eliminated.

In addition, in both countries an understanding of how this government-business relationship changed helps explain the differential impact of the financial crisis of 1997. In Korea, the very qualities that it pursued during its period of high growth – close ties between economic and political elites, rapid expansion, and a reliance on debt – were transformed by the 1990s to make Korea vulnerable to capital flows and moral hazard. In contrast, the Philippines, despite much slower growth in the previous four decades, had already begun to dismantle some of the cronyistic ties that had bedeviled it for so long, and it seemed – at least in the short run – poised to enjoy steady if not spectacular growth in the late 1990s.

[45] Antonio Lopez Manila, "Erap's Big Role," *Asiaweek* (October 9, 1998): 27–28.

7

Conclusion: Corruption and Development

By comparison with most underdeveloped countries, the basic economic position of the Philippines is favorable. . . . Through a comparatively high level of expenditure on education, transport, communications, and industrial plant over the past fifty years, the Philippines has achieved a position in the Far East second only to Japan . . . the prospects of the Philippine economy for sustained long-term growth are good.

– World Bank, 1957

There can be no doubt that this development program [the First Five-Year Plan] by far exceeds the potential of the Korean economy . . . it is inconceivable that exports will rise as much as projected.

– World Bank, 1961

This book has been about money politics in Korea and the Philippines. Money politics has been extensive, and consequential, in both countries. Although I have not focused on economic development, this book's argument leads to a natural question: why was there growth in Korea but not the Philippines? If both Korea and the Philippines were characterized by extensive political meddling into economic affairs, if influence peddling led to economic decisions made for political reasons, and if in both countries personal relationships mattered more than individual competence, then why did Korea grow so spectacularly whereas the Philippines did not? Although development is an entirely different dependent variable than money politics, it is fitting that this book concludes with a discussion of how the issues of corruption and development might relate to one another.

Money politics has always been a central aspect of the pattern of Korean and Philippine politics, and this study has shown that we cannot assume benevolence on the part of the state. This study has also cast doubt on the "hard" version of the developmental state. Massive corruption undermines the argument that the state is neutral, picks winners, and provides public goods because the civil service is insulated from social influences. A more limited version of the developmental state argues that governments can have a beneficial effect however the politics of government action is attained. And Korea *did* develop, and numerous studies have shown how the Korean state acted in a number of developmental ways to provide public goods and nurture investment. So how do we reconcile the politics and the economics? In Korea the mutual hostage balance kept corruption from swamping growth, whereas in the Philippines bandwagoning never allowed for the domestic stability that permits long-term growth.

I. Corruption and Development

The bulk of this book has focused on showing that institutions in Korea were not necessarily any more neutral, nor were subject to any less patronage or corruption, than those of the Philippines. Korea's loan policies, its import licensing, and its export-oriented policies were all driven by a rationale that emphasized personal, political connections rather than economic efficiency. However, the act of providing rents in exchange for bribes is only the middle of a chain of events that affects growth, and it is not the whole story. The creation of rents, the competition among actors to gain the rents (usually involving corruption), and the uses of rents, all have an impact on the economy.

The mutual hostage situation between elites in Korea reduced transaction costs and made investment and long-term agreements more efficient. In countries with weak legal and political institutions, long-term relationships may be difficult to create. The larger institutional environment in Korea – the balance of power among elites – reduced transaction costs, while bandwagoning in the Philippines tended to raise transaction costs. This argument can be broken into three specific mechanisms.

First, the mutual hostage situation in Korea was a key factor in keeping corruption from spinning out of control. The smaller the number of actors, and the less competitive the rent-seeking process, the lower the total costs arising from the process.[1] Competition for rents is not so great in situations involving few actors, and thus resources are not necessarily expended in obtaining rents. Much rent seeking entails competing with

---

[1] Gordon Tullock, "Rents and Rent-Seeking," in *The Political Economy of Rent-Seeking*, edited by C. Rowley, R. Tollison, and G. Tullock (Boston: Kluwer, 1988), p. 228.

Conclusion

other actors to win rents and then building entry barriers and other mechanisms to protect those rents. A group that has exclusive access to the rent markets has lower information costs and can collude over time with other rent seekers to lower costs.[2] The implication from this is straightforward: having smaller numbers of rent seekers reduces the total social cost because property rights over the rent are more secure. The balance of power meant that neither political nor bureaucratic elites could gain a decisive edge over the other. The bargain these elites struck was collusive – not cooperative – and both groups took as much advantage of the other as possible. But the process never spun out of control because the elites were vulnerable with respect to each other.

In the Philippines, the democratic era allowed society to overwhelm the state with its rent-seeking demands. The state was unable to design coherent economic policy and was unable to effectively limit the demands of society. The pendulum swung too far in the opposite direction during the authoritarian era, when Marcos and a relatively coherent state were able to extort and steal much of the domestic capital. Philippine money politics had looser limits on the amount of corruption that could occur.

Yet corruption is not the exclusive domain of poorly managed and unstable countries saddled with stagnant economies. Corruption can also flourish in emerging countries experiencing rapid increases in wealth. In these countries there exists a fluid institutional and political environment combined with pockets of inefficiencies that can be exploited by political or economic elites who have superior access to information, personal connections, or influence. Corruption in this sense is a function of growth rather than an inhibitor of growth. Although an imbalance between economic and political elites can lead to corruption spiraling out of control and choking off growth, where a rough balance does exist – as in the Korean case – corruption can be contained.

Second, bribes are transfers. As such, corruption does not necessarily imply any deadweight loss, and the political story I have told here does not necessarily affect the overall provision of public goods.[3] Indeed, corruption may arise from struggles over the distribution of state policy and goods rather than over the absolute level. The typical rent-seeking story

[2] Ha-joon Chang, *The Political Economy of Industrial Policy* (New York: St. Martin's Press, 1994), p. 120.
[3] Mushtaq Khan, "The Input-Output Function for Rent-Seeking: A Comparative Analysis of Differential Effects" (MS, University of London, 1997), p. 13.

begins with the standard neoclassical economic assumptions of a perfect market, numerous buyers and sellers, perfect information, and no transaction costs. In this world, assets are allocated efficiently according to their highest marginal return. All other factors being equal, rent seeking diverts these resources from their Pareto optimal use. Unsurprisingly, the conclusion arises that corruption (and rent seeking) is bad for the economy. Yet in reality, every society already has a distribution of rights that benefits some actors more than others, and thus bribery related to rent seeking is itself a mechanism that could lead to a more efficient distribution of rights than before. The relevant question is whether the resources will be put to more productive use in the possession of the seeker or the seekee, and theoretically only the lowest-cost firm could afford the highest bribe.[4] None of this necessarily entails rent seeking that would distort economic efficiency: if the transfer of wealth is from businessmen to politicians and results in productive investments, a nation may benefit even from machine-style politics.[5]

Finally, although the Korean state may have provided public goods and supported investment, that may not have been why those goods were provided. The Korean state intervened in the way it did because to do so was in the interests of a small group of business and political elites. The building of roads, apartment complexes, and power stations provides public goods, but it also provides private goods. Access to the private benefits of state resources was often contingent upon production of the public good.[6] Although enormous private benefits accrued to Samsung or Daewoo for having privileged access to state capital and policies, society benefited as well from improved infrastructure, employment, and opportunities. My

---

[4] Pranab Bardhan, "Corruption and Development: A Review of Issues," *Journal of Economic Literature* 35 (1997): 1322.

[5] For provocative essays that tackle this question, see Mushtaq Khan, "The Efficiency Implications of Corruption," *Journal of International Development* 8, no. 5 (1996): 683–696; Richard Doner and Ansil Ramsey, "Competitive Clientelism and Economic Governance: The Case of Thailand," in *Business and the State in Developing Countries*, edited by Sylvia Maxfield and Ben Ross Schneider (Ithaca: Cornell University Press, 1997); Andrei Shleifer and Robert Vishney, "Corruption," *Quarterly Journal of Economics* 108 (1993): 599–617; Robin Theobald, *Corruption, Development, and Underdevelopment* (Durham: Duke University Press, 1990); and Robert Klitgaard, *Controlling Corruption* (Berkeley: University of California Press, 1988).

[6] Mancur Olson, *The Rise and Decline of Nations: Economic Growth, Stagflation, and Social Rigidities* (New Haven: Yale University Press, 1982); and Lawrence Broz, *The International Origins of the Federal Reserve System* (Ithaca: Cornell University Press, 1997), pp. 2–7.

Conclusion

argument is complementary to Alice Amsden's argument that the state exchanged subsidies for performance.[7] The difference is that I provide a political story that explains the patterns of exchange, and I also show that the process based on money politics is heavily biased and not nearly as efficient as Amsden argues.

This study thus suggests that understanding even a developmental state requires knowing the political story. The Korean state made many decisions that fostered investment and growth over the past forty years, but politics played a major role. Economic policy choice is only one of many issues with which political elites must concern themselves. A political economy explanation must focus closely on how preferences emerge and on the institutions that direct the implementation of those preferences. Such an explanation must be sensitive to the nature of the political coalition that supported the elites, resource constraints, and the vulnerability that elites faced. Given that elites must constantly be concerned about retaining power, corruption and policy access can be powerful political tools.[8]

It is not clear, however, that corruption is one of the most important variables for growth. This study shows that the link is tenuous – many other factors were important in Korean development. As noted in Chapter 2, nations do not begin their race to development from the same starting line. Any true understanding of why some countries develop faster than other countries must be sensitive to all the factors involved and must weight them accordingly. The number of potential variables that influence growth is vast, and the real question is not whether, but how much, certain variables matter.[9]

Fostering economic growth requires much more than restraining corruption. The other major factor that I emphasize in this book was the role of the external threat. Korea was born on the frontlines of the Cold War, and throughout its existence has conducted its domestic politics within the

---

[7] Alice Amsden, *Asia's Next Giant* (Cambridge: Cambridge University Press, 1989).
[8] K. S. Jomo and Edmund Terence Gomez, "Rent Generation and Distribution, and Their Consequences in Malaysia" (Unpublished MS, 1998); Barry Weingast, "Constitutions as Governance Structures," *Journal of Institutional and Theoretical Economics* 149, no. 1 (1993): 286–311; and Hilton Root, *The Fountain of Privilege: Political Foundations of Markets in Old Regime France and England* (Berkeley: University of California Press, 1994).
[9] Jonathan Temple notes that "so many variables could be used to explain growth that it is difficult to find variables that are not only highly correlated with the endogenous variables but can also plausibly be excluded from the regression." Temple, "The New Growth Evidence," *Journal of Economic Literature* 37 (March 1999): 129.

looming shadow of a reclusive and potentially dangerous North Korea. In contrast, surrounded by an ocean and containing U.S. military bases, the sunny Philippines has never faced an appreciable external threat to its existence. Nor has the Philippines received the same level of financial transfers as did South Korea. In Korea, massive U.S. transfers allowed for increases in inputs that provided the capital for investment in heavy industrial projects. More generally, the international environment, and U.S. policies in particular, also provided a favorable and indeed formative environment within which Korea could develop. These contrasting external situations caused different domestic responses from both government and business in the two countries.

Initial conditions are also important for economic development. Contrasting colonial experiences set the stage for Korean development but Philippines underdevelopment. The United States had a formative – and opposite – impact on both countries. Whereas events tended to destroy the old order in Korea, in the Philippines they reinforced it. Philippine elites tended to be legitimized by having close relations to the U.S. imperialists, whereas Korean elites were delegitimized by their relations with the Japanese colonizers. Thus the U.S. colonization of the Philippines reinforced the existing structures, whereas Japanese colonialism caused the withering away of Korea's existing political structures.

Korea also benefited from a U.S. influence that included imposed land reform and from aid and funding policies that helped shape Korean economic policy in both the Rhee and Park eras. In Korea, thorough land reform was carried out in the early 1950s. This transformation of property rights in Korea was a critical factor helping to set the stage for growth and was originally enforced by the U.S. military government. Korea was also far more favored as a recipient of American largesse and attention over the postwar period than was the Philippines. Korea began its ascent with income distribution that was highly equitable by international standards due to the upheaval of war, the Japanese occupation, and the massive internal migration of the late 1940s and early 1950s, accompanied by a mindset that was hell-bent on catching up to the Japanese.

In contrast, U.S. policies concerning the Philippines were in the nature of "benign neglect." In the Philippines, the Americans never forced through land reform, and U.S. trade policies hindered the Philippines because the Bell Act gave U.S. firms special privileges that allowed them to dominate the domestic Philippine economy. Even into the 1990s, the absence of an external threat (and thus less pressure on domestic economic policies), an abortive Philippine land reform that kept (and continues to keep) peasants tied to the land, a series of islands that hindered the sense of national unity, and bad management all combined to make the Philippines during the postwar period a slow, although not poor, economic performer. Philippine distribution of income both before and after independence remained similarly inequitable, with a small proportion of elites owning much of the country's wealth.

A devastating but transformative war in Korea that preceded an enduring and severe external threat, different initial conditions and historical legacies in the two countries, and contrasting U.S. policies and attention all combined with the different patterns of domestic government-business relations studied in this book to cause different economic outcomes. This stew of reasons is not satisfying, and it is not easily generalizable. But it is probably fairly accurate.

II. Conclusion

The historical patterns of politics in Korea and the Philippines are essential to understanding the development trajectories of both countries. In both countries growth and corruption existed side by side for decades. Even in the period of rapid Korean growth, a political calculus, not economic efficiency, was the crucial factor. Yet because economic and political power was balanced, corruption never spiraled out of control. However, the configuration of actors that allowed rapid growth in Korea in the 1960s was undermined by its very success and eventually led to the crisis of 1997. In the Philippines, a different configuration of actors retarded development for decades. The imbalance between economic and political power led to abuses and corruption that were large enough to choke off growth. That pattern may finally be changing, and perhaps the strong growth of the 1990s is the beginning of an upward trend in the Philippines.

In making these arguments, I developed a model that explains these patterns of political influence. Concentrating on the government-business relationship, I showed how we would expect that excessive strength by either the government or the business sector would lead to an excess of rent seeking, whereas a balance between the two – although allowing corruption – would limit the discretion of both government and business. The approach in this book is plausibly applicable to other cases. What we have learned in this book may provide a way of thinking about the particular problems that other countries face. Indeed, a number of other cases fit my model.

Taiwan is an obvious example that deserves mention. Scholars have long grouped Korea and Taiwan in the same analytic category of newly industrializing countries. Although Taiwan and Korea are similar in terms of their successful developmental outcomes, their political and economic structures are fairly different on the surface. Taiwan is marked by an ethnic division between the mainland-dominated KMT and the indigenous Taiwanese. Taiwan has relied on long-term, stable, one-party rule by the KMT. Taiwan has no equivalent of the *chaebol* and instead is characterized by numerous small and medium-sized enterprises. Taiwan also avoided the high-debt growth model and largely avoided the Asian financial crisis.[10]

Yet although the two countries appear dissimilar, the pact between business and political elites in Taiwan was similar to that in Korea and resulted in a similar mutual hostages situation. The KMT and the indigenous Taiwanese exist in a prisoner's dilemma. They coexist by leaving each other alone, one to get rich, the other to hold political power and to plot for the return to the mainland. As Tun-jen Cheng writes, "[In] Taiwan . . . the separation between political power and wealth roughly parallels the sub-ethnic cleavage between the Mainlanders and the Taiwanese."[11] Indeed, largely because the KMT was financially self-sufficient through its ownership of state enterprises, the need to assail the business sector for donations was attenuated. And for the first four decades of KMT rule, as long as the Taiwanese got rich, the KMT largely left them alone. This situation resulted in a balance between economic and political strength, mediated through an ethnic division, that had similar results to the balance in Korea.

Corruption scandals have also been common in Taiwan, the black market economy comprising an estimated 40 percent of the entire economy.[12] Vote buying, a curb market for unregulated finance, and

[10] Hung-Mao Tien and Yun-han Chu, "Taiwan's Domestic Political Reforms, Institutional Change, and Power Realignment," in *Taiwan in the Asia Pacific in the 1990s*, edited by Gary Klintworth (Canberra: Allen & Unwin, 1994).
[11] Tun-jen Cheng, "Political Regimes and Development Strategies: South Korea and Taiwan," in *Manufacturing Miracles: Paths of Industrialization in Latin America and East Asia*, edited by Gary Gereffi and Donald Wyman (Princeton: Princeton University Press, 1990), p. 143.
[12] N.a., "Buried Treasure," *The Economist* (November 6, 1993): 37.

political meddling are all common features of Taiwanese life. Clientelism, in particular, local factions and vote brokers (known as *tiawaka*), mediate the formal institutions of democracy.[13] Thus even though Korea and Taiwan are not as similar as is commonly believed, my model can illuminate the central features of Taiwan's political economy.

Indonesia is another country that fits the model. From 1965 to 1997, General Suharto headed an authoritarian government. Spurred largely by oil revenues, an interventionist state was able to provide a measure of infrastructural investment and economic growth. The authoritarian regime restricted political participation and kept power in the hands of a small group of elites. The business sector, small and weak to begin with, never developed to the point that it could counter the regime's initiatives. Policy was determined by patrimonial and clientelist relations, with those close to Suharto or the ruling family receiving favorable treatment at the hands of the government. Andrew MacIntyre writes that "one consequence of Indonesia's state-structured and highly restrictive political framework is that it has encouraged traditional or patrimonial patterns of political participation that endure within the business community."[14]

As in the Philippines, favored supporters gained access to government largesse. The business sector as a whole was neither well developed nor large enough to press Suharto for fair treatment. As a result, Indonesia under Suharto looked very much like the Philippines under Marcos.[15] The financial sector remained dominated by the state banks, state-owned enterprises – many headed by members of Suharto's family – came to dominate large sectors of the economy, and the native Indonesian entrepreneurs remained sidelined in the political process. Chinese Indonesians became leading business figures, including Liem Sioe Liong of the Salim Group, Bob Hasan of the Hasan Group, and Goh Swie Kie of the Gunung Sewu

---

[13] Shelley Rigger, "Electoral Strategies and Political Institutions in the Republic of China on Taiwan," in *Harvard Studies on Taiwan: Papers of the Taiwan Studies Workshop*, vol. 1 (Cambridge, MA: Fairbank Center for East Asian Research, 1995).

[14] Andrew MacIntyre, "Power, Prosperity, and Patrimonialism: Business and Government in Indonesia," in *Business and Government in Industrialising Asia*, edited by Andrew MacIntyre (Ithaca: Cornell University Press, 1994), p. 245.

[15] Alex Irwan argues that in Indonesia different economic elites made their fortunes under the auspices of the political elites in power. When there was a shift in political power, the economic elites also changed. This led to a series of groups that would ascend to power, make their cash, and get out. Alex Irwan, "Business Patronage, Class Struggle, and the Manufacturing Sector in South Korea, Indonesia, and Thailand," *Journal of Contemporary Asia* 19, no. 4 (1989): 398–434.

Group.[16] As Richard Robison notes, "Political patronage and state protection afforded privileged access to bank credit, forestry concessions, trade and manufacturing monopolies . . . and state contracts for supply and construction."[17]

Excessive power concentrated in the hands of political elites and their cronies led to a state-dominated economy permeated by patronage and corruption. The business sector as a whole was unable to cohere. The Indonesian case is interesting because although its political structure was similar to that of the Philippines, Indonesia was able to experience moderate economic growth because of the fortunate happenstance of having large oil reserves. Oil revenues provided the means for economic growth and allowed a semblance of order for more than twenty-five years. However, the growth was never deep enough to become self-sustaining. An imbalance between political and economic power led to corruption, and growth occurred only for exogenous reasons. When the Asian financial crisis struck the region in 1997, the weaknesses of the system became exposed, and Suharto and his regime were toppled amid the widespread political turmoil.

The argument presented here also provides a useful reminder that we tend to have historical amnesia about countries that have successfully negotiated the path to development. The arc of economic development often includes experiences of corruption, nepotism, and patronage similar to those faced by Korea and the Philippines. But as nations develop further and their politics and business becomes more stable, we tend to forget that these countries experienced such situations in their recent past. In particular, both Japan and the United States have developed to the point that their business and politics appear at least somewhat professionalized. Both countries, however, have histories rife with the types of government-business corruption that I discuss in this book.

Japan became the first Asian nation to successfully pursue economic development, and its politics in the postwar era has been stable. Yet the history of prewar Japan is in many ways similar to what is currently facing Korea and was just as chaotic. For a brief period during the 1920s "Taisho democracy" provided a voice for the interests of Japanese society at large.

---

[16] Kunio Yoshihara, *The Rise of Ersatz Capitalism in Southeast Asia* (Oxford: Oxford University Press, 1988).
[17] Richard Robison, "Authoritarian States, Capital-Owning Classes, and the Politics of Newly Industrializing Countries: The Case of Indonesia," *World Politics* 41 (October 1988): 62.

Conclusion

However, by the early 1930s "government by assassination" had become the norm, with Prime Minister Inukai Takeshi assassinated in May 1932, and Finance Minister Junnosuke Inoue assassinated in 1931. Increasingly, the military and other political elites ran the country behind a façade of civilian leadership.[18] Corruption scandals such as that involving Teijin stock became commonplace as economic elites bribed influential politicians.[19] Powerful families created giant industrial conglomerates known as *zaibatsu*, among them Mitsui, Sumitomo, and Mitsubishi.[20] These *zaibatsu* wielded considerable political influence and continually sparred with the military and the government over policy.

During the postwar era Japanese politics retained the features of a tight relationship between business and politics. Corruption scandals have been endemic throughout the period of high growth, with Tanaka Kakuei being perhaps the most notorious but certainly not the only Japanese politician to have taken massive bribes in return for political influence.[21] Japan's political economy continues to be organized around large conglomerates, with favorable government policies being assured by a continual flow of political funds to important politicians and bureaucrats.

The United States at the turn of the century would also have been quite familiar to Korean or Philippines elites. Large conglomerates had massive market power and controlled large sectors of the economy. Standard Oil in petroleum, U.S. Steel, J. P. Morgan in banking, and the railroad magnates are a few examples of the concentration of economic power in America. Indeed, in relative terms, John D. Rockefeller was richer than Bill Gates is today. The financial system was fragile and largely unregulated, leading to episodic panics and runs on banks, perhaps the most notorious being the 1907 run that was staved off by the personal intervention of J. P. Morgan.[22] A small group of elites, mostly drawn from the "Eastern Establishment," ran politics. This political system was dominated by machines that ran the urban cities, Tammany Hall, Boss Tweed, and Huey

---

[18] James Thomson, Peter Stanley, and John Curtis Perry, *Sentimental Imperialists: The American Experience in East Asia* (New York: Harper and Row, 1981), Ch. 5.

[19] Yayama Taro, "The Recruit Scandal: Learning from the Causes of Corruption," *Journal of Japanese Studies* 16, no. 1 (Winter 1990): 93–114.

[20] Richard Samuels, *Rich Nation, Strong Army: National Security and the Technological Transformation of Japan* (Ithaca: Cornell University Press, 1994), p. 101.

[21] Jacob Shlesinger, *Shadow Shoguns: The Rise and Fall of Japan's Postwar Political Machine* (Simon and Schuster, 1997).

[22] Ron Chernow, *The House of Morgan: An American Banking Dynasty and the Rise of Modern Finance* (New York : Atlantic Monthly Press, 1990).

Long being prime examples of smoky backroom dealings and patronage politics.[23] The well-known phrases "vote early and often" and "robber barons" date from this period.

Yet half a century later, both politics and economics have become dispersed. Political power in the United States has become diffused, the Eastern Establishment is no longer as powerful as it once was, and machine politics has all but disappeared. The early 1900s saw a spate of legislation that reduced the discretion of the economic elites, from the Sherman Act of 1890 designed to limit monopolies, to the Clayton Act of 1914, which Congress enacted in order to outlaw a number of specific predatory tactics employed by American firms. Standard Oil itself was broken up in May 1911, "enshrining the principle that there are limits to the commercial power one man can legitimately accumulate."[24] Economic power is spread relatively evenly throughout the United States, with northern industrial concerns, midwestern farmers, and western high-technology firms. As a result, the ability of one group to dominate either political life or economic life is minimal. Corruption, although it exists, does not pay nearly as well as it did a century earlier.

This book has been an exploration of how money politics works in developing countries. More broadly, this book has looked at how politics and economics interact even in systems that we think are relatively depoliticized. So what have we learned?

There are three main implications arising from the argument presented in this book. First, the evidence presented here shows that a political story is essential to understanding how the developmental state functions. The logic described here shows how elite needs drove policy making, created enormous graft, and patterned the political and economic systems. More than any specific institution or policy, this larger institutional environment has been neglected in previous scholarship.

Second, increasingly microanalytical explorations of political economy must be balanced with an understanding of the larger institutional environment within which actors operate. Focusing too closely on the details of party organization or institutional and bureaucratic configurations may cause scholars to lose sight of the larger forces at play. Both approaches are valid, and they complement each other.

[23] Steven P. Erie, *Rainbow's End: Irish-Americans and the Dilemmas of Urban Machine Politics, 1840–1985* (Berkeley: University of California Press, 1988). See also Alan Brinkley, *Huey Long, Father Coughlin and the Great Depression* (New York: Vintage Books, 1983).
[24] John Cassidy, "Rich Man, Richer Man," *The New Yorker*, May 11, 1998, p. 98.

Conclusion

Finally, this study suggests that the contrasting Korean and Philippine developmental trajectories cannot be attributed mainly to differences in institutional structure and the consistent application of Korean performance standards in exchange for subsidies. Growth with corruption is an issue that needs to be explained, and until scholars directly address the issue of politics, our understanding of Asian development will remain incomplete.

Index

Aboitiz family, 131
Aboitiz Group, 135t, 179t
Aguinaldo, Emilio, 24, 26
amakudari, 72
Aquino, Benigno (Ninoy), 129, 143, 154
Aquino, Cory, 27, 154, 155
Aquino family, 137, 142–3
Asia
  economic growth in, 152
  skilled labor in, 176t
Asian financial crisis, 2–3, 152–3, 156–8
  corruption and, 5–6
  Korea and, 11, 156–7, 158–71
  Philippines and, 11, 157, 171
Ateneo de Manila University, 55
automobile industry
  in Korea, 109–11, 169–71
Ayala, Enrique Zobel de, 144
Ayala Group, 135, 178–9t

bailouts, 97, 113
balance of power, 3, 11
  in Korea, 116, 182
bandwagoning, 122, 125, 182
bank loans, to *chaebol*, 114–15
Bank of the Philippine Islands, 135t
bankruptcies, 170
banks. *See also* names of individual banks
  Asian financial crisis and, 157
  in the Philippines, 131t, 134–6
Bell Act, 31
Bell Commission, 76
Benedicto, Roberto, 139, 140–1
Benedicto family, 140

Bhargava, Vinay, 180
Board of Investments (BOI), 80
brain drain, reverse, 72n11
bribery, 1, 3, 183–4
  in Korea, 102, 105
build-operate-transfer (BOT) projects, 174
bureaucracy. *See also* civil service; state, the
  autonomy of, 3, 4n7, 62, 63
  developmental state and, 61–3
  efficiency of, 61–2
  in Korea, 163
    bifurcated, 9–10, 64, 87
    business subsidies and, 108
    military officials in, 85–7
    under Park Chung-hee, 9–10, 85–90,
      92
    patronage and politicization, 63–4
    politics within, 92
  in the Philippines, 76–7
    under Marcos, 9, 74–5, 80–4, 139, 148
    patronage in, 76–7
    reform of, 75
    size of, 77
    subordination to political regime, 63
  politicians and, 63
  role of, 8–9
business. *See also chaebol*
  diversified groups in, 14–15
  in Korea, 147
    borrowings of, 109, 113–14
    cf. with Philippines, 146
    false names in, 167–8
    intragroup transactions, 168
    personal relations in, 166–8

195

business *(cont.)*
  political donations from, 102–4,
    106–7, 162–3
  regulation of, 167–8
  size of, 107–9
  strength, 116–17
  in the Philippines, 131–6, 175
  cf. with Korea, 146
  concentration of ownership in, 175,
    177–80
  under Marcos, 136–7, 140–4
  relations with government, 2–3, 6–7
  relations with the state, 14–15, 180
  strength of, 17, 19–20
  weakness of, 17

car industry. *See* automobile industry
Central Bank (Philippines), 80, 174
chaebol, 9, 53, 54–5, 91–2. *See also* business;
  oligarchy
  bank loans to, 114–15
  bankruptcies, 170
  democratization and, 153–4
  donations from, 102–4
  expansion of, 164, 168–71
  groups, 168–9
  indebtedness of, 114, 115–16, 169–71
Chang Myon, 50
China-Rizal Banking, 135t
Chinese Indonesians, 189–90
chongsu, 166–7
Choson dynasty, 50
chun-chose, 102, 162–3
Chun Doo-hwan, 2, 50–1, 89–90, 96, 102,
  103, 119, 153
Chung Ju-yong, 163
  family, 53
Chung Tae-soo, 1
CIA (Korea), 89
civil servants
  education of
    in Korea, 56–7
    in the Philippines, 78, 79t
civil service. *See also* bureaucracy; state, the
  examinations
    in Korea, 61, 63, 67–70
    in the Philippines, 75, 76, 78, 79t
  in Korea, 65–74
  in the Philippines, 64, 74–84
Clayton Act, 192

coconut industry, 141
Cojuangco, Eduardo, 139, 141
Cojuangco, Ramon, 139
Cojuangco family, 51, 131, 136, 137, 139
Combined Economic Board (Korea), 70
Communist Party of the Philippines (CPP),
  32
conglomerates, 166
  in Korea, 117–18
  in the Philippines, 130–6
construction industry, in Korea, 164–5
convoy system, 169
corruption, 3, 18, 181–2
  bottom-up, 16–17, 138
  bureaucratic efficiency and, 62
  development and, 182–7
  economic growth and, 5–6, 185
  in emerging countries, 183
  in Korea, 3, 6, 96, 146, 150, 164
  measurement of, 18–20
  mutual hostage situation and, 182–3
  natural resources and, 46–7
  in the Philippines, 3, 75–6, 123, 146,
    148, 150
  scholarship on, 5–6
  in Taiwan, 188–9
  top-down, 16, 138
  types of, 15–18
Counter-Espionage Operations Command
  (*Bangch'opdae*), 102
cronyism, 3
  under Marcos, 138–41, 145
  under Park, 85–7
Cuenca family, 140

Daewoo, 94, 102, 110, 111
debt, business, 97, 114, 115–16, 169–71
De La Salle University, 55
Delta Motors, 140
democracy, 151–2
  in Korea, 10–11, 98–9, 151–2, 153–4,
    180
  in the Philippines, 152, 175, 180
Democratic Republican Party (DRP), 98,
  100, 104
developing countries
  government/business relations in, 6–7
  institutional structures in, 3
  policy making in, 7
  society's demands on the state in, 16

Index

development, and corruption, 182–7
developmental state, 6
  bureaucracy in, 61
  corruption in, 181–2
  organizational attributes, 62–3
Dewey, George, 24
Diokno, José, 143
Disini, Herminio, 139
Disini family, 140

economic growth, 2
  in Asia, 152
  corruption and, 5–6, 185
  external threats and, 185–6
  in Indonesia, 190
  in Korea, 4, 5, 11
  money politics and, 3
  in the Philippines, 4, 5, 11
Economic Planning Board (EPB), 92–3, 94,
    107, 108, 109, 110, 112, 114
economic policy
  elites and, 185
  in Korea, 9–10, 48–9
  in the Philippines, 10, 11, 49–50, 81–2
  types of, 9
education
  of civil servants
    in Korea, 56–7
    in the Philippines, 78, 79t
  of elites, 55–60
  importance of, in Asia, 57
  levels of, 59
  in the Philippines, 55–6, 57–8, 59
  spending on, 58
8-3 Decree, 113–14
elections
  in Korea, 99, 100, 159–61
  Korea cf. with Philippines, 149
  in the Philippines, 156
electrification, in the Philippines, 138
elites, 3, 185. *See also* bureaucracy; *chaebol*;
    oligarchy; politicians
  education of, 55–60
Enrile, Juan Ponce, 33, 141, 148, 154–5
Estrada, Joseph, 175
export-oriented industrialization (EOI), 48
expropriation, 148
Extended Fund Facility (EFF), 172
external threats
  domestic policy and, 29–30

economic growth and, 185–6
to Korea, 34–40, 185–6
to the Philippines, 30–4, 186

false names, in business, 167–8
families, 147. *See also chaebol*; oligarchy
  in Indonesia, 189
  in Korea, 53–5
  in the Philippines, 51–3, 124, 130–7
Far East Bank and Trust Company, 135t
Federation of Korean Industries (FKI),
    90–1, 113–14, 133
Fernandez and Yulo Group, 135t
fiscalizer, 125–6
Floirendo family, 131

Gatmaitan, Tony, 144
globalization, 175
Goh Swie Kie, 189
government/business relations. *See under*
    business; state, the
Gunung Sewu Group, 189–90

hacienderos, 132
haengsi. See civil service: examinations
Hanbo Steel Company, 1, 156, 165–6
Hasan, Bob, 189
Hasan Group, 189
Heavy and Chemical Industrialization Plan
    (HCIP), 105, 112
Honasan, Gregorio, 156
House Bill (HB) 1967, 28–9
Huk movement, 31–2, 51
Hyundai, 53, 102, 109, 110–11, 111–12,
    162

Ilhae Foundation, 102, 103
Illicit Wealth Accumulation Act, 118–19
import substitution policy, 48, 49
Indonesia, 189–90
influence peddling, measurement of, 19
Inoue, Junnosake, 191
institutional structures. *See also*
    bureaucracy; judiciary
  in developing countries, 3
  Korea cf. with Philippines, 145–6, 148–9,
    150
  money politics and, 4
  policies and, 7
Insular Bank of Asia and America, 135t

197

Index

Korean Military Advisory Group (KMAG), 35
Korean War, 36
Kukje group, 102–4
Kuomintang (KMT), 146, 188
Kyungbookgung Palace, 90

land reform
in Korea, 27–8, 186
in the Philippines, 28–9, 144, 155, 180, 187
Latin American countries
U.S. aid to, 44
Lee Byung-chull, 53, 55, 91
Lee Duck-soo, 101
Lee Hahn-been, 69–70, 91
Lee Hu-rak, 105
Lee Kun-hui, 165
Lee Pyong-hi, 106
Lee Se-ho, 106
Liberal Democratic Party (Japan), 157
liberalization, 175
Liberal Party (Philippines), 50, 123–4
Liem Sioe Liong, 189
Long, Huey, 191–2
Lopez, Eugenio, 52, 141
Lopez, Fernando, 52, 141
Lopez, Gerry, 143
Lopez family, 51, 52, 131, 137, 141–2
Lopez Group, 178t

Macapagal, Diosdado P., 144
MacArthur, Douglas, 27
Magsaysay, Ramon, 27, 31–2
Malaysia, in Asian financial crisis, 157
Manila Bank, 135t, 136
Manila Chronicle, 141, 142
Manila Electric Company (Meralco), 141, 142
manufacturing, in the Philippines, 132
Marcos, Ferdinand, 27, 52, 62, 122, 123
assassinations and, 128–9
bureaucracy under, 9, 74–5, 80–4, 139, 148
competitors of, 141–3
concentration of power by, 136
control of business, 136–7, 140–4
corruption under, 2, 148
cronies of, 138–41, 145
divide and conquer tactics, 138, 139f

downfall of, 11, 50, 144–5, 154–5
economy under, 154, 156
election of, 124
elimination of warlords by, 137
expropriation of business holdings, 141
judiciary under, 83–4, 148–9
land reform and, 28, 144
loyalty to, 138–41
martial law under, 32–3, 80–3, 136–45
New Society and, 137
the state under, 10, 83–4, 147–8
"survivors" under, 143–4
Marcos, Imelda, 2, 139, 147, 148
Marcos family, 137
martial law
in Korea, 22, 98, 119
Korea cf. with Philippines, 145
in the Philippines, 10, 80–3, 122, 136–45
Mexico, U.S. aid to, 44
Military Intelligence Agency (*Boan-sa*), 102
military officials, in Korea, 85–7
Ministry of Commerce and Industry (MCI) (Korea), 92
Ministry of Reconstruction (MOR), 70, 71–2
money politics, 2
economic growth and, 3
institutions and, 4
in Korea, 181–2
in the Philippines, 10, 181–2
state strength and, 9
Monopoly Regulation and Fair Trade Act (MRFTA), 167
moral hazard, 120, 158
Morgan, J.P., 191
Moro National Liberation Front (MNLF), 156
mutual hostages, 7, 9, 15f, 17–18, 152f, 154
in Korea, 116–20, 182–3
in Taiwan, 188

Nach, James, 155
Nacionalista party (Philippines), 50, 123–4
Nalundasan, Julio, 128
National Assembly (Korea), elections to, 159–62
National Defense Security Command (*poana*), 89–90
National Export Promotion Meeting (Korea), 73

199

Index

For EU product safety concerns, contact us at Calle de José Abascal, 56–1°,
28003 Madrid, Spain or eugpsr@cambridge.org.

www.ingramcontent.com/pod-product-compliance
Ingram Content Group UK Ltd.
Pitfield, Milton Keynes, MK11 3LW, UK
UKHW010044140625
459647UK00012BA/1594